Tiger McKee

THE BOOK OF TWO GUNS

The Martial Art of The 1911 Pistol and AR Carbine

Dedicated to Mark McKee
1963-2004

The purpose of this book is as reference material only and is not meant to be a substitute for training under a qualified instructor. Neither the author not the publisher assumes any responsibility for the use or misuse of information contained in this book.

The Book of Two Guns
The Martial Art of the 1911 Pistol and AR Carbine

Copyright 2004   ISBN: 1-4196-0180-6
Published by Shootrite LLC
95 Lois Lane
Langston, AL
35755
(256) 582-4777   www.shootrite.org

Forward

In the trying times of today it is rare to meet someone of youth who professes to be and is of a true warrior's mindset. I am aware of Tiger McKee as a student, adjunct instructor for Thunder Ranch, and fellow teacher of firearms and tactics. We have stood on range decks together and we have talked of and applied tactics and techniques that will serve and hopefully save our students and clients in potential times of conflict. Tiger is a young man in years, but yet wise in experience...he has never been a police officer, he has never been a military man...yet he has a firm grasp of these fields of endeavor. In my opinion he is not required to have done these things to teach and teach well in his personal chosen field of being a teacher of firearms and tactics. Yes he is in fact my friend...but most of all on his own merit he is a teacher of firearms and tactics.
I support and endorse him in this book and his life's work.

Clint Smith
Thunder Ranch, Inc.
Oregon
2004

SAMURAI IN FEUDAL JAPAN WOULD OFTEN UNDERTAKE A TRAINING PILGRIMAGE OF WARRIORSHIP CALLED A MUSHA-SHUGYO. TRAVELING FROM SCHOOL TO SCHOOL, TEACHER TO TEACHER, LEARNING AND GROWING AS SWORDSMEN. GENERALLY SPEAKING THERE WERE ALSO PLENTY OF OPPORTUNITIES TO TEST YOUR SKILLS AGAINST OTHERS IN LETHAL COMBAT.

IN 1994 I BEGAN MY MUSHA-SHUGYO TO LEARN AS MUCH AS POSSIBLE ON THE COMBATIVE USE OF FIREARMS. I CAN'T REMBER NOT SHOOTING. AS A CHILD MY EXPIREANCES INCLUDED LOTS OF SHOOTING/HUNTING WITH MY FATHER, A U.S. ARMY SPECIAL FORCES OFFICER. I GREW TO BELIEVE FIGHTING WITH FIREARMS WAS A MARTIAL ART AND AS I TRAINED AND STUDIED I ATTEMPTED TO BLEND WHAT I KNEW OF BOXING, KARATE, JU-JITSU, TAI CHI CHAUN, ETC INTO ONE ART. I THINK THE JAPANESE CALLED IT HOJUTSU, THE MARTIAL ART OF FIREARMS.

THIS "BOOK" WAS NEVER INTENDED FOR PUBLICATION. IT STARTED LIFE AS A TRAINING DIARY; A WAY TO RECORD MATERIAL FOR PERSONAL REFERANCE. THOSE WHO SAW THE BOOK SUGGESTED I PUBLISH IT. CLINT SMITH SAID IT SHOULD BE PUBLISHED WITH THE HAND DRAWN ILLUSTRATIONS AND WRITING.
THE ORIGINAL WAS FAIRLY ROUGH AND UNORGINIZED, SO I HAVE COPIED IT IN ORDER TO PUT MATERIAL INTO GENERAL CATAGORIES AND LEGIBLE. IT IS STILL FULL OF MIS-SPELLINGS AND GRAMMAR MISTAKES BUT I'M SURE YOU CAN FIGURE IT OUT.

AS I WROTE THE ORIGINAL THERE WOULD BE TECHNIQUES I WOULD RECORD, AND THEN LATER DECIDE I DIDN'T BELIEVE THEY WERE SOUND. IN RE WRITNG I DECIDED TO LEAVE THESE OUT. I HAVE RECORDED HERE TECHNIQUES AND PRINCIPLES I NOW TEACH AND BELIEVE IN.

THE FOCUS IS ON THE PISTOL, SPECIFICALLY THE 1911, AND THE AR/M16 WEAPONS. A GOOD PART OF THE MATERIAL WILL APPLY TO OTHER FIREARMS, AND SOME OF IT TO ANY FIGHT. REMEMBER THAT FIGHTING IS AN INDIVIDUAL ART SO ULTIMATELY YOU CHOOSE WHAT YOU BELIEVE IN.

I HAVE TRIED TO GIVE CREDIT WHERE DUE. A LOT OF
MATERIAL LEARNED FROM DIFFERENT INSTRUCTORS WAS
THE SAME. SOMETIMES I WOULD COME UP WITH A
TECHNIQUE ONLY TO SEE IT LATER FROM ANOTHER SOURCE.
THERE IS VERY LITTLE NEW, AND THE FORGOTTEN IS
CONSTANTLY BEING REDISCOVERED.

MY HOPE IS THAT NOBODY HAS TO USE THE MATERIAL
IN THIS BOOK. HOWEVER THE WORLD WE LIVE IN IS A
VIOLENT ONE, TROUBLE CAN STRIKE AT ANY TIME AND
WITHOUT WARNING. IT IS BEST TO BE PREPARED. AS
CLINT SMITH SAYS," IT IS DIFFICULT TO ACQUIRE NEW
SKILLS IN THE MIDDLE OF A FIGHT."

LEARNING ANY ART IS A LONG, DIFFICULT PROCESS AND
FIGHTING WITH FIREARMS IS NO EXCEPTION. ALONG THE
WAY I'VE BEEN ASSISTED BY MANY. CLINT SMITH HAS
BEEN A MAJOR INFLUENCE. I THANK HIM AND HIS WIFE
HEIDI FOR ALL THEY HAVE DONE FOR ME, AND COUNTLESS
OTHERS THEY HAVE HELPED. I'VE NEVER STOPPED LEARNING
UNDER CLINT, FIRST AS A STUDENT AND LATER WHEN I
TAUGHT FOR HIM. I ALSO HAVE TO THANK RAY COFFMAN,
JACK FURR, AND BILL MCLLECAN, THE 3 GUARDSMEN OF
THUNDER RANCH.

THANKS TO MY PARENTS, WHO TAUGHT ME WHAT IS IS TO BE
A MAN. THE BIG THANKS GOES TO MY WIFE, WHO HAS PUT
UP WITH BEING BROKE AND SUFFERED THROUGH LONG HOURS
BY HERSELF WHILE I WAS TRAVELLING TO TRAIN AND TEACH.

THE GREATEST THANKS TO GOD. WITHOUT ALL HE PROVIDES
NONE IS POSSIBLE.

THE BOOK OF TWO GUNS IS DEDICATED TO MY BROTHER,
MARK. HE WAS ONE OF THE BEST MARTIAL ARTISTS I
HAVE KNOWN, HE PROTECTED THE WEAK, STOOD BY HIS
FRIENDS AND FAMILY, AND FOUGHT TO THE DEATH AGAINST
HIS ATTACKERS.

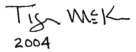

2004

2

THE DOCTRINE OF "URBAN RIFLE" WAS DEVELOPED BY CLINT SMITH; HE FIRST BEGAN TEACHING THE CONCEPT IN 1983. PRIOR TO THIS USE OF THE CARBINE WENT LARGELY UNNOTICED BY CONTEMPORARY LAW ENFORCEMENT, ESPECIALLY FOR SHORT TO MID RANGE CONFLICTS IN URBAN ENVIRONMENTS.
IT WASN'T UNTIL THE MIAMI FBI SHOOTOUT IN 1986 THAT INTEREST IN CLINT'S URBAN RIFLE CLASS DEVELOPED

INTEREST ROSE, THEN LEVELED OUT UNTIL THE NORTH Hollywood BANK ROBERY OCCURED AND THEN IT BUILT AGAIN.

F.B.I./Miami FireFight April 11, 1986

The bad guys, Platt and Matix, determined FBI agents were tailing them. Prior to this point Platt and Matix had pulled several robberies of banks and armored cars, killing several people in the process. As the bad guys and agents passed eachother in their cars one of the agents observed Platt loading a magazine into his MINI-14 and noted that Platt appeared to be "a man on a mission."

As the agents performed their car stop one agent, who was an excellent shooter, lost his glasses. Two agents lost their weapons during the collisions of the automobiles. The bad guys began shooting imediately.

Platt fired a total of 48 rounds from his .223 and three rounds from a .357 revolver. In the beginning of the fight he took a hit which passed through his right arm into his chest. Although this round would eventually kill him he continued to fight, killing two agents and wounding five others. Matix only fired one shot of #6 birdshot from his shotgun. FBI fired 70-78 rounds, scoring 12 hits on Platt and 6 on Matix.

JEFF Cooper on the "modern Technique" of the Pistol

"It is possible to say the revolution of pistolcraft in the 20th century began with Fairbain in China, although his efforts didn't receive wide acceptance.

In the 30's the F.B.I. created the "Practical Pistol course" which was a step forward. It was a departure from Bulls Eye Shooting and attempted to impart practical tactical skills.

In 1948 Cooper and Taft began to experiment with courses of fire related to the realistic use of the pistol — the result was the "Advanced military Combat Pistol Course," and the accompanying Army field manual.

In 1959 the "Bear Valley Gunslingers" began shooting in California, introducing realism into the sport of pistol competition. This lead to the establishment of the Southwest Combat Pistol League. IPSC was founded in 1976 and the "game" became priority.

Pistol craft is a fighting art. The "modern Technique" of the pistol is the evolution of combative art.

Jack weaver showed us the stance, Ray Chapman stylized it, John Plähn analyzed it and Jeff Cooper organized it.

➤——————————— –

It is my opinion that at the start of the 21st century we are entering the "Post modern" period of firearms training. New methods are being developed to address issues the modern Technique failed to cover.

We must take and borrow from all fighting arts to form the ultimate martial Art of combat with firearms.

4

In the past great gunfighters would gather on the edge of the west to discuss and demonstrate feats of gunplay. Today this is a thing of the past. Luckily deeds of the past are recorded and available for our examination. Time should be taken to inspect these works in depth; there is a lot of knowledge to be gained from studying the experiences of others.

"WAR ENDURES. AS WELL ASK MEN WHAT THEY THINK OF STONE. WAR IS ALWAYS HERE. BEFORE MAN WAS, WAR WAITED FOR HIM. THE ULTIMATE TRADE AWAITING THE ULTIMATE PRACTITIONER."

CORMAC McCARTHY
BLOOD MERIDIAN

ALWAYS WIN! ALWAYS CHEAT!

CLINT SMITH

CHARLES BECKWITH - You can't be unconvential until you're convential first.

THE FIREARM IS SIMPLY A TOOL USED TO ACCOMPLISH A TASK. ULTIMATELY WE FIGHT WITH OUR MINDS. FIGHTING IS 10% PHYSICAL - 90% MENTAL.

IN SOMILIA THE SMALL NUMBER OF U.S. TROOPS HELD OFF THOUSANDS OF STREET FIGHTERS. DUE TO THEIR TRAINING AND EQUIPMENT THEY WERE ABLE TO INFLICT THOUSANDS OF CASUALTIES AGAINST FIGHTERS WHO HAD SUPERIOR NUMBERS, THE HOME COURT ADVANTAGE, AND HAD BEEN FIGHTING ALL THEIR LIVES. THE BOOK "BLACKHAWK DOWN" SHOULD BE READ BY ALL.

FROM BLACKHAWK DOWN

CIVILIZED STATES HAD NON-VIOLENT WAYS OF RESOLVING DISPUTES, but depended on the willingness of everyone involved to back down. Here in the raw third world people hadn't learned to back down, at least not until after a lot of blood flowed. Victory was for those willing to fight and die.

> THIS CAN BE AN ISSUE IN ANY FIGHT. DON'T BELIEVE THAT JUST BECAUSE YOU HAVE A WEAPON THAT THE OTHER GUY WILL BACK DOWN. THEY MAY BE MENTALLY UNSTABLE, DRUNK OR HIGH, OR SIMPLY NOT CARE.

He blasted about a dozen rounds into him.
He shot another twelve rounds at the man, who never the less managed to crawl behind the tree.
NELSON squeezed off another long burst...
NELSON WAS SURPRISED HOW HARD IT COULD BE TO KILL A MAN.

> THE HUMAN BODY CAN ABSORB AN ENORMOUS AMOUNT OF DAMAGE AND STILL CONTINUE TO FUNCTION. REGARDLESS OF CALIBER OR VELOCITY YOU SHOULD BE PREPARED TO MAINTAIN FIRE UNTIL THE TARGET IS INCAPABLE OF CONTINUING THE FIGHT.

As they moved down the street it was one fluid process - scan for threats, find a safe place to go next, shoot, move, scan for threats... the key was to keep moving. The greatest danger was in getting pinned down.

> THIS IS TRUE WHEN FIGHTING AS AN INDIVIDUAL OR GROUP. THREE THINGS ARE NECESSARY DURING COMBAT - SHOOT, MOVE, COMMUNICATE

Howe was looking for people, focusing his eyes at mid torso first, checking the hands. THE HANDS TOLD YOU THE whole story.

> NORMALLY FOR SOMEONE TO BE A THREAT THEY MUST BE ARMED. THIS MEANS VISUALLY WE MUST FOCUS ON THE HANDS, WHICH GOES AGAINST OUR NATURAL TENDENCY OF LOOKING AT THE FACE.

THE GREEN TIP 5.56mm round had a tungsten tip and would punch holes in metal, but that very penetrating power meant his rounds were passing right through his targets. The bullet made a small, clean hole, and unless it happened to hit the heart or spine, it wasn't enough to stop a man in his tracks.

He drew a bead..., taking a progressive lead on them the way he learned... aiming several feet in front of them. He would squeeze two or three rounds, rapidly increasing his lead with each shot.

THIS IS THE LAW.
THE PURPOSE OF FIGHTING IS TO WIN.
THERE IS NO POSSIBLE VICTORY IN DEFEAT.
THE SWORD IS MORE IMPORTANT THAN THE SHIELD
AND SKILL IS MORE IMPORTANT THAN EITHER.
THE FINAL WEAPON IS THE BRAIN.
ALL ELSE IS SUPPLEMENTAL.   JHON STEINBECK

THE PRICE OF FREEDOM IS THE WILLINGNESS TO DO SUDDEN
BATTLE ANYWHERE, ANYTIME, AND WITH UTTER RECKLESSNESS.
                                   Robert Heinlein

KILL ONE, FRIGHTEN ONE THOUSAND.   SUN TZU

THE RULES OF THE MILITARY ARE FIVE: MEASUREMENT,
ASSESSMENT, CALCULATION, COMPARISON AND VICTORY. THE
GROUND GIVES RISE TO MEASUREMENTS, MEASUREMENTS
GIVE RISE TO ASSESSMENTS. ASSESSMENTS GIVE RISE TO
CALCULATIONS, CALCULATIONS GIVE RISE TO COMPARISONS,
COMPARISONS GIVE RISE TO VICTORIES.   SUN TZU

"THE WEAPON IS IN THE MAN"

FAST IS FINE   BUT ACCURACY IS FINAL   WYATT ERP

CARLOS MARIGHELLA - SEVEN SINS OF THE URBAN GUERRILLA

   INEXPERIENCE - UNDER OR OVERESTIMATES ENEMY
   BOASTING OF ACTIVITY
   VANITY
   DANGER OF EXAGGERATING FIGHTING STRENGTH
   PRECIPITOUS ACTING, ACTING TOO SOON
   ATTACKING WHEN ANGRY
   FAILING TO PLAN
         THESE RULES APPLY TO THE INDIVIDUAL AND GROUP.

7

MINDSET AND BODY LANGUAGE

STUDIES IN SOCIAL PSYCHOLOGY INDICATE THAT THE WAY HUMANS CARRY THEMSELVES - INCLUDING HOW THEY WALK, SPEAK, GESTURE, MOVE AND LOOK - COMMUNICATE VARIOUS MESSAGES. THESE NON-VERBAL MESSAGES CAN TRANSMITT WEAKNESSES THAT INDICATE OPPORTUNITY FOR HUMAN PREDATORS TO EXPLOIT.

WE MUST UNDERSTAND HOW OUR BEHAVIOR AND ACTIONS IMPACT OUR SURVIVAL EVEN WHEN PERFORMING THE MOST MUNDANE TASKS. WHEN PREDATORS OBSERVE WEAKNESS THEY WILL ATTACK.

> THE OFFENDER OBSERVED THE OFFICER FOR ONLY A SHORT TIME BEFORE HE "KNEW THIS WAS MY MAN" AFTER LOOKING AT THE FIRST OFFICER HE APPROACHED, "I KNEW HE'D BE A DIFFICULT TARGET," SO THE OFFENDER MOVED ON.

> KILLERS AND ASSUALTERS ALIKE STATED THAT IF THEIR VICTIMS GENERALLY GAVE THE IMPRESSION THAT THEY APPEARED AUTHORITATIVE, SEEMED RESOLUTE, OR ACTED PROFESSIONALLY, THEN THE OFFENDERS WERE RELUCTANT TO INITIATE AN ASSUALT.

> "OFFENDERS PERCEPTUAL SHORTHAND"
> FBI LAW ENFORCEMENT BULLETIN
> JUNE 1999 #6 ANTHONY PINIZZOTTO

NEVER BASE YOUR ACTIONS ON WHAT YOU FEEL THE THREAT'S INTENTIONS MAY BE; YOUR ACTIONS MUST BE BASED ON WHAT THE CAPABILITIES OF THE THREAT ARE. YOU MUST ASSUME THAT EVERYONE IS ARMED. IF THEY ARE NEAR YOU THEN THEY HAVE OPPORTUNITY. IF YOU ASSUME THEY ARE ARMED THEN THEY HAVE THE ABILITY. IF THEY DISPLAY INTENT THEN YOU SHOULD BE READY TO RESPOND WITH AGRESSIVE ACTION.

THE PURPOSE OF BEING IN A FIGHT IS TO WIN. THE PURPOSE OF SHOOTING IS TO HIT. ONLY HITS COUNT. HITS DON'T MEAN THAT YOU WIN, IT SIMPLY MEANS YOU'VE HAD YOUR TURN. JUST HIT THE TARGET UNTIL YOU WIN.

CLINT SMITH

TARGET INDICATORS

SOUND
    MOVEMENT
        REFLECTION
           OUTLINE
                CONTRAST
                    SMELL

REMEMBER THAT YOU ALSO GIVE OFF TARGET INDICATORS AS WELL AS THE BAD GUY.

METHODS OF CAMOUFLAGE
    BLENDING - TO BECOME PART OF THE ENVIRONMENT
    HIDING - CONCEALMENT
    DECEPTION - APPEAR AS SOMETHING ELSE

KEEP IN MIND THAT CAMO VARIES ACCORDING TO YOUR ENVIRONMENT ONE WOODED AREA IS DIFFERENT FROM ANOTHER, URBAN ARE DIFFERENT AND VARY FROM ONE TO ANOTHER. URBAN AREAS ARE COMPOSED OF BLOCKS AND STRAIGHT LINES MADE UP OF GRAYS, BROWNS AND MUTED COLORS US. THE ROUNDED INCONSISTENT SHAPES OF WOODED CAMO.

SUTEKAMARI NI JITSU (TECHNIQUES OF LYING DOWN AND BEING ABANDONED) DEVELOPED BY THE SHIMAZU CLAN OF SATSUMA AND INVOLVED LEAVING BEHIND SHARPSHOOTERS AS THE ARMY RETREATED.

IT IS THE RESPONSIBILITY OF THE PERSON WHO CARRIES A FIREARM TO BLEND INTO THE CROWD, AVOID ATTENTION AND CONFLICT. THE WEAPON IS ONLY DISPLAYED WHEN READY OR IN ANTICIPATION OF ITS USE.

THE HEIGHT OF EFFICIENCY IS TO MAKE CONFLICT UNNECESSARY THE SUPERIOR MILITARIST FOILS ENEMIES PLOTS   SUN TZU

PRACTICE AVOIDANCE!

The main elements of confrontations are well documented. The average distance will be 0-21 feet out to a max of 100 yards, lasting an average of 2.8 seconds, with an average of 12.5 rounds fired.

Target will be frontal or angular and moving. There is the possibility of body armor and mental condition will be questionable due to chemicals. Fifty percent of all encounters will include more than one opponent.

Deciding Factors
        Mental Condition & Preparation
        Tactics & Skills vs. Opponent
        Equipment
        Luck ?

Cartridge power, magazine capacity and the improved sight radius all combine to make the .223 AR carbine ideal for situations traditionally considered handgun confrontations. The rifle's accuracy at extended ranges is ideal in allowing you to maximize the distances between you and the threat while minimizing yourself as a target.

The pistol is defensive in nature, and is used because it can be carried with us at all times. If you knew you were going to a fight take a rifle) "the pistol," Clint reminds us, "is used to fight your way to the rifle you shouldn't have set down in the first place."

The advantage of magazine capacity is not being able to shoot more ammo but in not having to spend as much time reloading the weapon. The less time spent manipulating weapon the more time you are plugged into the fight. Another attribute is the ergonomic design.

During the fight you must stay plugged in constantly. While performing manipulations eyes must be kept up and on the target or threat environment. Weapon must be operated by feel without aid of eyesight.

THE SHOTGUN IS LIMITED DUE TO A VARIETY OF FACTOR. LIMITED MAG CAPACITY AND A COMPLICATED LOAD/RELOAD PROCEDURES MAKE IT A DIFFICULT WEAPON TO MAINTAIN OPERATIONAL

WITH SLUGS OR BUCKSHOT RANGE CAN BE EXTENDED OUT TO 100 yards, but ammo must be matched to weapon to achieve consistent results.

RECOIL IS HARD TO MANAGE FOR SOME SHOOTERS AND CAN INCREASE TIME FROM SHOT TO SHOT.

ADVANTAGES ARE ITS STOPPING POWER AND LIMITED PENETRATION.

IN MY OPINION IT IS MORE OF A SPECIFIC APPLICATION WEAPON AS OPPOSED TO A GENERAL PURPOSE WEAPON.

THE RIFLE IS A DYNAMIC WEAPON. ANYTIME IT IS EMPLOYED there should be movement and aggressive action. Defense is only an immediate response and should be followed closely by offensive actions. This is the purpose of the Rifle - to allow you ta actively engage the threat.

Introduction of a rifle into a hostile environment has a psychological advantage in addition to the tactical advantages. The rifle is very discouraging to the opponent facing it.

ELEMENTS OF SURVIVAL TACTICS - Jeff Cooper

... when the ball opens success will go to the artist more often than to the tactician — other things being roughly even.

The first principle of tactics is speed. The best fight is that which is over before the loser realizes that it has begun. The goal of the tactician is to ensure that the fight, when and where joined, is never "fair."

DEADLY FORCE MAY BE UTILIZED IF

    Someone's self-preservation is threatened

    There is no way to escape or avoid

    De-Escalation through other means isn't possible

ASK Yourself "IF I don't shoot now will someone be harmed?"

Weapon manipulations should be learned to the point that they are subconcious actions. The mind says reload and then the subconcious takes over to perform the sequence of actions. IF someone says "catch this ball," you don't actuely think to track the ball with your hands, open your hands and fingers, close your hands ... All this is a subconcious process that has been learned through thousands of repititions.

You should Never train to do things fast. Complicated sequences of actions should always be performed as pecisely as possible. Precision in action leads to speed because there is no excess/uncessary actions. SPEED IS THE ABSCENSE OF EXCESS!

Following Victory It Is Best To Reload
This applies to life as well as war.

WHEN PERFORMING PHYSICAL ACTIONS IT IS BETTER TO OPERATE AT 90% of your ability AS OPPOSED TO 100% - OR "ALL OUT" AT 100% YOU ARE PUSHED BEYOND THE COMPETANCE OF YOUR ABILITY. THERE IS NO ERROR OF MARGIN FOR MISTAKES - AND YOU WILL MAKE MISTAKES. BY FUNCTIONING AT 90% YOU HAVE MENTAL CONFIDENCE IN YOUR ABILITIES AND MISTAKES CAN BE CORRECTED OR compensated FOR.
IF YOU can't control your own actions then everything is out of control

12

MOVEMENT MUST BE MAINTAINED. TO ALLOW YOURSELF TO BECOME PINNED DOWN WILL RESULT IN DEFEAT DIRECTION IS AN ENVIRONMENTALLY DETERMINED ISSUE. FORWARD, BACKWARD, LEFT-RIGHT, DIAGONALS — ALL MUST BE USED TO AVOID BEING CONTAINED. ACCURATE SHOTS ON TARGET MUST BE COMBINED WITH MOVEMENT.

Caliber Choice is more important than pistol type, or number of rounds. Studies have shown that for pistols the 9mm comes up short, 45 is good, magnums kill a lot of people. But it won't matter what you shoot if you don't hit the target. ONLY HITS COUNT!

Although this book focuses on the 1911 pistol don't think I am not a fan of revolvers. Revolvers are great for fighting. They come in small size, of good calibers, and large size, with magnum rounds that work well against threats.

WHEN ENGAGING A THREAT WITH FIRE YOU ARE SHOOTING TO STOP THE THREAT — NOT KILL THEM. DUE TO THE AREAS WE MUST SHOOT TO STOP THE THREAT EFFECTIVELY — the center mass and head, the Threat may die. BUT THAT ISN'T the desired effects. Our Job is to STOP THE THREAT AS QUICKLY AS POSSIBLE — OR WE HURT THEM ENOUGH THAT THEY DECIDE TO LEAVE.

CLINT SMITH RECOMMENDS SAYING "DROP THE WEAPON!" vs. specifying what the threat is armed with. "Drop the Stick!" doesn't sound as though the threat is actually armed with a dangerous weapon.

13

THE SINGLE ACTION SEMI AUTO PISTOL IS EASIER
TO TRAIN, LEARN, AND EMPLOY DURING FIGHT.
THE SINGLE ACTION, BEING EASIER TO LEARN, IS
MORE CONSISTENT AND HIT PROBABILITY INCREASES
WITH THE DOUBLE ACTION, AND THE DIFFERENCE
BETWEEN FIRST PULL AND FOLLOWING SHOTS, WILL
CAUSE AROUND 60% MISSED SHOTS ON THE FIRST
TRIGGER PRESS.
WITH THE DA PISTOL YOU CAN PRESS THE FIRST
SHOT OFF QUICKLY, PROBABLY NOT GETTING A GOOD
HIT, AND GET TO THE SINGLE ACTION MODE OR
YOU HAVE TO BE REALLY CAREFUL ON THE FIRST
PRESS TO SCORE A GOOD HIT. EITHER CHOICE
TAKES MORE TIME TO GET A GOOD HIT.
ALSO THE SAFETY OR "DECOCKING" LEVERS ARE POORLY
POSITIONED AND DIFFICULT TO EMPLOY.

"COMMON SENSE TRAINING" COLLINS

"SUCCESS OR FAILURE DEPENDS ON IMMEDIATE ACTION."
THE OBJECTIVES ARE SPEED AND CO-ORDINATION.
QUICK REACTION, THE ABILITY TO ACCOMPLISH TACTICAL
JOBS QUICKLY, IS OFTEN THE KEY TO SUCCESS & SURVIVAL.

TO TRAIN DEMONSTRATE AND EXPLAIN ACTIONS. HAVE STUDENTS
PRACTICE SLOW, BY THE NUMBERS, DRY. THEN PRACTICE
LIVE FIRE AT HALF SPEED. CORRECT AND APPLY CONSTRUCTIVE
CRITICISM THEN LIVE FIRE AT FULL SPEED.

"A REALLY GOOD TRAINER CAN ALWAYS MAKE A CORRECTION
IN A CONSTRUCTIVE AND TEACHING FASHION."

"COMPLETING THE DRILL SHOULD GIVE THE STUDENT A SENSE
OF ACCOMPLISHMENT. HE SHOULD SEE POSITIVE RESULTS.

THREE MODES OF INFORMATION INTAKE

- AUDITORY - AUDITORY LEARNERS NEED SPECIFIC INSTRUCTIONS AND MAY OFTEN ASK QUESTIONS

- VISUAL - INSTRUCTOR SHOULD DEMONSTRATE AND SUPPLY CHARTS AND WRITTEN MATERIAL

- KINESTETIC - LEARN BY DOING. PRESENT MATERIAL THROUGH A VARIETY OF DRILLS WHICH TEACH THE SAME TECHNIQUE

MODES OF PERCEPTION

- GLOBAL - SEES THE "BIG PICTURE." MOVE FROM GENERAL PRINCIPLES TO SPECIFIC EXAMPLES. THEY STUDY THE WHOLE CONCEPT AND THEN CONSIDER THE DETAILS

- ANALYTIC - BEGINS WITH PARTS AND THEN ASSEMBLES THEM INTO A COMPLETE WHOLE

AS A student you should discover what type learner you are so you can get the most out of training.

PERFORMANCE GUIDELINES

ONLY HITS COUNT!

FUNCTION AT YOUR NATURAL BODY SPEED.

SPEED IS THE ABSCENCE OF EXCESS.

QUICKNESS DEVELOPES AS A RESULT OF PROPER PRACTICE.

RATE OF FIRE IS DETERMINED BY SIGHT PICTURE.

SHOOT ONE SHOT AT A TIME.

MUST APPLY YOUR SKILLS ON DEMAND.

FRONT SIGHT - PRESS - REPEAT AS REQUIRED.

DURING A VIOLENT ENCOUNTER THE ONLY THING YOU CAN CONTROL ARE YOUR OWN ACTIONS. IF YOU LOSE CONTROL OF YOUR ACTIONS, AND ARE SIMPLY REACTING, WINNING IS BASED ON LUCK. CONTROL YOURSELF, MAKE THE THREAT REACT TO YOU.

BEING SCARED OR AFRAID OF DYING WILL NOT DO YOU ANY GOOD. YOU MUST FIGHT AGGRESIVELY, MAKING SURE YOU DOMINATE THE ACTION AS SOON AS POSSIBLE.

PAY ATTENTION TO YOUR "GUT" FEELINGS OR INTUITION. SOMETHING HAS MADE YOU FEEL FUNNY. ACESS THE SITUATION AND YOUR ENVIRONMENT, FORM A PLAN OF RESPONSE, AND THEN IMPLEMENT AS SOON AS POSSIBLE MOST OF THE TIME THERE ARE SIGNALS THAT ALERT YOU TO DANGER. PAY ATTENTION! THESE SIGNALS ARE THE KEY TO WINNING THE ENCOUNTER.

TO PREPARE YOU MUST FIRST LEARN THE BASIC FUNDAMENTALS. THEN YOU PRACTICE UNTIL YOU CAN APPLY THESE SKILLS ON DEMAND. NEVER TRAIN JUST TO BE FAST! LET SPEED DEVELOPE AS A RESULT OF PROPER PRACTICE.

FUNDAMENTALS ⟶ CONSISTENCY ⟶ SPEED

NOTES FROM Col. Cooper's 1998 GENERAL PISTOL CLASS

THE PROBLEM IS SAVING YOUR LIFE IN A SHORT TIME SPAN WITHIN SHORT DISTANCES. START AT THE BEGINNING AND LEARN FROM THERE - BASIC GUNHANDLING, THE ABILITY TO HIT THE KILL ZONE IN A RESONABLE AMOUNT OF TIME, AND HOW TO COMMAND AND CONTROL YOUR ENVIRONMENT.

PROGRAM REFLEXES SO THAT RESPONSE IS AUTOMATIC, WITHOUT THOUGHT

Diligentia - PRECISION

Vis - POWER

Celeritas - QUICKNESS

FRONT SIGHT - PRESS! THIS IS ALL YOU MUST THINK

You must have the upper hand. You do this by taking the initiative away from the attacker.

If you shoot well you shouldn't require a large number of rounds. You must shoot to stop the threat - this is accomplished by heart or brain shots. (OVER 80% of people shot with pistols survive.)

You must decide in advance that you will take the shot. The moment of action is not the time to be debating the moral issues involved in taking a life.

Most victims RARELY RESIST.

Ammunition management is critical to the outcome of violent encounters. RELOAD WHEN YOU WANT TO - NOT WHEN YOU HAVE TO.

"THE TRANSFORMATION OF WAR" MARTIN VAN CREVELD

The three obstacles to warlike force are inflexibility, friction, and uncertainty. They exist wherever and whenever war is waged. War, according to Clausewitz, is "a mental and physical struggle conducted by means of the latter."

"In fact, war does not begin when some people kill others; instead it starts at the point where they themselves risk being killed in return." (159)

"In any war, the readiness to suffer and die, as well as to kill, represents the single most important factor." (160)

"SINCE HE WHO FIGHTS PUTS EVERYTHING AT RISK, WHATEVER HE FIGHTS FOR MUST BE DEEMED MORE PRECIOUS THAN HIS OWN BLOOD." (166)

WEAPONS ARE NOT JUST UTILITARIAN DEVICES BUT SYMBOLS OF MIGHT.

RYTHM

" SEEK TIMING, AS IT WILL OUTCLASS SPEED IN ALMOST EVERY CASE." KEN GOOD

IN COMBAT, AS WITH ALL ELSE, THERE IS A RYTHM THAT MUST BE CONSIDERED. YOU MUST LEARN TO RECOGNIZE THE TEMPO, AND THE WINDOWS OF OPPORTUNITY THAT EXIST WITHIN.

WHEN YOU ENGAGE YOU EITHER BLEND INTO THE OPPONENT'S ATTACK AND THEN COUNTER, OR YOU COUNTER IMMEDIATELY WITH A COMPLETELY DIFFERENT RYTHM — DISRUPTING HIS ATTACK. IF YOU ACCEPT THE TIMING AND LET THE ATTACK RUN ITS COURSE, LOSE ITS ENERGY, AND THEN COUNTER YOUR CHANCES OF SUCCESS INCREASE.

AN AGGRESSIVE ATTACK REQUIRES SUBSTANTIAL ENERGY, AND ALWAYS HAS OPENINGS ALLOWING YOU TO COUNTER.

FIREARMS - THE ULTIMATE MARTIAL ART

WITH MARTIAL ARTS THERE ARE 3 STAGES OF COMBAT. FIRST, YOU RECOGNIZE INTENT OR REACT TO THE ATTACK. SECOND, YOU MUST CLOSE THE GROUND REQUIRED TO EFFECTIVELY EMPLOY YOUR WEAPON. THIRD, YOU NEUTRALIZE THE ATTACKER.

MARTIAL ART HAVE ALWAYS BEEN CONCERNED WITH ECONOMY OF MOTION AND TECHNIQUE VS. STRENGTH. FOR THESE REASONS FIREARMS CAN BE CONSIDERED THE ULTIMATE MARTIAL ART. IT REDUCES THE TIME INVOLVED BY ELIMINATING THE NEED TO CLOSE THE GROUND. PROPER APPLICATION HAS A HIGH PROBABILITY OF STOPPING THE THREAT, AND FIREARMS REQUIRE LITTLE STRENGTH BUT RELY ON TECHNIQUE - MAKING IT POSSIBLE FOR ALMOST ANYONE TO EFFECTIVELY EMPLOY THEM.

IN COMBAT THERE IS DEFENSE OR ATTACK. DEFENSE IS EASIER BUT NEVER RESULTS IN VICTORY. TO ATTACK REQUIRES A CONCENTRATION OF EFFORT, CREATES RISK, BUT WILL PRODUCE VICTORY.

SLOW IS SMOOTH - SMOOTH IS FAST.

ACTION BEATS REACTION

PROXIMITY NEGATES SKILL

LUCK CAN BEAT SKILL AT ANY TIME

ATTACK WITHOUT RESERVATION. THEN IF YOU CAN THE AGGRESSION CAN BE REDUCED. IF YOU BEGIN TOO LOW ON THE SCALE YOU MAY FIND IT IMPOSSIBLE TO ACCELERATE YOUR ACTIONS.

ERICH HARTMAN - WWII GERMAN FIGHTER PILOT
Hartman described his attack system in 4 steps
See, Decide, Attack, Reverse - then evaluate and begin again
"The pilot who sees the other first has half the victory."

19

COLOR CODE OF AWARENESS
JEFF COOPER

WHITE - STATE OF COMPLETE UNREADINESS
OBLIVIOUS TO YOUR SURROUNDINGS

YELLOW - RELAXED ATTENTION, AWARE OF SURROUNDINGS

ORANGE - SPECIFIC PROBLEM NOTICED, POSSIBLE
PROBLEM DEVELOPING

RED - AWAITING MENTAL TRIGGER TO LAUNCH RESPONSE

BLACK - IN A FIGHT, STAY FOCUSED
(ADDED BY CLINT SMITH)

WHEN YOU LEAVE YOUR HOUSE YOU SHOULD BE IN YELLOW.

YOUR RESPONSE SHOULD BE INSTANTANEOUS AND DECIDED
ON BEFORE THE FIGHT BEGINS.

THE ENVIRONMENT WILL DETERMINE YOUR RESPONSE.

TO GO FROM ONE AWARENESS LEVEL TO ANOTHER IS
EASY. TO JUMP FROM WHITE ALL THE WAY TO RED IS
DIFFICULT. PAY ATTENTION AND ADJUST ACCORDINGLY.

PRINCIPLES OF SELF DEFENSE
JEFF COOPER

ALERTNESS - PRACTICE AVOIDANCE
DECISIVENESS - DO NOT DELAY
AGGRESSIVENESS - EXPLOSIVE ACTION
SPEED - QUICKNESS IS YOUR SALVATION
COOLNESS - CONTROL YOUR ACTIONS
RUTHLESSNESS - THERE IS NO OVER REACTION
SURPRISE - ATTEMPT THE UNEXPECTED

THE FIRST RULE OF TACTICS IS SPEED!

MINDSET

The Combat Triad
JEFF COOPER

Gunhandling   MARKSMANSHIP

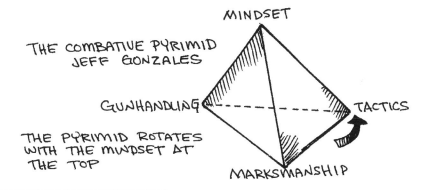

THE COMBATIVE PYRIMID
JEFF GONZALES

GUNHANDLING   TACTICS

THE PYRIMID ROTATES
WITH THE MINDSET AT
THE TOP

MINDSET

MARKSMANSHIP

ALL COMBAT BEGINS IN THE MIND.

YOU MUST HAVE THE ABILITY TO SIZE UP THE SITUATION,
MAKE AN INSTANT DECISION, SELECT THE APPROPRIATE
TACTICS AND ACT WITHOUT THE SLIGHTEST HESITATION
ABOUT USING LETHAL FORCE.   JEFF COOPER

Attacking completely without reservation is effective
within its limits. Outside the concentrated area
of effectiveness the attack's capcity to do damage
is greatly reduced or diminished completely.

MOST VICTIMS ARE ACTUALLY VOLUNTEERS

21

You must know the basics of shooting and be able to apply them under any conditions.

Limitations are more how you approach things rather than the degree of difficulty.

"There are no advanced shooting techniques, only advanced applications of the fundamentals."
Michael Plaxco

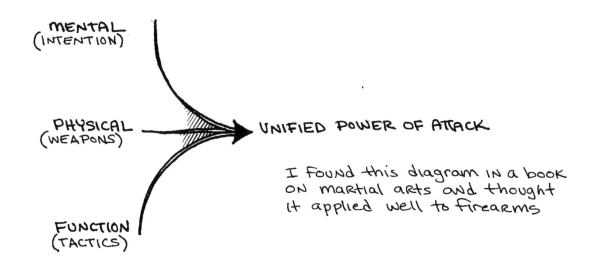

MENTAL
(INTENTION)

PHYSICAL
(WEAPONS) → UNIFIED POWER OF ATTACK

FUNCTION
(TACTICS)

I found this diagram in a book on martial arts and thought it applied well to firearms

"WHEN YOU ENTER A ROOM FULL OF ENEMY, KILL THE FIRST ONE THAT MOVES – HE HAS STARTED TO THINK AND IS THEREFORE DANGEROUS."   Paddy Mayne (SAS)

"A WARRIORS INSTINCTS MAKE HIM A STUDENT OF HIS CRAFT. THE BEST WARRIORS REGARD SKILL WITH THEIR WEAPONS AS HIGH ART. HOWEVER WE FREQUENTLY FIND TWO SUBSTITUTIONS FOR THIS BELIEF IN FUNDAMENTALS: FIRST, THE INVOLVEMENT WITH TECHNICAL SPECIALIZATION AT THE EXPENSE OF PERSONAL SKILL; AND SECOND THE COMPLACENT ASSUMPTION THAT THE BURDEN OF VICTORY RESTS ON THE WEAPON, NOT ITS WIELDER. THE FACT REMAINS THAT SKILL WITH WEAPONS IS THE ESSENCE OF THE WARRIOR'S CRAFT."   COMMANDER JOHN BYRON, USN

INCORRECT TECHNIQUES CAN BE LEARNED JUST AS EASILY
AS THE CORRECT TECHNIQUES. THE SUBCONSCIOUS - WHERE
YOU ACTUALLY LEARN- DOESN'T KNOW THE DIFFERENCE.

TRAINING IS MADE UP OF REPETITION - ANYTIME YOU DO
SOMETHING INCORRECTLY YOU ARE INCREASING THE CHANCE
YOU WILL DO IT WRONG WHEN YOUR LIFE DEPENDS ON
YOUR PERFORMANCE. IT IS HARDER TO RELEARN OR
BREAK A BAD HABIT THAN IT IS TO LEARN IT IN THE
START.

YOUR FIRST ATTEMPTS AT A NEW SKILL ARE THE MOST
CRITICAL. AT NO TIME SHOULD YOU WORRY ABOUT SPEED
THE BODY PERFORMS BETTER WHEN OPERATING AT A
NATURAL SPEED. WHEN TRAINING YOU SHOULD FOCUS
ON THE PERFORMANCE - NOT THE OUTCOME.

SELF TALK

You say to yourself "Don't Jerk The Trigger"
The subconscious mind processes this as "Jerk
the trigger" because it doesn't recognize
Negative qualifiers, therefor you are programming
the exact opposite of what you are striving for.

The proper statement would be "Press the trigger"
Eventually this could be shortened up to simply "press"

The concsious and subconscious work together
only by programming the positive.

If your thoughts move into concern with problems
you are imprinting a Negative image. All thoughts
and self talk should be focused on positive aspects.

"FEAR IS HAVING NO FAITH - PLAIN AND SIMPLE"
                                    KEN GOOD

MENTAL IMAGERY TRAINING

INTERNAL IMAGERY - PERSPECTIVE OF AN ACTIVE PARTICIPANT FROM THE BODY LOOKING OUTWARD

KINESTHETIC IMAGERY - IMAGERY OF MOVEMENT & MUSCULAR ACTIVITY, USE OF SENSE OF TOUCH & FEELING

VISUAL IMAGERY - THE SENSE OF SIGHT

The best success is obtained by making imagery as multi-sensory as possible, the more elements utilized the better

Firearms marksmanship requires a good deal of fine motor control, hand-eye coordination, and a high cognitive component. These task traits make it ideal for imagery training.

Imagery training has been used for a variety of activities when mental and physically components must operate in conjunction. Works well for sports, ect and is perfect for high stress conditions such as gunfighting.

PRIOR EXPOSURE TO THE TASK IS ESSENTIAL TO SUCCESS.

PRACTICE BEGINS BY FINDING A QUIET PLACE WHER YOU can relax without distractions. Then you will imagain a scenario to work through. It can be as simple as clearing a malfunctioned weapon to an actual fight.

After imagining the scenario the memory is stored in the subconscious mind which can't distinguish between what has actually occored and what was vividly imagined in your mind.

FEWER more detailed SCENARIOS are better than a greater number of QUICK SCENARIOS. Details are essential to success. Sights, sounds, smells, and physical sensations must be imagined.

Initial practice should begin with a perfected model of performance to be sure of accurately reproducing the process

AN INFINITE NUMBER OF "what if" SCENARIOS CAN be developed the key is to make it realistic, difficult, and INSURE that victory or success are the results.

CONTINUED...

24

TESTS HAVE SHOWN THAT IMAGERY PRACTICE IS VALUABLE
TO ACCELERATING, NOT MERELY ENHANCING TRAINING. It
is cost free and the potential is unlimited.

Vividness - colorful, realistic, and involving the appropriate
emotions

PRACTICE - LEARNING through short Repetitious sessions

Attitude & EXPECTATIONS - works best for those who believe
It is a legitimate experience

PREVIOUS EXPERIENCE - EXPERIENCED PARTICIPANTS WILL
BENEFIT MORE THAN BEGINNERS

RELAXED ATTENTION - must maintain a relaxed state of mind

Internal Imagery - view from an internal perspective

As mentioned 90% of our performance is based on mental
conditions. If the mind believes it has been in a type
situation before it WILL BE ABLE TO HANDLE THE CURRENT
EVENT BETTER SINCE IT HAS A PREVIOUS FRAME OF REFERENCE
TO ACCESS AND BASE DECISIONS ON.
Once we imagine something realistically it is filed away
into the subscious where it becomes a memory, ready
to be accessed when Necessary

Thomas Tutko - our psychological tendencies can help
or hinder us depending on how much we possess them
or they possess us.

FEAR AND ANGER ARE CLOSELY RELATED EMOTIONS. It IS VERY
BENEFICIAL TO TRANSFORM THE FEAR, AND ITS RELATED PHYSICAL
EFFECTS, INTO ANGER AND THE FIGHTING RESPONSE.

You must train and fight with the thought that
what you are doing is not going to be effective
and what are your Next actions going to be.
Just like in a chess game, in a fight you have
to be preparing actions in advance.

25

FIGHT - FLIGHT - POSTURE - SUBMIT - FREEZE

During a violent confrontation there are several options one may choose. Originally it was termed fight or flight, and described the pysiological stages the body goes through when preparing to fight or flee. However we sometimes posture, in an attempt to get the other to back down when we have no intention of actually fighting, or there are those who will submit to the demands of their attacker. Then there are those who will simply freeze, which although is a form of submission in the end it results from a total lack of response.

PHYSICAL	MENTAL
SHORTNESS OF BREATH	DISTRACTING ANXIETY
BLURRED VISION	MAKES YOU GIVE UP
TENSE MUSCLES	HALTS DEVELOPMENT
MUSCLE FATIGUE	HYPNOTIC EFFECTS
DISRUPTED COORDINATION	RUINS TACTICAL JUDGEMENT
PRONENESS TO INJURY	MAKE YOU PHYSICALLY SICK

Success depends on moral more than physical qualities. Offensive action is the forerunner to victory.

Surprise is the most effective and powerful influence, and results in returns beyond the effort. The elements of surprise are speed, deception, originality, and audacity.

Concentration is a matter of timing vs pace.

The objectives in a gunfight are to live and either capture or kill your opponent.

At times the right action is "sensed" against all logic and the wise man follows his hunch and lives.

Almost invariably a man, provided he does not have too long to think, will automatically do what he has been trained to do.

> "If you get in a gunfight don't let yourself feel rushed. TAKE your time, fast."
> Captain John Hughes

Be sure you have correctly identified your target, then lock on and keep with it. Don't switch as long as your original target is available without a very good reason.

Keep moving around ... A moving target is harder to hit even if you are caught out in the open. It is generally better to move toward your left due to the tendency of most people to "milk" their shots low and left.

Don't wear light colored clothing, particularly at night.

You can keep on fighting even if you are hit.

27

THE BOOK OF FIVE RINGS   MIYAMOTO MUSASHI

I began reading this book at the age of 15 and 30 years later I still consider it one of the best studies on the art of individual combat.

"When in a fight to the death, one wants to employ all one's weapons to the utmost. I must say that to die with one's sword still sheathed is most regrettable."

> This applies to any weapons you have access to, including the most important one you possess; your brain.

"As for body posture, do not raise or lower the head or lean it to one side.
Lower both shoulders, hold the back straight, and do not stick out the buttocks."

> Posture and balance are critical to being able to fight effectively.

"Steady your gaze and try not to blink; Narrow your eyes a little more than usual.
Vigilance in combat means keeping one's eyes wide open."

> Narrowing the eyes slightly helps us to see more by bringing things into focus at different distances. Keep eyes up and maintain visual contact with environment.

"It is essential to make the everyday stance the combat stance and the combat stance the everyday stance."

"Victory is achieved in the Heihō of conflict by ascertaining the rythm of each opponent, by attacking with a rythm not anticipated by the opponent, and the use of knowledge of the rythm of the abstract."

"what is meant by the three intial attacks"

The first of the "three intial attacks" is where you make the intial move. The second is where your intial move takes place instantly after the opponent makes the first move. The third one is made when you and the opponent attack at the same time. In all conflict there can be no other intial attacks other than these three."

"There is rythm in all."
"The spirit to be able to win no matter what the weapon, this is the teaching of my school of Heihō.

"Where you hold your sword (or weapon) depends on your relationship to the opponent, depends on the environment, and must conform to the situation; wherever you hold it, the idea is to hold it so that it will be easy to kill your opponent."

"The teacher is the needle and the disciple is the thread."

"Although your stride may be long or short, slow or fast, according to the situation, it is to be normal. Complementary stepping is essential, do not move just one foot alone.

It is bad to go too far or not far enough; take the mean. When you go too quickly it means you are scared or flustered. When you go too slowly it means you are timid or frightened.

To delibertly hold back a spontaneous action means the mind is more disturbed than the mind that would act. To try not to move is to haved moved.

29

THE READY POSITION

Whatever "ready" position you use do not think of it as being on "guard," but think of it as part of the act of attacking. As opposed to being on "guard"- an act of defense- we must think in aggresive terms. Therefore "ready"- ready to attack.

The ready position is based on environment. If you are going down a set of stairs it will be low; if you are a long distance from the theat - on level ground- it will be higher. The ideal position is with arms low enough to see everywhere in the threat environment, or the hands of a specific threat and in the "middle" where you can attack in any direction of the threat environment. When addressing 2 possible threats you will want to set the ready between the two so you can engage either one - as long as the threats are of equal valve.

For a Specific threat ready allows you to SEE THE HANDS OF THREAT

Going down stairs the ready would be lowered to be able to see the entire area below you.

In the ready position I keep the safety on. This insures that everytime I come up to fire I am in the habit of releasing safety. Engaging the safety in the ready also tells you if there is a problem with gun when safety won't engage.

30

READY POSITIONS

THERE MAY BE SITUATIONS WHERE YOU WOULD WANT TO ALREADY HAVE YOUR WEAPON IN YOUR HAND, BUT NOT YET ADVERTISE THE FACT.

YOU COULD HIDE IT BEHIND YOUR BODY, OR TUCK IT INSIDE YOUR COAT OR COVER IT WITH A JACKET OVER YOUR ARM.

MY GRANDFATHER, WHO WAS POLICE, WOULD APPROACH WITH PISTOL IN HAND AND HAND IN THE POCKET OF HIS COAT.

YOU CAN ALSO DO THE SAME THING WITH THE RIFLE, IF IT IS COMPACT ENOUGH. HIDE THE WEAPON BY BLADING YOUR BODY TO THE TARGET.

THE MAIN THING TO REMEMBER IS THAT YOUR READY POSITION IS DICTATED BY THE SITUATION AND ENVIRONMENT. REMAINING HIDDEN, OR APPEARING UNARMED, MAY BE TO MY ADVANTAGE DEPENDING ON THE SITUATION.

USE OF THE SAFETY

I LIKE TO ENGAGE THE SAFETY WHENEVER THE SIGHTS ARE OFF THE TARGET. SIGHTS ON THE TARGET- SAFETY OFF AND FINGER ON TRIGGER. SIGHTS OFF TARGET- FINGER OFF TRIGGER AND SAFETY ON. WORKING THE SAFETY OFF & ON PROVIDES A SYSTEM CHECK - IF SAFETY WON'T ENGAGE MY FIREARM HAS A PROBLEM. PLUS IT INSURES SAFETY IS OFF WHEN I ATTEMPT TO ENGAGE A TARGET.

31

DURING STRESSFUL SITUATIONS 90% OF SENSORY INPUT IS ACQUIRED VISUALLY. IF YOU DON'T KEEP EYES UP AND SEARCHING/SCANNING, OR ALLOW YOURSELF TO BECOME VISUALLY FIXATED ON ONE SPECIFIC THING, YOU WILL MISS SOMETHING IMPORTANT.

UNPREPARED OR POORLY TRAINED PERSONS WILL EXPERIENCE A CHAIN REACTION OF ESCALATING STRESS THAT INCREASES HEART RATE, CREATES A LOSS OF MOTOR SKILLS, AND RESTRICTS YOUR PERIPHERAL VISION AND DEPTH OF FOCUS. MANAGING STRESS IS ACCOMPLISHED BY CONTROLLING HEARTRATE.

BY UTILIZING VISUALIZATION YOU CAN PREDICT THREAT CUES, PROGRAM THE PROPER RESPONSE AND PREPARE BACK UP PLANS. MENTALLY YOU DISCARD INEFFECTIVE RESPONSES IN ADVANCE. BY LIMITING RESPONSE OPTIONS YOU REDUCE REACTION TIMES.

Auditory cues are generally reacted to quicker than visual cues, but they are NORMALLY NON-SPECIFIC and we can't shoot at sounds - except for military type engagements. What you should do is focus your attention on general movements - as opposed to waiting and watching one part of the body you should look for any MOVEMENT IN the whole body while at the same time paying attention to the hands. It is like looking at nothing so you can see everything.

MAINTAIN CONSTANT VISUAL CONTACT WITH YOUR ENVIRONMENT.

INSTRUCTING TIPS

BAD PERFORMANCE SHOULD BE IMPROVED BY SUPPLYING TECHNIQUES TO CORRECT PROBLEMS, NOT JUST POINTING OUT WHAT THE STUDENT IS DOING WRONG. INTENSIVE AND CONTINUOS PRESSURE HAS A NEGATIVE EFFECT ON MOST STUDENTS.

VERBAL AND NON-VERBAL FORMS OF COMMUNICATION MUST BE USED. YOU SHOULD DESCRIBE, DEMONSTRATE, DRILL IT DRY & THEN RUN IT LIVE FIRE.

SKILLS MUST BE OVERLEARNED, WHICH REQUIRES A VARIETY OF DRILLS TO REINFORCE THE SAME SKILLS.

RANKING INDIVIDUAL PERFORMANCE SEEMS TO HAVE A NEGATIVE EFFECT ON STUDENTS. AFTER FINISHING INSTRUCTION THE STUDENTS SHOULD FEEL AS THOUGH THEY HAVE ACHIEVED SUCCESS. AT THE SAME TIME THEY SHOULD UNDERSTAND THAT THERE IS MUCH TO PRACTICE, AND MORE TO LEARN, REGARDLESS OF THEIR SKILL LEVEL.

KEEP IN MIND THERE IS A LOT OF DIFFERENCES BETWEEN INSTRUCTORS AND TEACHERS. AN INSTRUCTOR CAN SHOW YOU HOW TO DO SPECIFIC TECHNIQUES OR ACCOMPLISH GENERAL TASKS. A TEACHER WILL ALSO EXPLAIN WHY YOU DO IT THAT WAY, WHEN AND WHERE PLUS ALTERNATIVE TECHNIQUES. A TEACHER WILL ALSO PASS ON THEORIES AND PRINCIPLES OF COMBAT THAT WILL APPLY TO A VARIETY OF SITUATIONS. THEY ALSO TEACH YOU TO THINK FOR YOURSELF.

IN THE BEGINNING AN INSTRUCTOR IS FINE BUT AT SOME POINT IN TIME YOU MUST SEEK OUT A TEACHER TO STUDY UNDER.

THE MORE TEACHERS, AND EXPOSURE TO IDEAS YOU RECEIVE, THE BETTER YOU WILL BE ABLE TO JUDGE WHAT YOU WILL USE WHEN YOUR LIFE DEPENDS ON THE CHOICES YOU MAKE.

OODA LOOP

OBSERVE THE THREAT, ORIENT TO THE THREAT, DECIDE ON A COURSE OF ACTION, ACT ON DECISION. WHOEVER PROCESSES THE CYCLE FIRST HAS THE ADVANTAGE.

ONEE THE DECISION HAS BEEN MADE YOU MUST PROCEDE AGGRESIVELY. Although YOU ARE ACTING IN DEFENSE YOU MUST APPLY OFFENSIVE TACTICS.

——————————————— ·· —— ·

CAPTAIN S.J. Cuthbert "WE SHALL FIGHT IN THE STREETS" CONDITIONS DICTATE METHODS: THE FITTEST SURVIVE, BECAUSE THEY UNDERSTAND AND ADAPT THEMSELVES TO THE CONDITIONS IN WHICH THEY LIVE.

STREET FIGHTING IS CARRIED ON IN UNIQUE, UNNATURAL CONDITIONS. It IS ABOVE ALL NECESSARY TO ANALIZE AND UNDERSTAND THE PECULIAR FEATURES OF GROUND WHICH GO to MAKE STREET FIGHTING SUCH A HIGHLY SKILLED FORM OF WARFARE.

——————————————— ·· — ·

THE GOOD FIGHTER IS ALWAYS TRYING TO FORCE HIS OPPONENT INTO CHOICE MAKING SITUATIONS THAT WILL SLOW THE OPPONENTS REACTIONS.

——————————— ·· —· ·

The time to launch an attack is when the opponent is preparing his attack. As Forrest said you get there first with the most.

——————————— ·· —

Action beats reaction but pro-action beats action. Being aware allows you to prepare your response in advance.

Also consider the difference between reaction time and response time. There isn't a lot we can do about reaction time but we can train to reduce our response time

TAKEN FROM JEFF GONZALES

34

OUR MENTAL STATE EFFECTS OUR PHYSICAL ACTIONS, BUT WE MUST ALSO REMBER THAT THE PHYSICAL INFLUENCES THE MENTAL. AN AGGRESSIVE MENTAL STATE MUST BE ACCOMPANIED BY AN AGGRESSIVE PHYSICAL STATE - UNLESS OF COURSE YOU ARE ATTEMPTING TO HIDE OR MASK YOUR INTENTIONS.

IF YOU ASSUME A FIGHTING STANCE IT WILL HELP PUT YOUR MIND INTO A COMBATIVE STATE.

MENTAL STATE

PHYSICAL ACTIONS

EACH INFLUENCES THE OTHER ONE

YOU CONTROL THE PHYSICAL BY CONTROLLING THE MIND, AND THE MORE YOU CONTROL THE MIND THE EASIER IT IS TO REGULATE THE PHYSICAL.

CONTROL THE SITUATION INSTEAD OF ALLOWING THE SITUATION TO CONTROL YOU. YOU MUST ACT INSTEAD OF ALWAYS REACTING

YOUR PHYSICAL CONDITIONING IS IMPORTANT TO THE ACT OF FIGHTING. ALTHOUGH MOST FIGHTS ARE SHORT IN DURATION THERE ARE ALWAYS EXCEPTIONS, AND EVEN SHORT DURATION FIGHTS ARE EXTREMELY PHYSICALLY DEMANDING.

EDUCATING NEUROMUSCULAR SKILLS

1) Acquire the feeling of being relaxed

2) Practice until this feeling can be reproduced at will and under all conditions

3) Reproduce the feeling during tension or stressful situations

FACTORS AFFECTING FIRING PLATFORM

- WEAK HAND & ELBOW UNDER THE RIFLE HAND SUPPORTS RIFLE BUT APPLIES NO GRIPPING PRESSURE
- STRONG HAND APPLIES PRESSURE TO REAR
- STRONG ELBOW UP TO CREATE POCKET FOR STOCK, UNLESS TACTICALLY UNSOUND
- BUTTSTOCK HIGH IN POCKET
- STOCKWELD - CHEEK ON STOCK, EYES ON THE TARGET
- BREATH CONTROL
- RELAXED NATURAL POINT OF AIM

ELEMENTS OF MARKSMANSHIP

- AIM - ACQUIRE A SIGHT PICTURE
- HOLD - MAINTAIN SIGHT PICTURE
- PRESS - SMOOTH BREAK ON THE TRIGGER

THE TRIGGER PRESS IS EXTREMELY IMPORTANT TO MAKING GOOD HITS. EVEN IF THE SIGHTS ARE PERFECTLY ALIGNED, IF YOU JERK THE TRIGGER YOU WON'T HIT. YOUR JOB IS TO FOCUS ON FRONT SIGHT AND PRESS THE TRIGGER. LET THE WEAPON DO ITS JOB AND FIRE WHEN IT IS READY.

CHECK NATURAL POINT OF AIM BY GETTING A SIGHT PICTURE, CLOSING YOUR EYES AND TAKING SEVERAL DEEP BREATHS. WHEN YOU OPEN YOUR EYES IF SIGHTS HAVE MOVED THEN REPOSITION YOUR BODY - DON'T JUST USE MUSCLES TO REALIGN THE SIGHTS.

BREATH CONTROL

- FULL LUNGS - INHALE, FILLING LUNGS COMPLETLY INCONSISTENT DEPENDING ON STRESS
- HALF FULL - HARD TO JUDGE WHAT IS HALF
- EMPTY LUNG - MOST CONSISTENT, ALLOWS BODY TO COLLASPE TO SKELETAL SUPPORT
- OR YOU CAN TAKE A POSITION, INHALE AND THEN EXHALE UNTIL THE SIGHTS ALIGN, HOLD THE BREATH & FIRE

THE KEY IS TO USE THE METHOD THAT FITS YOUR SITUATION

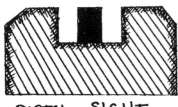

PISTOL SIGHT

FOCUS ON
THE FRONT
SIGHT!

AR SIGHT

DUE TO THE WAY THE EYE IS DESIGNED IT IS NOT POSSIBLE FOR US TO FOCUS ON THE REAR & FRONT SIGHT AND THE TARGET AT THE SAME TIME. THE SOLUTION IS TO FOCUS ON THE FRONT SIGHT, WHICH IS THE MIDDLE OF THOSE THREE POINTS.

BY FOCUSING ON THE FRONT SIGHT THE TARGET WILL APPEAR BLURRY BUT YOU WILL STILL BE ABLE TO KEEP THE FRONT SIGHT CENTERED ON THE TARGET. THE SAME APPLIES TO THE REAR SIGHT.

SO AS YOU BEGIN YOUR TRIGGER PRESS YOU SHOULD VISUALLY FOCUS ON THE FRONT SIGHT. THE AMOUNT OF PRECISION REQUIRED OF SIGHT PICTURE, AND AMOUNT OF FOCUS, IS DETERMINED BY THE DISTANCE TO THE TARGET. MORE DISTANCE - MORE PRECISION MORE DISTANCE - MORE TIME AVAILABLE TO ACQUIRE A MORE PRECISE SIGHT PICTURE.

IF YOUR SHOTS ARE SCATTERED ABOUT THE TARGET IT MEANS YOU ARE LOOKING AT THE TARGET INSTEAD OF FOCUSING ON THE FRONT SIGHT.
THE PROBLEM IS THAT THE EYE IS ATTRACTED TO MOVEMENT, SO IF THE THREAT IS MOVING - HIGHLY LIKELY DURING A FIGHT - WE HAVE A NATURAL TENDENCY TO LOOK AT THE THREAT. YOU MUST FIGHT THIS AND FOCUS ON THE FRONT SIGHT, REGARDLESS OF WHAT IS HAPPENING.

THERE IS NO WAY TO PREDICT WHAT AN ATTACKER WILL LOOK LIKE. THEY MAY BE OLD, YOUNG, MALE FEMALE OR ANY RACE. WE SHOULD ALSO BE PREPARED FOR THE HORRIBLE POSSIBILITY THAT IT MAY BE SOMEONE FAMILIAR TO US - FAMILY OR WELL KNOWN TO US FOR YEARS. IT COULD BE A NEIGHBOR OR FELLOW CO-WORKER.

REGARDLESS OF WHO IT IS WE MUST BE READY TO RESPOND TO ANYONE AT ANYTIME. YOU MUST BE ABLE TO INSTANTLY SWITCH INTO AN EMOTIONAL STATE THAT WILL ALLOW YOU TO DEFEND WITH AGGRESSIVE ACTIONS.

NOTES FROM CLASS WITH GABE SUAREZ

WHEN APPLYING TACTICS YOU MUST HAVE A SPECIFIC MISSION OR OBJECTIVE - DON'T LOSE SIGHT OF YOUR PURPOSE DURING THE FIGHT.

TACTICS ARE 50% HUNTING - 50% BEING HUNTED.

THE CURRENCY OF TACTICS IS PERSONAL RISK.

HAGAKURE, THE BOOK OF THE SAMURAI
YAMAMOTO TSUNETOMO

It is a mistake to put forth effort and obtain some understanding and then stop at that. At first putting forth great effort to be sure that you have grasped the basics, then practicing so that they may come to fruition is something that will never stop for your whole lifetime. Do not rely on following the degree of understanding that you have discovered, but simply think, "THAT IS NOT ENOUGH."

One should search throughout his whole life how best to follow the way. And he should study, setting his mind to work without putting things off. Within this is the Way.

"I'm a coward." "At that time I'll probably RUN" "How frightening" "How painful" These are words that should never be said in jest, on a whim, or without thinking. If a person with understanding hears such things he will see to the bottom of the speaker's heart.

38

FACTORS DETERMINING WOUND POTENTIAL
     MASS OF BULLET   VELOCITY OF BULLET
     DIAMETER OF BULLET   DEFORMATION OF BULLET
     BULLET SHAPE

INCAPACITATION FACTORS
     BULLET PLACEMENT
     TISSUE DAMAGE
     PSYCHOLOGICAL RESPONSE

FOR IMMEDIATE RESULTS THE BULLET MUST DAMAGE THE CENTRAL NERVOUS SYSTEM. BLOOD LOSS MAY TAKE SEVERAL SECONDS TO MINUTES.

THE BULLET CAUSES "PERMANENT CAVITY" DAMAGE BY TISSUE DESTRUCTION. "TEMPORARY" EFFECTS ARE DUE TO THE ELASTIC NATURE OF TISSUE, AND MAY NOT BE PERMANENT AND DEPEND A LOT ON THE VELOCITY OF BULLET. THE HYDRAULIC SHOCK WAVE CAN CAUSE PERMANENT DAMAGE SOME DISTANCE FROM THE WOUND TRACK.
FRAGMENTATION OF THE BULLET, AND BONE PARTICLES ADD TO DAMAGE. THE MORE FLUID IN THE TISSUE THE MORE EFFECT THE HYDRALICS WILL HAVE.

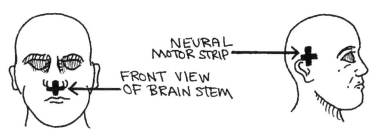

NEURAL MOTOR STRIP ➤
FRONT VIEW OF BRAIN STEM ➤

IMMEDIATE INCAPACITATION IS ACHEIVED BY DESTROYING THE BRAIN STEM (MEDULLA OBLONGTA) OR THE NEURAL MOTOR STRIPS ON EITHER SIDE OF THE BRAIN.
BOTH ARE DIFFICULT TO ACHEIVE WITH A PISTOL ROUND SINCE THEY ARE EASILY DEFLECTED

IN COMBAT THE MAJORITY OF LETHAL WOUNDS OCCUR TO THE HEAD AND NECK REGIONS.

39

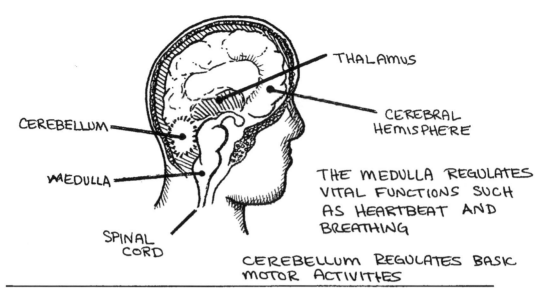

THALAMUS

CEREBRAL HEMISPHERE

CEREBELLUM

MEDULLA

SPINAL CORD

THE MEDULLA REGULATES VITAL FUNCTIONS SUCH AS HEARTBEAT AND BREATHING

CEREBELLUM REGULATES BASIC MOTOR ACTIVITIES

TO INSURE PENETRATION INTO THE BRAIN CAVITY ON A FRONTAL SHOT IT MUST BE PLACED IN THE OCULAR CAVITY, WHICH IS BELOW THE EYEBROWS AND ABOVE THE NOSE

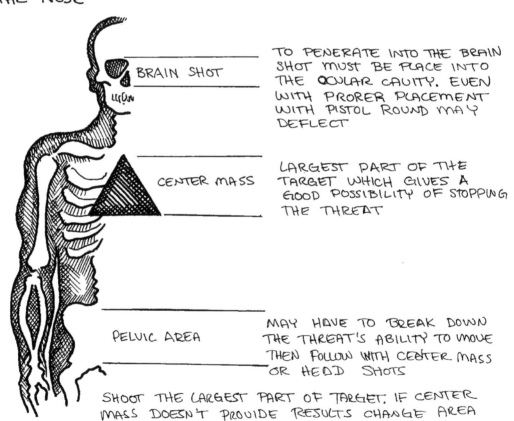

BRAIN SHOT

TO PENERATE INTO THE BRAIN SHOT MUST BE PLACE INTO THE OCULAR CAVITY. EVEN WITH PRORER PLACEMENT WITH PISTOL ROUND MAY DEFLECT

CENTER MASS

LARGEST PART OF THE TARGET WHICH GIVES A GOOD POSSIBILITY OF STOPPING THE THREAT

PELVIC AREA

MAY HAVE TO BREAK DOWN THE THREAT'S ABILITY TO MOVE THEN FOLLOW WITH CENTER MASS OR HEAD SHOTS

SHOOT THE LARGEST PART OF TARGET; IF CENTER MASS DOESN'T PROUIDE RESULTS CHANGE AREA BUT ENGAGE UNTIL TARGET IN NO LONGER A THREAT OR LEAVES.

DEPENDING ON WHAT ANGLE THE
THREAT IS YOU MAY HAVE TO
ADJUST YOUR POINT OF AIM

FRONT
SHOT

ANGLE
SHOT

IF THE THREAT IS WEARING
LOOSE OR BULKY CLOTHING
IT WILL BE MORE DIFFICULT
TO PLACE SHOTS PROPERLY.

IT WILL BE HARD TO SEE ON THE THREAT
WHERE YOUR SHOTS HIT, SO YOU HAVE
TO KNOW WHERE SIGHTS ARE WHEN THE
SHOT FIRES.

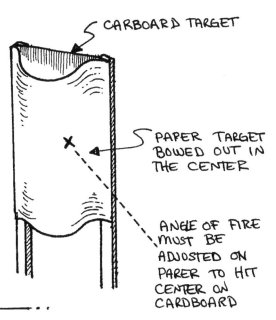

CARBOARD TARGET

BY USING A PAPER TARGET
WHICH IS BOWED OUT IN
THE CENTER YOU CAN GET
AN IDEA OF HOW TO ADJUST
YOUR POINT OF AIM TO
STILL HIT VITAL AREA OF
THE CARDBOARD BACKER.

THIS SIMULATES A 3-D
TARGET, AND WHERE YOU
SHOOT TO PENETRATE INTO
THE CENTER MASS.

PAPER TARGET
BOWED OUT IN
THE CENTER

ANGLE OF FIRE
MUST BE
ADJUSTED ON
PAPER TO HIT
CENTER ON
CARDBOARD

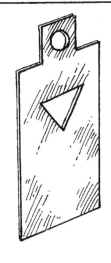

"NEGATIVE" TARGETS ARE ALSO USEFUL.
THE IDEA IS TO PUT SHOTS INTO THE
HOLES, OR NEGATIVE AREAS, NOT THE
SURROUNDING AREA. THIS SOMETIMES
WILL WORK GOOD TO BREAK PEOPLE
OF THE HABIT OF LOOKING TO SEE
WHERE THEIR SHOTS GO

41

PISTOL MODIFICATIONS

The 3 most important elements to a fighting pistol are sights you can see, a general dehorning job and a crisp trigger (4.5 lbs is recommended) Sights should be easily seen by your eyes, and be smooth enough so that manipulating the weapon doesn't cut your hands up. A low mount thumb safety works well for smaller hands, and beavertails keep the web between thumb and first finger from getting beat up.

TRITIUM SIGHTS ARE NICE, BUT CERTAINLY NOT A NECESSITY.

CONTOURED REAR SIGHTS KEEP HANDS FROM BEING CUT UP.

COMMANDER HAMMERS KEEP HANDS FROM BEING BITTEN

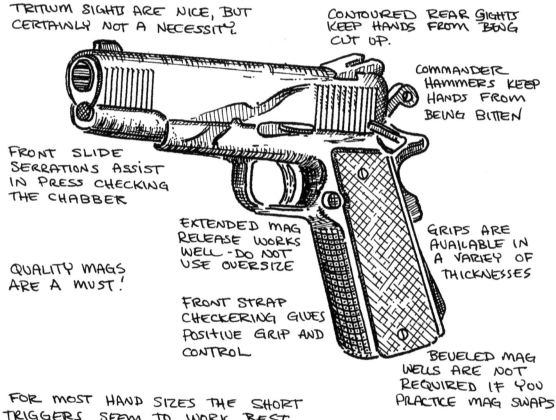

FRONT SLIDE SERRATIONS ASSIST IN PRESS CHECKING THE CHABBER

EXTENDED MAG RELEASE WORKS WELL - DO NOT USE OVERSIZE

GRIPS ARE AVAILABLE IN A VARIETY OF THICKNESSES

QUALITY MAGS ARE A MUST!

FRONT STRAP CHECKERING GIVES POSITIVE GRIP AND CONTROL

BEVELED MAG WELLS ARE NOT REQUIRED IF YOU PRACTICE MAG SWAPS

FOR MOST HAND SIZES THE SHORT TRIGGERS SEEM TO WORK BEST

MAINSPRING HOUSINGS, FLAT-WEDGED-OR CURVED-ARE A PERSONAL CHOICE AND YOU SHOULD USE WHICHEVER FITS YOUR HAND BEST.

SIMPLICITY IS BEST, AND THE KEY TO REALIABILITY. YOU MUST DEMAND 100% FROM A WEAPON USED TO DEFEND YOUR LIFE!

COMMUNICATION

Vebral commands, Along with the prescence of a firearm, can be extremely effective. We also will need to communicate with the people arownd us or other members of family.

Succesful communications require

Clear, concise and accurate messages
The recipient must be capable of
understanding the message. Remember
communications are a two way street
and you must respond to confirm
recipt of message.

Screaming makes it difficult for others to understand you, plus it is a manifestation of fear. Whispering makes it difficult for others to understand you, and normally carries further than you think.

SPEECH CONSUMES A LARGE PART OF THE BRAIN, AND THERE ARE TIMES WHEN YOU WON'T WANT TO TAKE THE TIME TO SPEAK OR GIVEAWAY YOUR POSITION. OFTEN TIMES IF YOU ARE IN THE MIDDLE OF SPEAKING YOU WILL HESITATE AND WON'T FIRE UNTIL YOU HAVE FINISHED SPEAKING, EVEN WHEN THERE IS A NEED TO SHOOT. YOU CAN ALSO MAKE SOMEONE SPEAK, FOR EXAMPLE GET THEM TO ANSWER A QUESTION, CREATING A WINDOW FOR YOU TO ACT WHEN THEY DELAY REACTION DURING SPEECH.

ALSO REMEMBER A LOT OF OUR COMMUNICATION IS NON-VERBAL. BODY LANGUAGE - HOW WE MOVE, FACIAL EXPRESSIONS, HOW WE PERFORM ACTIONS - TRANSMITS A LOT OF INFORMATION. YOU CAN EXAMINE SOMEONE PERFORMING A TASK AND JUDGE FAIRLY WELL WHETHER OR NOT THEY ARE EXPERIENCED OR COMPETANT AT WHAT THEY ARE DOING.

TALKING TO OURSELVES IS ALSO A GOOD WAY TO LEARN A NEW TECHNIQUE OR PRACTICE YOUR SKILLS. STUDIES HAVE SHOWN THAT VERBALLY COACHING YOURSELF IS INGRAINED INTO YOUR SUBCONCIOUS AND WE RETAIN MORE MATERIAL MENTALLY.

BALANCE - SPEED & ACCURACY

ONE OF THE MOST DIFFICULT THINGS TO LEARN WHEN TRAINING TO FIGHT WITH FIREARMS IS THE BALANCE BETWEEN SPEED AND ACCURACY. MOST STUDENTS HAVE THE TENDENCY TO GO TOO FAST - SHOOTING BEFORE THEY HAVE A SIGHT PICTURE AND JERKING ON THE TRIGGER AS THEY ANTICIPATE RECOIL, ATTEMPTING TO SHOOT QUICKER. THE OTHER TENDENCY IS TO GO TOO SLOW, ATTEMPTING TO MAKE EACH SHOT PERFECT. THE IDEA IS TO GO AS QUICKLY AS POSSIBLE, SINCE WE ARE IN A LIFE THREATENING SITUATION, AND STILL MAKE GOOD HITS TO STOP THE THREAT. 2 GOOD HITS WILL DO THE JOB QUICKER THAN FIRING 6 SHOTS AND ONLY GETTING A GOOD HIT AT THE LAST.

A LARGE PORTION OF TRAINING WITH FIREARMS IS LEARNING WHAT IS AN ACCEPTABLE SIGHT PICTURE AND TRIGGER PRESS FOR THE DISTANCES INVOLVED, INCLUDING EXTENDED DISTANCES. THEN YOU MUST MENTALLY REGULATE YOURSELF AND APPLY YOUR SKILLS, ON DEMAND, IN ANY CIRCUMSTANCES.

"OUT OF EVERY 100 MEN, TEN SHOULDN'T EVEN BE HERE. EIGHTY ARE JUST TARGETS. NINE ARE THE REAL FIGHTERS, AND WE ARE LUCKY TO HAVE THEM, FOR THEY MAKE THE BATTLE. AH, BUT THE ONE, ONE IS A WARRIOR. AND HE WILL BRING THE OTHERS BACK."   HERICLETUS, 500 BC

According to research BY THE FBI of ALL PEOPLE SHOT 10% die. OF all people stabbed 30% die. INJURIES SUSTAINED by LE OFFICERS - 30.2% from firearms, 30.5% by edged weapons. IN most fatal cuttings depth of wound is 1-1½ inches through rib cage. most defenders fail to see knife until after attack has begun. KNIVES are concealable, silent, never malfunction or run out of ammo and can be used by almost anyone.

44

CROSS DRAW HOLSTERS HAVE A COUPLE OF DISADVANTAGES. IT IS SLIGHTLY SLOWER THAN THE STRONG SIDE HOLSTER. IF THE THREAT IS CLOSE IT IS EASY FOR THEM TO JAM YOU, PREVENTING YOU FROM GETTING THE PISTOL INTO THE FIGHT. IF YOU'RE NOT CAREFUL YOU CAN SWEEP BYSTANDERS WITH THE MUZZLE AS YOU PRESENT THE PISTOL. POSITION OF THE HOLSTER MAKES IT EASIER FOR SOMEONE TO DISARM YOU.

THE SHOULDER HOLSTER HAS THE SAME DISADVANTAGES.

THE STRONG SIDE HOLSTER IS THE BEST OPTION.

IT IS EASIEST TO PROTECT

IT IS SHORTEST MOVEMENT TO THE TARGET

QUALITY HOLSTER, BELT AND MAG POUCH ARE ESSENTIAL - DON'T SCRIMP ON COST!

HOLSTER MUST BE HELD TIGHTLY AGAINST THE BODY AND NOT SLIDE AROUND.

HOLSTER SHOULD BE REINFORCED AT THE MOUTH SO IT DOESN'T COLLASPE WHEN PISTOL IS DRAWN AND WEAPON CAN BE REHOLSTERED WITHOUT USE OF THE SUPPORT HAND.

MAG POUCH IS CARRIED ON SUPPORT SIDE OF THE BODY

SUPPORT HAND ACCESSES SPARE MAGS FOR RELOADS

INSIDE THE WAISTBAND HOLSTERS ARE GREAT FOR CONCEALMENT

45

CONCEPTION OF DEFENSE – VON Clausewitz

What is defense in conception? The warding off a blow. What is then its characteristic? The state of expectancy (or waiting for the blow)

But as we must return the enemy's blows if we are really to carry on battle on our side, therefore this offensive act in defensive war takes place more or less under the general title defensive... We can, therefore, in a defensive campaign fight offensively ...

What is the object of defense? To preserve. To preserve is easier to acquire; from which follows at once that the means on both sides being supposed equal, the defensive is easier than the offensive.

If the defensive is the stronger form of conducting war, but has a negative object, it follows of itself that we must only make use of it so long as our weakness compells us to do so, and that we must give up that form as soon as we feel strong enough to aim at that positive object.

... the natural course in war to begin with the defensive, and to end with the offensive.

... three which appear to us of decisive importance: surprise, advantage of ground, and the attack from several quarters.

"The SPIRIT TO BE ABLE TO WIN NO MATTER WHAT THE WEAPON   THIS IS THE TEACHING OF MY SCHOOL OF HEIHŌ.   MUSASHI

WHEN MUSASHI SPEAKS OF FIGHTING WITH 2 SWORDS HE IS REFERRING TO USING ALL OF ONES FACILITIES - BOTH MENTAL AND PHYSICAL.

46

The Human Body HAS 3 ENERGY SOURCES

Adenosine Triphosphate/Phosphocreative (ATP/PC) consists of energy stored in muscles. Used during high strength activities. 100% performance for 10-15 seconds then approx 50% decrease in output

Lactic Acid System (LAS) Provides about 45 seconds of intermediate level performance after ATP/PC burns off.

Aerobic System (AS) final and dominate feul system. Oxygen, carbohydrates and free fatty acids combine for long output. Performance depends on body conditioning. Length of time decreases output.

The optimum heart rate for complex motor skills, reaction times, and cognitive skills is 115-145 BPM.

KINESTHETIC PERCEPTION - BRUCE LEE
The ability to feel contraction and relaxation, to know what a muscle is doing, is called kinesthetic perception. Kinesthetic perception is developed by consciously placing the body and its parts in a given position and getting the feel of it. This feeling of balance or imbalance, grace or awkwardness, serves as a constant guide to the body as it moves.

Relaxation is a physical state but it is controlled by the mental state.

"FEAR IS HAVING NO FAITH"
KEN GOOD

AIMED VS INSTINCTIVE SHOOTING

- AIMED - USING SIGHTS TO ALIGN BORE OF WEAPON WITH THE TARGET AND SHOOTER'S EYES

- INSTINCTIVE - RELYING ON NATURAL POINTING ABILITY TO INDEX SIGHTS ONTO THE TARGET

INSTINCTIVE SHOOTING IS MORE DIFFICULT TO LEARN, REQUIRING MORE TIME AND EFFORT TO DEVELOPE ANY DEGREE OF SKILL. IT IS NOT AS ACCURATE AS SIGHTED FIRE. INSTINCTIVE SHOOTING ALSO DOESN'T WORK WELL ON MULTIPLE TARGETS OR TARGETS AT SEVERE ANGLES AND DIFFERENT PLANES FROM THE SHOOTER SUCH AS WHEN ELEVATED OR LOWER LEVEL.

SIGHTED FIRE WORKS IN ALL SITUATIONS, IS MORE ACCURATE AND IS EASIER AND QUICKER TO LEARN. EVEN AT EXTREMELY CLOSE DISTANCES THE SIGHTS ARE USED TO SOME EXTENT. DISTANCE DETERMINES THE PRECISION REQUIRED IN THE SIGHT PICTURE TO GURANTEE HITS.

DURING VIOLENT ENCOUNTERS THE MAJORITY OF OUR INPUT IS OBTAINED VISUALLY. IF YOU DON'T USE THE SIGHTS AND THE EYES IT IS LIKE BOXING WITH YOUR EYES CLOSED.

IF YOU TRY TO TRAIN WITH BOTH SIGHTED AND UNSIGHTED FIRE IT WILL CAUSE CONFUSION, AND DELAY YOUR RESPONSE, WHILE YOU DECIDE ON WHICH METHOD TO EMPLOY.

OUR MIND FUNCTIONS MUCH FASTER THAN THE BODY IS EVER CAPABLE OF PERFORMING, ESPECIALLY WHEN PEFORMING SEQUENCED PROCEDURES UNDER STRESS. WHILE YOUR BODY IS STILL ON STEP 3 YOUR BRAIN IS ON STEP 10. THEN WE THINK WE ARE BEHIND, START TRYING TO GO FASTER, AND END UP FUMBLING THE TASK AND MAKING MISTAKES, WHICH FRUSTRATES THE MIND EVEN MORE. YOU MUST REGULATE THE MIND SO IT ALLOWS THE BODY TO OPERATE AT THE SPEED IT CAN PERFORM COMFORTABLY.

DISTANCE AND FIGHTING

DISTANCE IS A MAJOR FACTOR WHEN DECIDING HOW TO SOLVE A LETHAL CONFRONTATION. REGARDLESS OF WHAT WEAPON WE ARE FIGHTING WITH — THE DISTANCE BETWEEN US AND THE THREAT? WHAT OPTIONS ARE AT OUR DISPOSAL TO SOLVE THE PROBLEM?

DISTANCE EQUALS TIME. NORMALLY THE MORE DISTANCE THE MORE TIME, AND THE MORE OPTIONS. IF THERE IS DISTANCE, AND TIME, I MIGHT BE ABLE TO AVOID THE FIGHT COMPLETELY. IF THERE IS NO DISTANCE, AND NO TIME, THERE MAY NOT EVEN BE A CHANCE TO GET MY WEAPON OUT AND IN THE FIGHT UNTIL I CAN CREATE TIME AND DISTANCE. BY CREATING DISTANCE I CAN CREATE TIME.

IF THERE ARE DISTANCE AND TIME I WOULD WANT TO USE COVER FOR PROTECTION. I MAY BE ABLE TO USE MY COVER AS AN AID TO ACCURACY, STABILIZING MY WEAPON ON THE COVER TO MAKE A LONGER SHOT FROM EXTENDED DISTANCES. AT EXTREMELY CLOSE DISTANCES I MAY HAVE TO SHOOT FROM WHATEVER POSITION I FIND MYSELF IN, INCLUDING FIGHTING FROM THE GROUND.

TO UNDERSTAND WHAT OUR OPTIONS ARE WE MUST DISCOVER WHAT AMOUNT OF TIME RESPONSES REQUIRE. THIS DOESN'T MEAN TRAINING FOR SPEED, BUT TIMING YOURSELF SO YOU KNOW HOW LONG A CERTAIN ACTION WILL TAKE. THEN YOU KNOW WHAT YOU CAN OR CAN'T GET DONE WHEN AN ATTACKER, ARMED WITH A KNIFE, IS ONLY 20 FT AWAY, WHICH WE KNOW FROM STUDY HE CAN COVER 20 FT IN LESS THAN 1.5 SECONDS. IF IT TAKES ME 1.5 SECONDS TO GET MY WEAPON OUT, PLUS .25 SECOND TO SIMPLY REACT, THEN I AM ALREADY BEHIND.

UNDERSTANDING THE RELATIONSHIP BETWEEN DISTANCE AND TIME IS CRITICAL TO MAKING THE RIGHT CHOICE.

BRUCE LEE - TAO OF JEET KUNE DO

BODY FEEL IN ATTACK

PHYSICAL

- CONSIDER BALANCE BEFORE, DURING, AFTER
- CONSIDER AIRTIGHT DEFENSE BEFORE, DURING, AND AFTER
- LEARN TO CUT INTO THE OPPONENT'S MOVING TOOLS AND LIMIT THE GROUND FOR HIS AGILITY
- CONSIDER ALIVENESS

MENTAL

- ALLOW THE "WANTING" TO SCORE THE TARGET
- BACK YOURSELF BY ALERTNESS, AWARENESS TO SUDDEN CHANGE TO DEFENSE OR COUNTER
- KEEP A NEUTRAL WATCHFULNESS AT ALL TIMES, ALWAYS OBSERVING THE OPPONENT'S ACTIONS AND REACTIONS TO FIT IN
- LEARN TO RELAY DESTRUCTIVENESS (LOOSENESS, SPEED, COMPACTNESS, EASE) TO MOVING TARGETS

USE ALL MEANS AND BE BOUND BY NONE. USE ANY TECHNIQUE OR MEANS WHICH SERVE ITS END.

READY POSITION - THE POSITION ADOPTED SHOULD BE THE ONE FOUND TO GIVE MAXIMUM EASE AND RELAXATION, COMBINED WITH SMOOTHNESS OF MOVEMENT AT ALL TIMES.

TRAINING IS MORE A MATTER OF LEARNING COORDINATION, TRAINING THE NERVOUS SYSTEM, NOT A QUESTION OF TRAINING THE MUSCLES. THE TRANSITION TO THE HIGHEST PERFECTION IS A PROCESS OF DEVELOPING THE CONNECTIONS IN THE NERVOUS SYSTEM.

TRAINING FOR SKILL (COORDINATION) IS PURELY A MATTER OF FORMING PROPER CONNECTIONS IN THE NERVOUS SYSTEM THROUGH PERFECT PRACTICE.

THE MASTERY OF PROPER FUNDAMENTALS AND THEIR PROGRESSIVE APPLICATION IS THE SECRET OF BEING A GREAT FIGHTER.

BREATHING, AND CONTROLLING BREATH, CALMS THE MIND. WHEN THE MIND IS CALM IT CAN DIRECT THE BODY. WHEN THE BODY PERFORMS PROPERLY IT ALLOWS THE MIND TO STAY CALM. KEEP BREATHING.

────────────── .

IN A ONE ON ONE FIGHT THERE ARE THREE POSSIBLE OUTCOMES

- YOU WIN
- HE WINS
- YOU BOTH KILL EACHOTHER

ONLY ONE OF THESE IS ACCEPTABLE. WHEN YOU HAVE MULTIPLE OPPONENTS THE OUTCOMES STACK AGAINST YOU EVEN MORE.

THE LONGER THE FIGHT LASTS THE MORE DIFFICULT VICTORY BECOMES. END THE FIGHT AS QUICKLY AS POSSIBLE, WITH THE LEAST AMOUNT OF EFFORT NECESSARY.

────────────── .

ALTHOUGH THERE IS A DISTINCT DIFFERENCE BETWEEN A COMBATIVE AND DEFENSIVE MINDSET, AND PHYSICAL ACTIONS, IT IS RARELY DISCUSSED. IN A DEFENSIVE ENCOUNTER YOUR JOB IS TO ESCAPE WITHOUT HARM, USING YOUR WEAPON ONLY IF THERE IS NO OTHER ALTERNATIVE. IN A COMBATIVE SITUATION YOU MUST ATTACK WITHOUT RESERVATION, APPLYING AGGRESIVE ACTIONS TO DESTROY THE THREAT(S). SOMETIMES THE LINES BETWEEN DEFENSIVE AND OFFENSIVE ARE CROSSED SEVERAL TIMES IN ONE CONFLICT. IT MAY BEGIN AS A DEFENSIVE ENCOUNTER, THEN THE ONLY OPTION TO VICTORY BECOME OFFENSIVE ACTIONS. VICTORY IS NEVER ACHEIVED THROUGH DEFENSE. YOU MUST TRAIN FOR BOTH DEFENSE AND OFFENSE TO BE PREPARED FOR ALL.

3 SECOND PRINCIPLE

THE 3 SECON RULE APPLIES TO A VARIETY OF SITUATIONS. FOR INSTANCE IT NORMALLY TAKES ABOUT 3 SECONDS, OR A LITTLE LESS, FOR SOMEONE TO SEE YOU, DECIDE THEY ARE GOING TO ATTACK, AND THEN INITIATE THEIR ATTACK. SO IF YOU WERE MOVING FROM COVER TO COVER YOU WOULD WANT TO LIMIT YOUR EXPOSURE IN THE OPEN TO NO MORE THAN 3 SECONDS.

TRY NOT TO REMAIN IN THE SAME LOCATION FOR LONGER THAN 3 SECONDS. IN AN ACTIVE FIGHT YOU MIGHT NOT WANT TO LEAVE YOUR FLASHLIGHT ON FOR LONGER THAN 3 SECONDS. WORKING COVER WHERE THERE IS INCOMING FIRE YOU WILL WANT TO LIMIT YOUR EXPOSURE TIME. (TOM GIVENS TEACHES THIS)

DEPENDING ON YOUR ENVIRONMENT, AND OPPONENTS, IT MIGHT BE THE 2 SECOND RULE. APPLY LOGIC.

TACTICAL GUIDELINES

- USE YOUR EYES AND EARS
- NEVER TURN YOUR BACK ON ANYTHING YOU HAVEN'T CHECKED OUT
- MAXIMIZE THE DISTANCE BETWEEN YOU AND THE THREAT
- MINIMIZE YOURSELF AS A TARGET
- MAINTAIN BALANCE - PHYSICALLY AND MENTALLY
- FOCUS ON THE FRONT SIGHT- PRESS TRIGGER SMOOTHLY
- ALWAYS CHEAT! ALWAYS WIN! (CLINT SMITH)

THE HEAD IS HELD ERRECT SO YOU DON'T RESTRICT AIR FLOW THROUGH THE NECK. TILT HEAD SLIGHTLY DOWN AT THE CHIN SO PARIPHERAL VISION WORKS BEST.

FEET SHOULD BE SHOULDER WIDTH APART. TOO WIDE AND IT'S DIFFICULT TO MOVE; TOO NARROW AND YOU ARE UNSTABLE. LEFT FOOT IS POINTED TOWARDS THE THREAT WITH 60% OF WEIGHT ON IT. RIGHT FOOT IS POSITIONED WITH THE TOES EVEN WITH HEEL OF LEFT FOOT. RIGHT FOOT IS SLIGHTLY AT AN ANGLE. THE HEEL OF THE RIGHT FOOT SHOULD BE LIFTED SLIGHTLY OFF THE GROUND SO THAT YOU CAN MOVE QUICKLY, AND THIS WILL SHIFT WEIGHT TO THE LEFT FOOT, WHICH HELPS WITH THE RECOVERY OF RECOIL, AND GIVES YOU AN AGGRESSIVE FIGHTING STANCE.

WITH THE LEFT FOOT LEADING THE UPPER BODY IS ANGLED. THIS ALLOWS THE RIGHT ARM TO BE STRAIGHT AND LEFT ARM

TO HELP ON RECOIL YOU NEED TO BUILD ISOMETRIC TENSION BETWEEN THE ARMS. WITH THE RIGHT ARM YOU PUSH FORWARD SLIGHTLY FROM THE SHOULDER. WITH THE LEFT ARM PULL BACK WITH THE SAME AMOUNT OF TENSION. THIS HELPS WITH THE RECOIL RECOVERY.

THE FIGHTING STANCE IS THE SAME REGARDLESS OF WHETHER I'M FIGHTNG WITH HANDS, KNIFE, IMPACT INSTRUMENT OR FIREARMS. WHEN FIGHTNG WITH FIREARMS YOU MAY FIND YOURSELF FIRING FROM A VARIETY OF POSITIONS, BUT IF POSSIBLE THIS STANCE WORKS BEST.

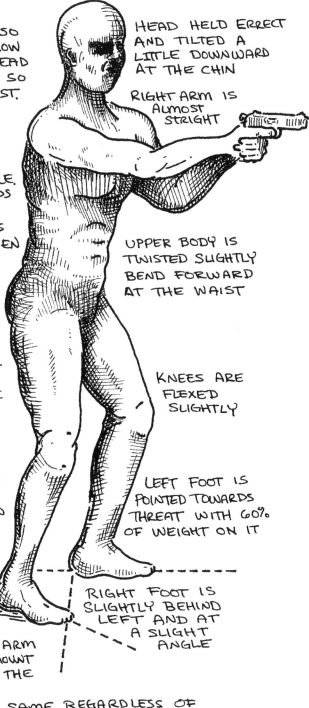

HEAD HELD ERRECT AND TILTED A LITTLE DOWNWARD AT THE CHIN

RIGHT ARM IS ALMOST STRIGHT

UPPER BODY IS TWISTED SLIGHTLY BEND FORWARD AT THE WAIST

KNEES ARE FLEXED SLIGHTLY

LEFT FOOT IS POINTED TOWARDS THREAT WITH 60% OF WEIGHT ON IT

RIGHT FOOT IS SLIGHTLY BEHIND LEFT AND AT A SLIGHT ANGLE

WITH THE CARBINE THE STANCE IS THE SAME. ALTHOUGH WITH SOME PEOPLE THE PRIMARY SIDE FOOT MAY BE A LITTLE MORE TO THE REAR, WITH THE BODY BLADED MORE.

ELBOW OF THE SHOOTING HAND SHOULD BE HELD UP, TO CREATE POCKET FOR THE STOCK, EXCEPT WHEN WORKING OUT TO THE RIGHT OF COVER IT IS A GOOD IDEA NOT TO EXTEND IT OUT PAST COVER. WITH THE LIGHT RECOIL OF .223 THIS ISN'T A PROBLEM.

THE SUPPORT SIDE ELBOW SHOULD BE HELD DOWN, AS CLOSE TO UNDERNEATH THE WEAPON AS POSSIBLE. WHEN ENGAGING MULTIPLE TARGETS YOU CAN TRANSITION FROM TARGET TO TARGET SLIGHTLY QUICKER IF THE SUPPORT ELBOW IS HELD OUT SLIGHTLY TO THE SIDE. THEN YOU CAN USE THE SUPPORT ARM TO PULL OR PUSH THE MUZZLE LEFT OR RIGHT. THIS IS QUICKER SINCE I DON'T HAVE TO MOVE MY WHOLE UPPER BODY.

THE SHOOTING HAND SHOULD APPLY A SMALL AMOUNT OF PRESSURE TO THE REAR TO SEAT STOCK INTO SHOULDER. THE SUPPORT HAND CRADLES THE RIFLE WITHOUT APPLY GRIPPING PRESSURE, OR LIGH PRESSURE AT MOST.

IT IS A GOOD IDEA TO PICK UP THE SLING IN THE LITTLE FINGER OF THE SUPPORT HAND. IF IT IS DANGLING DOWN IT COULD SNAG OR CATCH ON SOMETHING IN YOUR ENVIRONMENT.

THERE ARE A LOT OF DISADVANTAGES TO "TACTICAL" SLINGS, THOSE THAT LOOP AROUND YOUR BODY, TYING YOU TO THE RIFLE. THERE ARE SOME SHOOTING POSITIONS THAT WON'T WORK. IF YOU HAVE A STUCK CASE YOU HAVE TO UNSLING TO CLEAR IT, AND THERE ARE RETENTION ISSUES. THIS IS ALL DISCUSSED IN DETAIL LATER.

AR CONFIGURATION

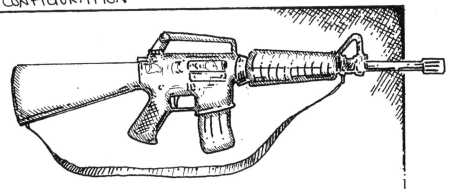

WHEN IT COMES TO THE AR I'VE FOUND THAT SIMPLICITY IS THE KEY. STARTING WITH THE STOCK - A FIXED STOCK IS BEST. THE COLLASPABLE STOCK CAN COME APART, HAS A SMALL HEEL WHICH DOESN'T FIT INTO THE SHOULDER WELL, MOST PEOPLE - WHEN UNDER STRESS - FAIL TO EXTEND THE STOCK, AND WHEN CLEARING A STUCK CASE IT MUST BE COLLASPED, THE CASE CLEARED, AND THEN EXTENDED - WHICH CONSUMES MORE TIME. I PREFER THE A-1 STOCK BECAUSE IT IS ABOUT A ½ INCH SHORTER THAN THE A-2 STOCK WHICH WAS DEVELOPED FOR COMPETITION SHOOTING. THE SHORTER A-1 MAKES A QUICK HANDLING RIFLE.

I THINK A SIMPLE 1 INCH SLING IS BEST. (THIS IS DISCUSSED THROUGHOUT THE BOOK.)

IRON SIGHTS ARE BEST. THEY WORK WELL A SHORTER RANGES AND EXTENDED RANGES. MOST RIFLE FIGHTS TAKE PLACE AT 30 yds AND CLOSER, BUT WE KNOW THERE IS A CHANCE WE MIGHT HAVE TO MAKE LONGER DISTANCE SHOTS. A TRADITIONAL SCOPE MAGNIFIES TOO MUCH AT CLOSE DISTANCES, WHICH MAKES ACQUIRING A SIGHT PICTURE SLOWER, AND THEY RESTRICT YOUR ABILITY TO SEE AROUND YOU WHEN THE EYE IS FOCUSED ON THE EYE PIECE OF THE SCOPE. "RED DOT" SCOPES DON'T WORK AS WELL AT EXTENDED DISTANCES. ANY THING WITH BATTERIES ISN'T GOOD SINCE THE BATTERIES CAN GOOD DOWN, AND PROBABLY WHEN YOUR LIFE DEPENDS ON IT. IF YOU DO HAVE OPTICS YOU SHOULD HAVE IRON SIGHTS AS BACK-UP SYSTEM.

CONTINUED NEXT PAGE

SOMETIMES OPTICS ARE REQUIRED, FOR SPECIFIC APPLICATIONS OR TO COMPENSATE FOR VISION HANDICAPS, BUT FOR GENERAL USE IRON SIGHTS ARE BEST. FOR THE REAR SIGHT I USE ONE WHICH HAS THE SAME PLANE FOR BOTH LARGE AND SMALL APPERTURES. ON THE STANDARD REAR SIGHT THE SMALL HOLE RAISES THE POINT OF IMPACT. IT WAS DESIGNED TO SHOOT AT LONG DISTANCES AND IMPROVES ACCURACY WHILE COMPENSATING FOR BULLET DROP. I TEND TO USE THE SMALL HOLE ALL THE TIME, ALTHOUGH WITH SOME SHOOTERS THEY SAY IT SLOWS THEM DOWN WHEN TRYING TO SHOOT QUICKLY AT CLOSE DISTANCES.

I DON'T THINK TRITIUM SIGHTS ARE NECESSARY.

A WEAPON MOUNTED LIGHT IS A GOOD ADDITION. IT SHOULD BE CONFIGURED WITH MOMENTARY AND CONSTANT SWITCH. THIS ALLOWS A CONSTANT ON WITH OPTION OF FREEING UP SUPPORT HAND FOR TASKS SUCH AS OPENING DOORS OR CLEARING MALFUNCTIONS. EVEN IF YOU DO HAVE A WEAPON MOUNTED LIGHT YOU MUST BE FAMILIAR WITH OPERATING HAND HELD LIGHT AS BACKUP SYSTEM.

FLASH SUPPRESOR IS NECESSARY. WITHOUT IT THE RIFLE WILL CREATE A HUGE FIREBALL—DEPENDING ON AMMUNITION.

THE LIGHTER THE WEIGHT OF THE RIFLE THE BETTER. THIN LIGHTWEIGHT BARRELS WORK BEST. THE HEAVY BARRELS ARE ANOTHER MODIFICATION DEVELOPED FOR COMPETITION AND ARE NOT NECESSARY FOR FIGHTING.

16 INCH BARRELS WORK BEST, ESPECIALLY FOR BUILDING CLEARING, AND THEY REDUCE WEIGHT.

A SIMPLE 1 INCH SLING WORKS BEST. I PREFER TO MOUNT THEM TO THE SIDE OF THE REAR STOCK SO THAT THE RIFLE HANGS FLAT WHEN SLUNG.

I LIKE 30 RD MAGS. LESS TIME RELOADING, AND THE MAG CAN BE USED AS A MONOPOD WHEN FIRING FROM PRONE.

• TRIPOD THEORY

THE TRIANGLE IS AN EXTREMELY STABLE BASE, WILL STAND ON UNEVEN SURFACES, AND SUPPORT EMMENSE LOADS. BUT IF YOU REMOVE ONE OF THE LEGS OR CORNERS INSTABILITY RESULTS.

THE HUMAN BODY IS LIKE A TRIPOD MISSING A LEG. BALANCE REQUIRES CONSTANT ATTENTION, AND THE SLIGHTEST PROBLEM CREATES INSTABILITY.

WHEN FIGHTING SOMEONE LOOK AT THEM AS A TRIPOD MISSING A LEG. IF YOU CAN DIRECT THEIR MASS TOWARDS THE THIRD POINT OF THE TRIANGLE YOU UPSET THEIR BALANCE, WHICH REDUCES THEIR ABILITY TO FIGHT. FOR EXAMPLE IF YOU HAVE A WRIST LOCK, AND WANT TO TAKE YOUR OPPONENT TO THE GROUND, THEN YOU DIRECT THE WRIST TOWARDS THE THIRD POINT AND THEIR BODY FOLLOWS. IF YOU DIRECT THE HEAD TOWARDS THAT POINT THE BODY FOLLOWS. BY USING YOUR OPPONENTS ARMS OR WEAPONS YOU INCREASE THE LEVERAGE, OR THE HIGHER UP ON THEIR BODY YOU APPLY PRESSURE THE BETTER. THIS IS SIMPLE GEOMETRY.

TO OVERCOME THIS ACTION YOUR OPPONENT MUST REACT IMMEDIATELY. IF YOU HAVE THE ELEMENT OF SURPRISE IT IS EASY TO TOPPLE SOMEONE.

YOU MUST ALSO BE AWARE THAT THE SAME PRINCIPLE CAN BE APPLIED AGAINST YOU. BE CONCERNED WITH BALANCE AT ALL TIMES.

TO FIGHT EFFECTIVELY YOU MUST BE BALANCED BOTH MENTALLY AND PHYSICALLY.

THIRD POINT EXISTS IN THE FRONT AND REAR.

THIS PRINCIPLE APPLIES TO ALL TYPES OF SITUATIONS, AND AS MUSASHI SAID, IT CAN BE APPLIED TO ONE OR ONE THOUSAND.

57

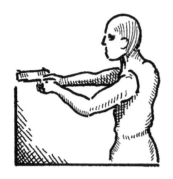 

THE DISTANCE FROM YOUR BODY AND ARMS TO THE MUZZLE WITH PISTOL OR 16 INCH BARREL RIFLE IS ROUGHLY THE SAME, SO WORKING AROUND COVER OR CORNERS ISN'T ANY PROBLEM.

WHEN MOVING THE RIFLE IS MORE DIFFICULT TO SHOOT ACCURATELY SINCE IT IS MOUNTED INTO THE SHOULDER SO MOVEMENT OF THE BODY IS TRANSFERED TO THE SIGHTS. WITH A PISTOL THE HANDS CAN MOVE TO MAINTAIN A SIGHT PICTURE.

THE PISTOL IS SOMETIMES EASIER TO FIRE FROM UNCONVENTIAL POSITIONS, UNSUAL STANCES, AND OF COURSE IS EASIER TO FIRE AND MANIPULATE WITH ONLY ONE HAND, OR FIRE TO EXTREME ANGLES TO THE LEFT OR RIGHT SIDES.

A LOT OF PEOPLE WILL GRIP THE RIFLE AT THE MAG WELL BUT THIS WILL CREATE MORE MOVEMENT TO THE SIGHTS DUE TO THE EXTENDED RADIUS, OR DISTANCE, FROM HAND TO SIGHTS. IT ALSO MAKES THE RIFLE "HEAVIER" BECAUSE OF THE GEOMETRY.

THE RULES OF GEOMETRY APPLY TO ALL ASPECTS OF FIGHTING AND SHOULD BE CONSIDERED AT ALL TIMES DURING COMBAT.

PRESENTATION ACCORDING TO CLINT SMITH

- STEP 1 - SLAP & GRIP THE FIRING HAND ACQUIRES A GRIP ON THE PISTOL. IT SHOULD BE A FIRING GRIP SO YOU DON'T HAVE TO REPOSITION THE HAND LATER. SUPPORT HAND IS POSITIONED IN THE CENTER OF UPPER BODY. THIS KEEPS IT FROM BEING COVERED BY MUZZLE AND PREPS IT FOR COMPLETING THE GRIP.

- STEP 2 - CLEAR, ROCK & LOCK PISTOL CLEARS HOLSTER AND ELBOW ROCKS SO THE WEAPON IS POSITIONED AGAINST THE SIDE. CAN BE FIRED FROM HERE IN RETENTION POSITION.

VIEW FROM SIDE

- STEP 3 - GRIP LEFT HAND THE SUPPORT HAND GRIPS THE PISTOL AFTER PUSHING PISTOL JUST FAR ENOUGH FORWARD TO ALLOW LEFT HAND TO ACQUIRE A FIRING GRIP.

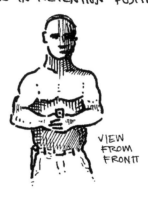

VIEW FROM FRONT

- STEP 4 - EXTEND PISTOL IS PUNCHED OUT TOWARDS TARGET TO ACQUIRE A SIGHT PICTURE. AS IT IS PUNCHED OUT FINGER GOES TO THE TRIGGER AND SAFETY IS DEPRESSED.

SIDE VIEW

- STEP 5 - FRONT SIGHT AND PRESS VISUAL FOCUS IS SHIFTED TO FRONT SIGHT AND THE TRIGGER IS PRESSED SMOOTHLY.

HOLSTERING IS THE SAME STEPS IN REVERSE. AS YOU HOLSTER YOU SHOULD STOP AT EACH STEP TO SCAN THE ENVIRONMENT AND ASSESS THE SITUATION.

PRESENTATION SHOULD BE PRACTICED OVER AND OVER, SLOWLY. LETTING SPEED DEVELOPE NATURALLY.

59

DURING THE FIRST TWO STEPS
THE SUPPORT HAND SHOULD BE
HELD IN THE CENTER OF THE
BODY SO THAT IF NECESSARY
IT CAN BE USED TO STRIKE
OR WARD OF THREATS.

IF THE WEAPON IS FIRED FROM
THIS POSITION IT IS CRITICAL TO
BRING THE SUPPORT HAND BACK
INTO THE CENTER OF THE BODY

WEAPON CAN ALSO
BE FIRED FROM
POSITION THREE OF
THE PRESENTATION

THE SUPPORT HAND CAN ALSO
BE BROUGHT UP TO THE SIDE
OF THE HEAD TO SERVE AS
A SHIELD TO BLOCK BLOWS

DURING A CLOSE QUARTER BATTLE
YOU WILL PROBABLY FLOW FROM
ONE TECHNIQUE TO ANOTHER

DON'T GET TIED INTO ONE TECHNIQUE
BUT EMPLOY WHATEVER THE SITUATION DICTATES.

SUPPORT HAND
CAN STRIKE OR
BLOCK

UNDER JEFF COOPER YOU LEARN A DIFFIERNT PRESENTATION.
AT STEP 2, WHERE CLINT SMITH HAS THE ROCK & LOCK
IN THE RETENTION POSITION, COOPER TEACHES AS SOON AS
THE PISTOL CLEARS THE HOLSTER IT GOES TO THE TARGET
IN A STRAIGHT LINE TOWARDS THE TARGET. THE SUPPORT
HAND ACQUIRES A GRIP AS THE PISTOL IS PUSHED
FORWARD.

DURING A PRESENTATION AN AGGRESSIVE STANCE SHOULD
BE EMPLOYED. THE "SPEED ROCK" WHERE YOU LEAN BACK
TO DISTANCE YOURSELF FROM THE THREAT, PUTS YOU OFF
BALANCE AND SHOULDN'T BE USED.

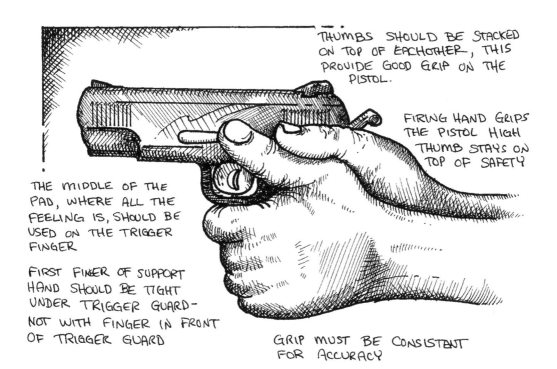

THUMBS SHOULD BE STACKED ON TOP OF EACHOTHER, THIS PROVIDE GOOD GRIP ON THE PISTOL.

FIRING HAND GRIPS THE PISTOL HIGH THUMB STAYS ON TOP OF SAFETY

THE MIDDLE OF THE PAD, WHERE ALL THE FEELING IS, SHOULD BE USED ON THE TRIGGER FINGER

FIRST FINGER OF SUPPORT HAND SHOULD BE TIGHT UNDER TRIGGER GUARD — NOT WITH FINGER IN FRONT OF TRIGGER GUARD

GRIP MUST BE CONSISTANT FOR ACCURACY

GRIPPING PISTOL IS CRITICAL TO ACCURACY AND BEING ABLE TO SHOOT QUICKLY. GRIP PRESSURE SHOULD BE MODERATE. SIMILAR TO USING A HAMMER TO DRIVE NAILS — YOU USE JUST ENOUGH GRIP TO HOLD HAMMER AND KEEP IT FROM BOUNCING AROUND IN YOUR HAND, BUT NOT A WHITE KNUCKLED DEATH GRIP. SAME IS TRUE WITH PISTOL. MOST PEOPLE GRIP IT WAY TOO TIGHTLY

THE FOREARM, WRIST, AND HAND SHOULD FORM A STRAIGHT LINE WITH THE BARREL OF THE PISTOL. WEB OF THE HAND SHOULD BE HIGH ON THE PISTOL. THE HIGHER UP THE MORE RECOIL IS ABSORBED BY HAND AND ARM. THE LOWER THE GRIP THE MORE THE PISTOL WILL FLIP UPWARD.

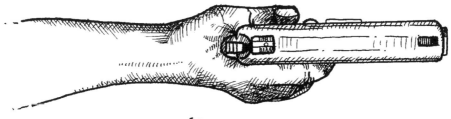

61

THE GRIP ON PISTOL IS ESSENTIAL TO ACCURACY AND SPEED. IF THE GRIP ON PISTOL IS DIFFERENT FROM TIME TO TIME OR SHOT TO SHOT ACCURACY SUFFERS. THE PROPER GRIP ON PISTOL SHOULD BE ACQUIRED BEFORE PISTOL IS PULLED FROM THE HOLSTER.

PRESSURE ON THE PISTOL SHOULD BE APPLIED TO THE FRONT AND REAR OF THE FRAME. AS LITTLE PRESSURE AS POSSIBLE IS APPLIED TO THE SIDES OF THE WEAPON. THE FINGERS APPLY PRESSURE TO THE FRONT STRAP WHICH FORCES THE BACK OF THE FRAME AGAINST THE HAND. FINGERS SHOULD PRESS STRAIGHT BACK AND NOT PUSH OR PULL TO ONE SIDE OR OTHER.

MOST PEOPLE APPLY GRIPPING PRESSURE WITH SUPPORT HAND. WITH POSITION OF HAND THIS GRIPS ON SIDES OF WEAPON AND FIRING HAND. THIS CAN EASILY FORCE THE WEAPON'S MUZZLE TO ONE SIDE OR THE OTHER. THE TRUE USE OF SUPPORT HAND SHOULD BE TO APPLY A PULLING ACTION TO FRONT OF FIRING HAND, BUT WITHOUT ACTUAL GRIPPING PRESSURE OR SQUEEZING THE FIRING HAND.

THE RECOIL OF PISTOL IS TO FLIP THE MUZZLE UP. TO CONTROL THE WEAPON, AND GET THE SIGHTS BACK ONTO THE TARGET FOR FOLLOW UP SHOTS, WE NEED TO KEEP MUZZLE FROM FLIPPING. THIS REQUIRES CONTROLLING FRONT AND REAR OF PISTOL FRAME, NOT THE SIDES OF THE PISTOL- WHERE THE "GRIPS" ARE LOCATED.

DON'T ATTEMPT TO CONTROL THE RECOIL, BUT STRIVE TO RECOVER FROM IT AS QUICKLY AS POSSIBLE.

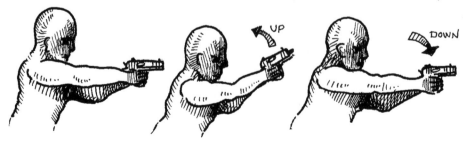

REALISM MUST BE FACTORED INTO YOUR TRAINING
YOU WILL FIGHT AS YOU HAVE TRAINED
SCENARIOS MUST REFLECT ACTUAL ENCOUNTERS

> SHORT DISTANCES
> SHORT DURATIONS OF TIME
> MULTIPLE MOVING TARGETS
> CONDITIONS OF LOW LIGHT

THE MILITARY REQUIRES 3 THINGS FOR SUCCESS
DURING COMBAT — SHOOT, MOVE, AND COMMUNICATE.
CLINT SMITH SHIFTED THESE IN SEQUENCE —
ESPECIALLY FOR CIVILIAN ENCOUNTERS — COMMUNICATE,
MOVE, AND SHOOT WHEN NECESSARY.

DEFEAT IN DETAIL

ATTACK THE ENEMY AT ITS WEAKEST POINT, DEFEAT
THAT POINT AND MOVE TO THE NEXT POINT OF
ATTACK

AS FORREST SAID, ARRIVE FIRST WITH THE MOST

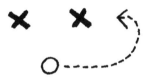

MULTIPLE TARGETS
SHOULD BE "STACKED"

ATTACKING THE CORNER
• EASIER TO ATTACK
• CONFUSING TO MULTIPLE
  OPPONENTS
• GREATEST POSSIBILITY OF
  CREATING MOST DAMAGE

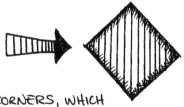

ATTACK AND WEAKEN THE CORNERS, WHICH
WEAKENS THE UNIT AS A WHOLE

SINGLE THREAT
2 PARTNERS

63

LOADING

MAGAZINES SHOULD BE POSITIONED IN POUCH SO
THE BULLET IS FACING FORWARD. AS THE MAG IS
BROUGHT OUT OF THE POUCH
IT SHOULD BE HELD SO THE
FIRST FINGER IS TOUCHING
THE TOP ROUND IN THE MAG.
BASEPAD OF MAG SHOULD BE
IN CONTACT WITH THE HEEL
OF THE PALM.

CHECK TOP
ROUND WITH
FINGER. IF
ROUND IS
STICKING OUT,
WHICH WILL
PREVENT IT FROM
BEING INSERTED
YOU FLICK IT OUT
WITH FINGER

MAG POUCH IS ON
SUPPORT SIDE —
MAG RIDES WITH
BULLET FACING
FORWARD

PISTOL SHOULD BE HELD UP. IN A
SAFE DIRECTION OR POINTED AT THREAT

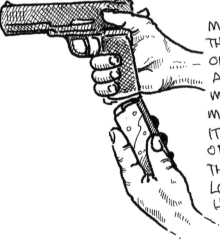

MAGAZINE IS BROUGHT UP TO
THE PISTOL. INDEX THE FLAT
ON THE BACK OF THE MAG
AGAINST THE BACK OF THE
MAG WELL. THEN ALIGN THE
MAG, INSERT IT, AND SEAT
IT FIRMLY WITH THE PALM
OF HAND. THE WHOLE TIME
THE BASE OF THE MAG NEVER
LOSES CONTACT WITH THE
HEEL OF PALM.

THE SLIDE IS THEN CYCLED BY GRASPING THE
REAR OF THE SLIDE BETWEEN PALM AND FINGERS
WITH THUMB FACING TO THE REAR.
GRASPING SLIDE THIS WAY IS WHERE
YOUR GRIPPING POWER IS BEST
REMEMBER AFTER LOADING PISTOL THE MAG IS ONE ROUND
SHORT. TOP IT OFF OR SWAP IT FOR A FULL ONE!

YOU HAVE NO WAY OF PREDICTING HOW THE THREAT WILL REACT TO THE SHOTS YOU FIRE. YOU SHOULD ALWAYS BE THINKING WHAT YOUR NEXT ACTIONS WILL BE - MORE SHOTS TO DIFFERENT PARTS OF THE BODY, RELOADING, MOVING TO BETTER COVER, ...

IN THE CA BANK ROBBERY, WHERE THE BAD GUYS WORE ARMOR, THE POLICE FIRED UNDERNEATH A CAR, HITTING THREAT IN ANKLES AND DROPPING HIM TO HIS KNEES. THEN HE WAS SHOT IN LEGS, CAUSING HIM TO FALL TO SIDE, AND THEN BODY SHOTS. NUMEROUS THREATS HAVE TAKEN LETHAL HITS AND CONTINUED TO FIGHT. THIS IS WHAT YOU MUST EXPECT, SAYING TO YOURSELF, "THIS SHOT ISN'T GOING TO WORK, WHERE WILL I AIM FOR MY NEXT SHOT?" YOU ALWAYS REACQUIRE THE SIGHTS, RESET THE TRIGGER AND PREPARING TO SHOOT AGAIN. OVER 80% of PEOPLE SHOT WITH PISTOL ROUNDS SURVIVE THE INCIDENT. LESS THAN 20% of THOSE SHOT WITH RIFLE ROUNDS SURVIVE.

WE. ENGAGE UNTIL THE THREAT EITHER CAN'T FIGHT ANYMORE, DUE TO PHYSICAL DAMAGE, OR HURT THEM SO MUCH THEY DECIDE TO LEAVE, OR BETTER YET - YOU DON'T HAVE TO FIRE BECAUSE YOU USE VERBAL COMMANDS, COUPLED WITH THE PRESENCE OF YOUR PISTOL, CONVICES THE THREAT TO LEAVE YOU ALONE.

REMEMBER THAT OUR FIRST AND BEST OPTION IS TO NOT HAVE TO PHYSICALLY ENGAGE THE THREAT. THE ACTUAL BATTLE BEGINS LONG BEFORE THE ATTACK BEGINS. IF YOU ARE MENTALLY AWARE, AND YOU RESPOND PRIOR TO THE ATTACK, YOU THWART THE ATTACK, AND WIN THE "WAR".

65

<u>RELOADS</u>   APPY TO PISTOLS & RIFLES

• EMPTY - WHEN I TRAINED UNDER JEFF COOPER LETTING
  YOUR WEAPON RUN EMPTY WAS CONSIDERED A "SIN".
  CLINT SMITH TAGHT THAT AN EMPTY WEAPON IS A
  REALITY OF FIGHTING AND YOU SHOULD RELOAD AND GET
  BACK INTO THE FIGHT. YOU WON'T/CAN'T COUNT THE
  NUMBER OF ROUNDS FIRED.

• SPEED LOAD - THIS IS WHERE YOU DO AN EMPTY RELOAD
  BEFORE THE WEAPON RUNS EMPTY. THE PARTIALLY
  FULL MAG DROPS TO THE GROUND, WHICH MEANS YOU
  WON'T PROBABLY BE ABLE TO PICK IT UP IF YOU
  NEED IT SINCE CHANCES ARE YOU BE MOVING AND
  LEAVING IT ON THE GROUND. IF YOU ARE SHOOTING
  YOU WON'T BE TRYING OR STOPPING TO LOAD UNTILL
  THE WEAPON IS EMPTY. IF YOU HAVE TIME TO RELOAD
  THEN DO A TACTICAL LOAD AND MAINTAIN POSSESION OF
  THE PARTIALLY FULL MAG IN CASE YOU NEED IT.

• TACTICAL RELOAD - THE TACTICAL RELOAD ALLOWS YOU
  TO GET A FULL MAG INTO THE WEAPON AND RETAIN
  PARTIAL MAG. IT IS PERFORMED ONLY WHEN THERE
  IS OPPORTUNITY - <u>NOT</u> IN THE MIDDLE OF A FIGHT.

ADMINSTRATIVE RELOAD - THE PISTOL stays w the
holster. Your holster should be designed so you
can press the mag release. Remove the partial
mag and either replace it with a full one or
reload the partial to full capacity and put it
back into the pistol.

TUG ON MAG TO
MAKE SURE IT'S
SEATED

TO SEAT THE
MAG I GET A
HOLD ON THE GRIP
WITH MY FIRST
TWO FINGERS AND
PRESS MAG IN WITH
YOUR THUMB.

66

EMPTY RELOAD - AS SOON AS YOU REALIZE THE
WEAPON IS EMPTY YOU NEED TO DO SEVERAL THINGS
AT ONCE. THE WEAPON SHOULD BE HELD UP AND
INDEXED ON THE THREAT. THE SUPPORT HAND GOES
FOR THE FRESH MAGAZINE. THE PRIMARY HAND
PRESSES THE MAGAZINE RELEASE. LET THE EMPTY
MAG DROP TO THE GROUND! IF YOU'RE DOING AN
EMPTY LOAD YOU PROBABLY HAVE A THREAT TO SHOOT
AND YOU DON'T HAVE TIME TO PUT THE EMPTY MAG
INTO YOUR POCKET. IF THE EMPTY MAG DOESN'T
DROP FREE YOU PULL IT OUT WITH THE SUPPORT
HAND - BUT ONLY AFTER THE SUPPORT HAND HAS
SECURED THE NEW/FULL MAG.

CHECK THE TOP ROUND OF NEW MAG WITH FIRST
FINGER OF SUPPORT HAND. BRING THE MAG TO
THE WEAPON, INDEX, INSERT, AND SEAT. SEAT
IT WITH EXTRA FORCE TO MAKE SURE IT
SEATS. IT MIGHT MAKE IT EASIER TO INDEX
MAG IF YOU ROTATE THE PISTOL SLIGHTLY
CLOCKWISE, FOR A RIGHT HANDED SHOOTER, BUT
KEEP WEAPON POINTED TOWARD THREAT.

AFTER SEATING THE MAG THE SUPPORT HAND
CYCLES THE SLIDE. DON'T USE SLIDE "RELEASE"
THIS LEVER IS ONLY A SLIDE LOCK - NOT A RELEASE.
PLUS THE LEVERS ARE LOCATED IN DIFFERENT
LOCATIONS, AND UNDER STRESS OR WITH SLIPPERY/
COLD/ OR GLOVED HANDS IT CAN BE HARD TO
HIT. CYCLING THE SLIDE WORKS ALL THE TIME
WITH ANY PISTOL (OR RIFLE)

KEEP YOUR EYES ON THE TARGET! DON'T
LOOK AT YOUR PISTOL OR RIFLE. PRACTICE UNTIL
YOU CAN DO IT WITH YOUR EYES CLOSED.

TACTICAL RELOAD - PISTOL

THE TACTICAL RELOAD IS PERFORED ONLY WHEN THERE IS A LULL IN THE FIGHT. IF POSSIBLE YOU SHOULD EMPLOY COVER. PURPOSE OF THE TACTICAL RELOAD IS TO GET A FULL MAGAZINE INTO THE WEAPON AND RETAIN POSSESION OF THE PARTIALLY FULL MAG.

• SEARCH & SCAN YOUR ENVIRONMENT TO MAKE SURE THERE ARE NO ADDITIONAL THREATS.

• SUPPORT HAND SECURES FRESH MAG. CHECK TOP ROUND POSITION WITH FIRST FINGER.

• AS YOU BRING THE FRESH MAG UP TO THE PISTOL PLACE THE MAG IN BETWEEN FIRST AND SECOND FINGERS. THIS FREES UP THE THUMB AND FIRST FINGER TO GRAB THE PARTIAL MAG

• REMOVE OLD MAG, INSTALL NEW MAG. IT MAY BE NECESSARY TO TWIST PISTOL SLIGHTLY TO HIT MAG RELEASE WITH YOUR THUMB

NEW MAG

PARTIAL MAG

• SECURE PARTIAL MAG - I LIKE TO PUT THEM IN MY MAG POUCH. IF I HAVE A DUAL MAG POUCH I WILL TAC LOAD FROM REAR MAG SO I KNOW THE FRONT ONE IS FULL, THE REAR IS PARTIAL

IF YOU PUT IT IN YOUR POCKET USE REAR POCKET. IF YOU PUT IN IN FRONT POCKET YOU CAN'T GET TO IT WHEN KNEELING OR SQUATTING.

• RELOAD WHEN YOU CAN NOT WHEN YOU HAVE TO

THE MOST COMMON PROBLEMS ARE RELOADING WITHOUT SEARCHING/SCANNING AND LOOKING AT YOUR WEAPON.

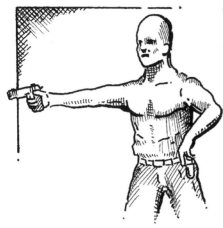

DURING ANY WEAPONS MANIPULATION PISTOL IS KEPT EXTENDED OUT AND POINTED TOWARDS THREAT WITH YOUR HEAD AND EYES UP.

AS SOON AS RELOAD OR CLEARANCE IS COMPLETED YOU ARE READY TO FIRE IF NECESSARY, WITHOUT THE TIME REQUIRED TO REBUILD YOUR SHOOTING PLATFORM IF THE ARM AND WEAPON ARE LOWERED DOWN OR BROUGHT IN CLOSE TO YOUR BODY. PLUS IF YOU NEED TO GLANCE AT THE WEAPON YOU CAN WITH IT HELD UP AT EYE LEVEL.

AFTER YOU DO YOUR TACTICAL RELOAD, BUT PRIOR TO STOWING THE PARTIAL MAG, YOU SHOULD CHECK THE TOP ROUND WITH FIRST FINGER. IF THE ROUND IS NOT SEATED YOU CAN PUSH IT BACK INTO THE MAG OR FLIP IT OUT. IF THERE IS NO ROUND THERE MAG IS EMPTY- GET RID OF IT. PLUS YOU MIGHT WANT TO DO A PRESS CHECK TO MAKE SURE THE SLIDE JUST DIDN'T FAIL TO LOCK BACK ON THE EMPTY MAGAZINE.

YOU SHOULD GET INTO THE HABIT OF PERFORMING A TACTICAL RELOAD BEFORE HOLSTERING SO THAT IF THE FIGHT CONTINUES OR ESCALATES YOU WILL HAVE A FULLY LOADED PISTOL TO CONTINUE.

IF YOU ARE DOING A TAC RELOAD AND DROP A MAG THEN PUT THE ONE BACK INTO THE PISTOL AND RETRIVE THE ONE DROPPED BY SQUATTING DOWN, WITH HEAD AND EYES UP. THEN YOU CAN LOAD OR SECURE DEPENDING ON WHICH MAG YOU DROPPED.

IF YOU KNOW IN ADVANCE YOU ARE ENTERING INTO A TARGET RICH ENVIRONMENT YOU MIGHT WANT TO HAVE A MAG READY TO RELOAD AS QUICKLY AS POSSIBLE (TIP LEARNED FROM SUAREZ)

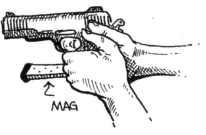

MAG

PRESS
CHECK

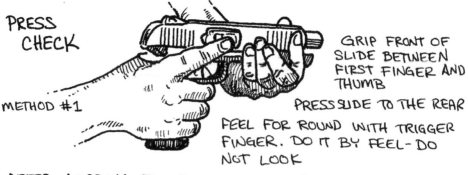

GRIP FRONT OF
SLIDE BETWEEN
FIRST FINGER AND
THUMB

METHOD #1

PRESS SLIDE TO THE REAR

FEEL FOR ROUND WITH TRIGGER
FINGER. DO IT BY FEEL- DO
NOT LOOK

AFTER LOADING THE PISTOL, OR BEFORE ENTERING INTO
A POSSIBLY VIOLENT SITUATION, IT IS CHEAP INSURANCE
TO PRESS CHECK TO MAKE SURE THERE IS A ROUND
IN THE CHAMBER.

DO THIS BY FEEL. YOU NEED TO KEEP YOUR EYES
ON THE ENVIRONMENT, AND IF IT IS DARK YOU WON'T
BE ABLE TO SEE ANYWAY.

THERE ARE A COUPLE OF TECHNIQUES YOU CAN USE
BUT REGARDLESS OF WHICH ONE YOU EMPLOY MAKE
SURE TO KEEP YOUR FINGERS BEHIND THE MUZZLE.

WITH TECHNIQUE #1 YOU MAY HAVE TO LOSE YOUR
GRIP OFF THE PISTOL TO GET THE TRIGGER FINGER
UP TO THE CHAMBER.

TECHNIQUE #2

PINCH THE FRONT
OF THE SLIDE WITH
THE LAST THREE
FINGERS AND THUMB
AND PRESS THE SLIDE
TO THE REAR.
WITH THE FIRST FINGER
YOU FEEL THE CHAMBER

THE ADVANTAGE OF
THIS METHOD IS THAT
YOU MAINTAIN A FIRING
GRIP ON THE WEAPON

WITH SOME OF THE DOUBLE ACTION PISTOLS IT IS
EASIER TO PRESS CHECK IF YOU COCK THE HAMMER
FIRST, PRESS CHECK, AND THEN DECOCK THE WEAPON

TO DO A COMPLETE SYSTEM CHECK YOU PERFORM
A PRESS CHECK AND THEN CHECK THE MAGAZINE
TO MAKE SURE IT IS FULL OF AMMO

─── SIGHT PICTURE ───

FOR ANYTHING FARTHER THAN A FEW FEET THE
SIGHTS ARE REQUIRED FOR ACCURATE HITS. THE
DIFFERENCE IS THE AMOUNT OF PRECISION IN THE
SIGHT PICTURE AND HOW LONG YOU ACTUALLY SPEND
LOOKING AT THE SIGHTS. THE FARTHER THE SHOT
THE LONGER YOU LOOK AT THE SIGHTS.
ACQUIRE THE TARGET AND FOCUS ON THE EXACT
SPOT YOU WANT THE SHOT TO GO. AS THE SIGHTS
COME UP ONTO THE TARGET YOU ALIGN THE SIGHTS
WITH THE POINT OF AIM. THE PRECISION REQUIRED
IN ALIGNING THE SIGHTS DEPENDS ON THE DISTANCE
TO THE TARGET. ONCE YOU HAVE THE SIGHT PICTURE,
AND BEGIN TO PRESS THE TRIGGER YOUR VISUAL
FOCUS SHIFTS TO THE FRONT SIGHT.

AT CLOSE RANGE YOU USE THE
FLASH SIGHT PICTURE. THIS IS
JUST A QUICK CONFIRMATION
THAT THE SIGHTS ARE INDEXED
ONTO THE TARGET AND YOU
PRESS THE TRIGGER.
THE SECOND AND FOLLOW UP
SHOTS ARE PRESS AS SOON
AS YOUR BODY FEEL TELLS
YOU YOU'RE BACK ON TARGET.

TEST YOUR WEAPON AT VARIOUS
DISTANCES TO SEE WHERE THE
WEAPON WILL SHOOT WITH THE
FRONT SIGHT SET TO ONE SIDE
OR THE OTHER WHEN POSITIONED
IN THE REAR SIGHT. YOU'LL FIND THAT THE
SHOTS WILL GO ON TARGET, ACCURATE ENOUGH
FOR COMBATIVE USE, EVEN WITH THE FRONT
SIGHT OFF CENTER.

MALFUNCTIONS

WHEN I LEARNED TO WORK MALFUNCTIONS THERE WAS A DIFFERENT CLEARING PROCEDURE FOR EACH TYPE MALFUNCTION. SO YOU WOULD FIRST HAVE TO DETERMINE WHAT TYPE MALFUNCTION YOU HAD, THEN CHOOSE THE CORRECTIVE MEASURE, AND THEN APPLY THE CLEARANCE.

EVENTUALLY EVERYONE SHIFTED TO A NON-DIAGNOSTIC APPROACH. INSTEAD OF GOING THROUGH THE ABOVE MENTIONED PROCESS YOU SIMPLY APPLY A CORRECTIVE SET OF PROCEDURES THAT WILL CLEAR ALL TYPE MALFUNCTIONS.

THERE ARE THREE TYPE MALFUNCTIONS THAT CAN OCCUR. THE TYPE 1 IS DUE TO EITHER A BAD ROUND OF AMMO, OR MOST LIKELY NO ROUND OF AMMO. THIS IS USUALLY CAUSED BY A FAILURE TO SEAT THE MAGAZINE AND THEN WHEN YOU CYCLE THE SLIDE IT DOESN'T FEED AMMO INTO THE CHAMBER. REGARDLESS OF THE CAUSE THE RESULT IS THAT WHEN YOU PRESS THE TRIGGER YOU GET A CLICK INSTEAD OF BANG.

TYPE 2 IS A FAILURE TO EJECT - SOMETIMES CALLED A STOVE PIPE BECAUSE THE EMPTY PIECE OF BRASS IS STUCK IN THE EJECTION PORT LOOKING LIKE A STOVE PIPE.

THE TYPE 3 IS A DOUBLE FEED DUE TO EITHER A FAILURE TO EXTRACT AN EMPTY PIECE OF BRASS FROM THE CHABER AND THE FRESH ROUND FEEDS AGAINST IT OR TWO ROUNDS POP OUT OF THE MAGAZINE AT ONCE.

THE KEY TO CLEARING MALFUNCTIONS QUICKLY IS TO PRACTICE THEM UNTIL THE RESPONSE BECOMES AUTOMATIC. YOUR CLEARING PROCEDURES MUST BE SUBCONCIOUS. FOR EAMPLE WHEN THE CONCIOUS MIND SAYS MALFUNCTION THE SUBCONCIOUS TAKES OVER AND ACTUALLY CLEARS THE WEAPON. THIS LEVEL OF SKILL ONLY OCCURS AFTER THOUSANDS OF REPITITIONS.

MALFUNCTIONS

WITH A NON-DIAGNOSTIC APPROACH TO MALFUNCTIONS IT DOESN'T MATTER WHAT MALFUNCTION YOU HAVE. AS SOON AS YOU REALIZE THE WEAPON ISN'T WORKING YOU GO INTO THE CLEARANCE PROCEDURE. THIS IS A CLEARANCE SEQUENCE THAT IS EASIER TO LEARN - AND EASIER TO TEACH.

WHEN YOU ATTEMPT TO FIRE AND THE WEAPON DOESN'T THE IMMEDIATE RESPONSE IS TO TAP TO SEAT THE MAGAZINE, CYCLE THE SLIDE, AND ATTEMPT TO FIRE. WE TAP TO MAKE SURE THE MAG IS SEATED SINCE THE MOST COMMON CAUSE OF NOT FIRING IS THAT MAG WASN'T SEATED SO WHEN THE SLIDE WAS CYCLED NO ROUND WAS CHAMBERED. THEN, AFTER TAPPING THE MAG WE CYCLE THE SLIDE TO EITHER GET RID OF A BAD ROUND OF AMMO OR, MORE LIKELY TO CHAMBER A ROUND INTO THE EMPTY CHAMBER. WHEN YOU'VE TAPPED AND RACKED YOU ATTEMPT TO FIRE - BUT ONLY IF THE SLIDE HAS GONE INTO BATTERY. OBVIOUSLY IF YOU TAP & RACK AND THE SLIDE DOESN'T GO INTO BATTERY THE WEAPON WON'T FIRE SO DON'T WASTE THE TIME BRINGING THE WEAPON UP AND TRYING TO PRESS THE TRIGGER.

IF THE FIRST STEP OF THE PROCESS DOESN'T CLEAR THE WEAPON THEN THE PROCEDURE IS FOLLOWED BY UNLOAD, CLEAR, AND RELOAD. YOU PRESS THE MAG RELEASE WHILE STRIPPING THE MAG OUT OF THE PISTOL. THIS IS WHERE BASEPADS ON YOUR MAGS ARE AN ADVANTAGE. YOU WILL PROBABLY HAVE TO REALLY TUG ON THE MAG SINCE THE SPRING PRESSURE ON THE ROUNDS STUCK IN THERE WILL BE TIGHT. IF IT IS IMPOSSIBLE TO STRIP THE MAG OUT THEN YOU WILL HAVE TO LOCK THE SLIDE TO THE REAR TO TAKE SPRING PRESSURE OFF. ONCE MAG IS OUT YOU SHOULD CYCLE THE SLIDE TO CLEAR OUT OBSTRUCTION. MAG GOES BACK INTO PISTOL, CYCLE THE SLIDE, AND FIRE IF NECESSARY.

SO IF THE WEAPON WON'T FIRE - TAP AND RACK. THIS WILL CLEAR TYPE 1 & 2 MALFUNCTIONS. IF THIS DOESN'T WORK THEN STRIP THE MAG, CLEAR OBSTRUCTION BY CYCLING THE SLIDE, AND RELOAD.

WITH THE NON-DIAGNOSTIC APPROACH THERE IS NO TIME WASTED DETERMINING WHAT MALFUNCTION YOU HAVE OR WHICH CLEARANCE TO APPLY.

WHEN MANIPULATING THE PISTOL DON'T BRING IT INTO YOUR BODY BECAUSE THE NEXT THING YOU DO WILL BE TO LOOK DOWN AT IT. KEEP HEAD & EYES UP!

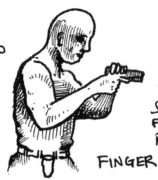

KEEP MUZZLE ON TARGET AND LOOK AT FRONT SIGHT, WITH ARMS EXTENDED SO YOU'RE READY TO FIRE IMMEDIATELY IF REQUIRED.

FINGER OFF THE TRIGGER!

ANYTIME THE MAG COMES OUT OF THE PISTOL, REGARDLESS OF THE REASON, IT SHOULD GO INTO THE PINKIE FINGER OF THE PRIMARY HAND. YOU CAN THEN MANIPULATE WITH THE SUPPORT HAND FREED UP. THEN THE MAG IS RIGHT THERE WHEN YOU ARE READY TO RELOAD. EVEN WHEN YOU ARE DOING AN ADMINISTRATIVE UNLOAD YOU GET INTO THE HABIT OF DOING THIS.

EVERY TIME YOU MANIPULATE THE WEAPON YOU MUST USE CORRECT TECHNIQUE. REMEMBER TRAINING IS MADE UP OF REPETITION. IF SOMETIMES YOU DO IT RIGHT, SAY DURING RANGE PRACTICE, THEN YOU GET SLOPPY, AT HOME UNLOADING TO CLEAN YOUR WEAPON, YOU ARE TRAINING YOURSELF TO DO SOMETHING IN TWO WAYS - THE RIGHT WAY AND THE WRONG WAY. DO IT RIGHT - ALL THE TIME.

SOMETIMES YOU WILL GET A ROUND STUCK INTO THE CHAMBER. TO CLEAR IT YOU WILL HAVE TO GRAB THE SLIDE WITH THE SUPPORT HAND, PULL THE STRONG HAND BACK, AND STRIKE THE GRIP WITH THE WEB OF THE HAND BETWEEN THUMB & FIRST FINGER.

74

MORE ON MALFUNCTIONS

THERE ARE A LOT OF VARIATIONS THAT PEOPLE TEACH WHICH I DON'T THINK IS A GOOD IDEA. FOR EAMPLE SOME TEACH ON A TYPE 3 MALFUNCTION, THE DOUBLE FEED, TO GET RID OF THE MAGAZINE IN THE PISTOL. THEIR THEORY IS THAT THE MAG MIGHT BE THE CAUSE OF THE MALFUNCTION. IF YOU HAVE A BAD MAG GET RID OF IT! PRIOR TO A FIGHT! THERE MAY BE TIMES THE MAG IN YOUR WEAPON IS THE ONLY ONE YOU HAVE. 3AM IN THE MORNING, YOU HEAR A NOISE, SO YOU GRAB YOUR LIGHT AND PISTOL TO INVESTIGATE IN YOUR UNDERWEAR - CHANCES ARE YOU WON'T HAVE AN EXTRA MAG AND IF YOU TRAIN TO DUMP THAT MAG IT WON'T BE GOOD.

ONE SCHOOL OF THOUGHT BELIEVES YOU CAN PULL THE MAG DOWN SLIGHTLY, NOT REMOVING IT, DURING A DOUBLE FEED CLEARANCE. THE PROBLEM WITH THIS IS THAT A LOT OF TIMES THE MALFUNCTION IS DUE TO A FAILURE TO EXTRACT RESULTING FROM A BROKEN OR WEAK EXTRACTOR. THE EXTRACTOR IN THIS CONDITION MAY BE ABLE TO PULL THE ROUND OUT BUT NOT ENOUGH FORCE TO EJECT THE ROUND. IF THE MAG IS REMOVED YOU CREATE A BIG HOLE WHICH THE ROUND OR BRASS CAN DROP OUT OF. THE IDEA OF NOT REMOVING THE MAG, I BELIEVE, IS A RESULT OF WORKING MALFUNCTIONS WITH A WEAPON THAT IS ACTUALLY FUNCTIONING PROPERLY.

TO SET UP MALFUNCTIONS FOLLOW THESE PROCEDURES

TYPE 1 - REMOVE MAG, EMPTY THE CHAMBER, AND REINSTALL MAG WITHOUT CYCLING THE SLIDE. OR YOU CAN PRESS MAG RELEASE & LET IT DROP DOWN ENOUGH SO IT WON'T FEED A ROUND AFTER FIRING THE ROUND IN THE CHAMBER.

TYPE 2 - WITH A ROUND IN THE CHAMBER PULL THE SLIDE BACK SLIGHTLY AND PLACE A PIECE OF BRASS INTO THE EJECTION PORT. LET THE SLIDE GO FORWARD SO THAT IT TRAPS THE BRASS.

TYPE 3 - REMOVE THE MAG AND LOCK THE SLIDE TO THE REAR. TAKE A LOOSE ROUND OF AMMO AND DROP IT INTO THE CHAMBER. INSTALL MAG AND LET THE SLIDE GO FORWARD.

YOU CAN ALSO LOAD MAGS WITH DUMMY AMMO AND SPENT BRASS, ALONG WITH LIVE ROUNDS, TO PROVIDE UNEXPECTED MALFUNCTIONS OF VARIOUS TYPES.

IT IS CRITICAL TO REMEMBER THE AMOUNT OF TIME REQUIRED TO CLEAR A MALFUNCTION, AND THE FACT THAT THE AVERAGE PERSON CAN COVER 21 FEET IN 1.5 SECONDS - OR LESS. THIS MEANS IF YOU ARE 30 FEET AWAY FROM SOMEONE AND YOU HAVE SOME TYPE MALFUNCTION, WHICH TAKES 3 SECONDS FOR YOU TO CLEAR, PLUS A HALF SECOND TO FIGURE OUT YOU'VE EVEN GOT A MALFUNCTION, THE BAD GUY CAN CLOSE THE GROUND AND ATTACK YOU BEFORE YOU CAN GET YOUR WEAPON BACK INTO THE FIGHT.

DISTANCE EQUATES TO TIME, AND TIME IS A HUGE FACTOR IN ANY FIGHT.

———————————————————————

MANIPULATING YOUR WEAPON MUST BECOME A PART OF YOUR REGULAR TRAINING. THE BEST WAY TO PRACTICE IS DRY FIRE PRACTICE. TO PRACTICE MAKE SURE WEAPON IS UNLOADED, AND THAT THERE IS NO LIVE AMMO ANY-WHERE NEAR WHERE YOU ARE PRACTICING. MAKE SURE YOU HAVE A SAFE DIRECTION TO AIM YOUR WEAPON. USE DUMMY AMMO ONLY. WITH THE DUMMY AMMO YOU CAN SET UP MALFUNCTIONS TO CLEAR, AND WORK ON RELOADS. PRACTICE YOUR PRESENTATION AND SIGHT WORK. YOU DON'T EVEN NEED A WEAPON TO PRACTICE HOLDING A SIGHT PICTURE WHILE MOVING - JUST HOLD UP YOUR HANDS AND USE YOUR THUMB FOR A SIGHT.

———————————————————————

WHEN IT COMES TIME TO SHOOT IN YOUR MIND YOU SHOULD BE SAYING "FRONT SIGHT - PRESS" AFTER THE SHOT IS FIRED YOU MUST FOLLOW THE SIGHT WITH YOUR EYES, RECOVER AND GET ANOTHER SIGHT PICTURE, AND RESET THE TRIGGER BY ONLY LETTING IT GO FAR ENOUGH FORWARD TO REENGAGE. DON'T LET YOUR FINGER LOSE CONTACT WITH THE TRIGGER. TRIGGER RESET IS ESSENTIAL TO SHOOTING - AND HITTING - QUICKLY.

DON'T TRY TO CONTROL THE RECOIL — CONCENTRATE ON RECOVERING FROM IT AS QUICKLY AS POSSIBLE.

76

WHEN CYCLING THE SLIDE ALWAYS GRAB IT BETWEEN YOUR PALM AND FINGERS, WITH THE THUMB POINTING TOWARDS YOU. THEN, AS THE SUPPORT HAND SPRINGS INTO ACTION BY BRISKLY PULLING THE SLIDE TO THE REAR THE GUN HAND PUSHES FORWARD. THE ACTION USED SHOULD BE LIKE YOU'RE TRYING TO RIP THE SLIDE OFF THE FRAME.

TRIGGER FINGER SHOULD BE OFF THE TRIGGER AND MUZZLE POINTED TOWARDS THREAT OR IN A SAFE DIRECTION.

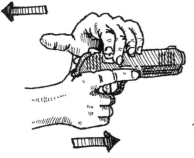

NORMALLY YOU WILL BE CYCLING THE SLIDE AFTER YOU SEAT THE MAG. I'VE FOUND THAT WHEN SEATING THE MAG WITH THE HEEL OF THE PALM, WHICH IS THE HARD PART OF THE PALM AND PROVIDES THE RESISTANCE NEEDED TO SEAT MAG, YOU CAN USE THAT SAME UPWARD MOMENTUM TO LET THE HAND GO UP TO CYCLE THE MAG. YOU SHOULD ACT AS THOUGH YOU ARE TRYING TO CATCH A FLY THAT HAS LANDED ON TOP OF THE SLIDE.

1
AS THE HAND SEATS THE MAG IT BEGINS TO TWIST SO THUMB IS POINTING TOWARDS YOU.

2
AND THEN THE HAND SPRINGS UP TO "CATCH THE FLY" ON TOP OF THE SLIDE.

3 THEN THE HAND PULLS SLIDE TO THE REAR.

WHEN PRACTICING IT IS A GOOD TRAINING AID TO RELATE YOUR ACTION WITH THE PISTOL TO SOMETHING YOU ARE ALREADY FAMILIAR WITH. THAT'S WHY "CATCH THE FLY" WORKS WELL. WE KNOW HOW QUICK, YET RELAXED, OUR MUSCLES MUST WORK TO CATCH A FLY. THE SAME APPLIES TO MANIPULATIONS.

SEARCHING IS DONE AFTER THE THREAT IS DOWN OR GONE. IT IS ACCOMPLISHED BY CHECKING WITH THE EYES AND MUZZLE WORKING AS ONE UNIT. THE WEAPON SHOULD BE IN LOW READY POSITION SO IT AND YOUR HANDS/ARMS WON'T BLOCK YOU FROM SEEING ANYTHING IN YOUR ENVIRONMENT. SCANNING IS WHEN YOU TURN YOUR HEAD ONLY, LOOKING BEHIND YOU AND TO THE SIDES. WHEN SCANNING THE MUZZLE SHOULD STAY POINTED TOWARDS THE THREAT OR THREAT ENVIRONMENT.

IF I HAD A THREAT DOWN I WOULD KEEP MUZZLE INDEXED TO THREAT AND SCAN. SHOULD I FIND ADDITIONAL THREATS THEN OBVIOUSLY WEAPON IS INDEXED TO THE THREAT.

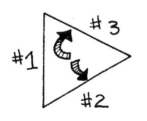

WHEN SEARCHING, OR INVOLVED IN A VIOLENT SITUATION YOU WILL BE ABLE TO SEE MORE TO YOUR SIDES IF YOU TILT YOUR HEAD DOWN SLIGHTLY AS OPPOSED TO STRAIGHT UP.
DON'T BRING YOUR HEAD DOWN, TUCKING THE CHIN, BECAUSE THIS WILL RESTRICT YOUR AIRFLOW THROUGH THE THROAT. JUST ROTATE THE HEAD.

WHEN SEARCHING YOUR ENVIRONMENT, PRIOR TO LOCATING A SPECIFIC THREAT, THINK ABOUT YOUR ENVIRONMENT AS A 3 SIDED TRIANGLE INSTEAD OF A 360° CIRCLE. WITH THIS CONCEPT YOU CAN COVER FRONT AREA, WHICH IS CONSIDERED PRIORITY #1, THEN SEARCH OR SCAN AREAS #2 & 3, WITHOUT TOTALLY LOSING VISUAL ON AREA #1 OR TURNING YOUR BACK.

CHECK AREA #3 WITHOUT MOVING. STEP SLIGHTLY BACK WITH LEFT FOOT AND CHECK AREA #2. STEP BACK WITH LEFT TO ORIGINAL POSITION.

#3
#1
#2

END UP IN YOUR ORIGINAL STANCE

CLOTHING CONSIDERATIONS

WITH A SWEATSHIRT, WHICH IS EXCELLENT FOR CONCEALING PISTOL, THE SUPPORT HAND PULLS BOTTOM OF SHIRT, ON RIGHT SIDE, UP AND OVER PISTOL. RIGHT HAND GRIPS THE WEAPON.

ANOTHER TECHNIQUE WHICH WORKS WELL, AND CLEARS THE SHIRT OVER THE SPARE MAG ON THE LEFT SIDE, IS FOR BOTH HANDS TO PULL BOTH SIDES OF SWEATSHIRT. THIS WAY THE SHIRT ROLLS UP AND STAYS IN POSITION.

WITH A JACKET OR A SPORTCOAT THE RIGHT HAND SWEEPS JACKET OUT OF THE WAY TO ALLOW ACCESS TO PISTOL.

YOUR CLOTHING SHOULDN'T ATTRACT ATTENTION. DULL, DARK COLORS WORK BEST IN LOW LIGHT ENVIRONMENTS, BLACK STILL STANDS OUT IN LOW LIGHT

PRACTICE WITH ALL TYPES OF CLOTHING

CLOTHES MUST ALLOW YOU TO CONCEAL WEAPON AND ALLOW EASY ACCESS. SHOULD BE LOOSE ENOUGH TO ALLOW FREEDOM OF MOVEMENT.
ALSO CONSIDER SHOES. DO THEY GRIP ON WET GRASS OR SLIPPERY CONCRETE?

ONE OF THE QUICKEST DRAWS IS TO HAVE PISTOL JUST OFF CENTER OF FRONT ON LEFT SIDE. PUT LEFT SIDE OF THE BODY TO THE THREAT. PISTOL IS PULLED UP AND OUT AND THIS ACTION POINTS IT AT THE THREAT.

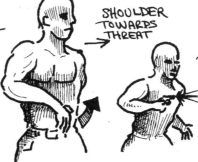

SHOULDER TOWARDS THREAT

PISTOL IS PULLED INTO BODY AND POINTED TO THREAT

MAKE SURE BODY CLEARS MUZZLE!

WHEN FIRING WITH THE LEFT
HAND ONLY THE THUMB SAFETY
SHOULD BE DEPRESSED WITH
THE THUMB. TO ENGAGE SAFETY
THE PRESS UPWARD IS ACCOMPLISHED
WITH THE TRIGGER FINGER.

SAME TECHNIQUES ARE USED IF YOU ARE LEFT HANDED
AND USING BOTH HANDS TO FIRE WEAPON. THE TRIGGER
FINGER IS USED TO PRESS THE MAGAZINE RELEASE.

DURING A FIGHT IT ISN'T RECOMMENDED THAT YOU
SWAP HANDS TO FIGHT USING THE OPOSITE SIDE.
UNLESS YOU CAN TRULY USE EACH HAND EQUALLY
WELL YOU ARE HAMPERING YOUR ABILITIES TO
FIGHT. REMEMBER MOST FIGHTS WILL CONTAIN
NO TIME TO FUMBLE A MANIPULATION OR MISS
A SHOT. YOUR JOB IS TO STOP THE ATTACKER AS
QUICKLY AND THERE IS NO TIME FOR MISTAKES.
FIGHT WITH THE WEAPON AS EFFICIENTLY AS POSSIBLE,
AND THIS MEANS WITH THE STRONG, OR PRIMARY, OR
WHATEVER TERM YOU WANT TO USE.

WHEN FIRING WITH ONE HAND ONLY
YOU CAN BLADE YOUR BODY MORE
TO LEAN INTO IT, USING
YOUR BODY WEIGHT TO
HELP WITH RECOIL RECOVERY.

THE PROBLEM WITH THIS IS THAT IT
MAKES MOVING, IN ANY DIRECTION,
MORE DIFFICULT.

IF YOU DO USE THIS POSITION MAKE
SURE TO ASSUME IT BY STEPPING
TO THE REAR, TO BLADE THE BODY,
INSTEAD OF STEPPING FOWARD.

Step back,
not foward

80

SLIGHTLY ROTATE

SHOOTING WITH ONE HAND IS EASIER IF YOU SLIGHTLY ROTATE THE HAND. THIS ALLOWS THE ELBOW JOINT AND MUSCLES TO FUNCTION EFFICIENTLY TO RECOVER FROM RECOIL.

Always Avoid positioning the weapon with muzzle up. If the attacker is able to get hold of the weapon there is no way to get the muzzle down to be able to engage the threat with fire.

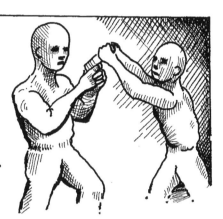

IF SOMEONE IS ATTEMPTING TO GET HOLD OF YOUR WEAPON YOU SHOULD CONSIDER THEM A LETHAL THREAT. MOST PEOPLE WHO ARE DISARMED ARE THEN SHOT WITH THEIR WEAPON. MAINTAIN CONTROL OF YOUR WEAPON AT ALL COSTS. NEVER CLOSE THE GROUND OR DISTANCE TO THE THREAT. YOU SHOULD STRIVE TO KEEP OR INCREASE THE DISTANCE WHENEVER POSSIBLE!

ONE INTIAL DEFENSE AGAINST A DISARMING MOVE SHOULD BE TO STEP BACK WITH RIGHT FOOT AS YOU EXTEND YOUR ARMS. RELAX THE ARMS AND LET THE ARMS EXTEND.

VIOLENTY JERK ARMS

THEN YOU VIOLENTLY PULL THE ARMS IN TOWARDS CENTER OF CHEST, AND FIRE.

AS SOON AS YOU CAN, MOVE BACK AND GO TO NORMAL FIGHTING STANCE.

THIS ACTION NORMALLY WILL JERK PISTOL FREE OF THE THREAT

81

DEFENSIVE TACTICS, WHETHER WEAPON RETENTION, DISARMING MOVES, OR EMPTY HANDED RESPONSES, MUST BE ACCOMPLISHED WITH EXPLOSIVE ACTIONS THAT APPEAR TO COME FROM NOWHERE AND SURPRISE THE OPPONENT. ACTION MUST SPRING FROM YOUR BODY. IF YOU TELEGRAPH YOUR ACTIONS, BY SETTING YOUR FEET, SHIFTING YOUR SHOULDERS ETC. YOU GIVE YOUR OPPONENT TIME TO COUNTER. IF YOU TRY TO USE ONLY MUSCLE POWER YOU BECOME INVOLVED IN A PHYSICAL STRUGGLE - AND THEY MAY BE STRONGER THAN YOU. PROPER TECHNIQUE AND SURPRISE ARE THE ESSENTIAL ELEMENTS FOR SUCCESS.

ANOTHER RETENTION TECHNIQUE IS TO SIMPLY SQUAT DOWN. IF THE THREAT CONTINUES TO HOLD ONTO THE WEAPON THIS ACTION WILL CENTER THE MUZZLE ONTO THEIR BODY. THIS WORKS REGARDLESS OF WHICH HAND OR HANDS THEY GRAB WITH. ONCE MUZZLE IS ON THEM YOU CAN SHOOT. KEEP IN MIND THAT IF THEY ARE HOLDING THE PISTOL IT WILL NOT CYCLE WHEN SHOT.

THIS ACTION THROWS THE ATTACKER OFF BALANCE, BOTH MENTALLY AND PHYSICALLY.

IF YOU SQUAT AND FIRE BUT THE THREAT CONTINUES TO COME FORWARD YOU SHOULD CONTINUE WITH THE DOWNWARD ACTION OF THE SQUAT AND ROLL ONTO YOUR BACK. AT THE SAME TIME YOU KICK YOUR FEET UP TO KEEP THE THREAT OFF OF YOU. CONSTANTLY APPLY PRESSURE WITH THE LEGS TO KEEP THREAT FROM COMING AROUND YOUR SIDES.

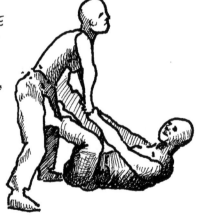

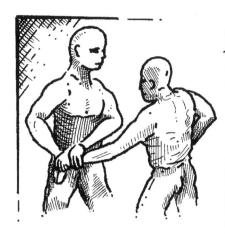

IF SOMEONE ATTEMPTS TO GRAB THE PISTOL IN THE HOLSTER THE FIRST STEP IS TO TRAP THE PISTOL SO THEY CAN'T REMOVE IT FROM THE HOLSTER.

AS YOU TRAP THE PISTOL YOU SHOULD BEGIN TO TWIST IN A DIRECTION THAT TAKES THE PISTOL AWAY FROM THE THREAT.

AS YOU TWIST YOU SQUAT QUICKLY.

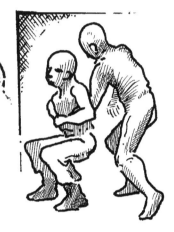

THIS ACTION WHEN PERFORMED SUDDENLY AND VIOLENTLY WILL THROW THE ATTACKER OFF BALANCE AND OFF THEIR FEET. IT IS IMPORTANT TO KEEP THEIR HANDS TRAPPED AS YOU EXECUTE THE TECHNIQUE. (YOUR ELBOW SHOULD BE OUTSIDE THEIR ARM, TRAPPING THE ARM IN A LOCKING ACTION)

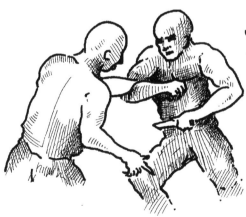

YOU CAN ALSO LOCK THEIR ARM BY WRAPPING YOUR'S AROUND AND HOLDING IT TIGHT AGAINST YOUR BODY WHILE BRINGING OUT YOUR EDGED WEAPON TO ENGAGE AND CUT THEM OFF.

THIS IS A GOOD REASON TO HAVE YOUR BLADE ON THE OPPOSITE SIDE OF THE PISTOL.

IF YOUR HOLSTER IS EXPOSED YOU CAN PREVENT PISTOL FROM BEING PULLED OUT BY GRABBING THE BOTTOM OF THE HOLSTER AND PULLING IT UP. AS IT ROTATES ON THE BELT THE PISTOL GRIP IS WEDGED AGAINST YOUR SIDE. THE PISTOL WON'T COME OUT OF THE HOLSTER UNTIL YOU RELEASE THE LIFT ON THE BOTTOM OF HOLSTER.

TACTICAL MOVEMENT

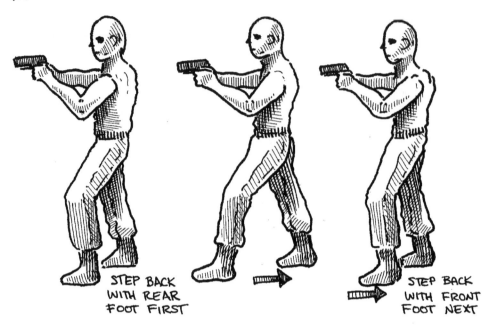

STEP BACK WITH REAR FOOT FIRST

STEP BACK WITH FRONT FOOT NEXT

TACTICAL MOVEMENT IS ACHEIVED BY SHUFFLING THE FEET WITHOUT CROSSING THE LEGS. THE REAR FOOT MOVES FIRST, RIGHT FOR RIGHT HANDED SHOOTER. THEN LEFT FOOT MOVES BACK. YOU STEP LARGE WITH RIGHT FOOT AND A HALF STEP WITH LEFT FOOT. THE KEY IS THAT AFTER EACH SEQUENCE OF STEPS YOU END UP IN THE FIGHTING STANCE YOU BEGAN WITH.

FROM THE WAIST UP NOTHING SHIFTS. BEND THE KNEES SO THEY ACT AS SHOCK ABSORBERS AND ALLOW THE BODY FROM WAIST UP TO REMAIN STEADY. DO NOT CROSS FEET, OR ALLOW FEET TO WIND UP CLOSE TOGETHER — BOTH WILL CREATE AN UNSTABLE POSITION.

IDEALLY YOU WANT TO BE ABLE TO MOVE AND SHOOT AT THE SAME TIME. YOU HAVE TO LET YOUR SIGHT PICTURE TO DICTATE THE RATE OF FIRE. DO NOT SHOOT UNLESS YOU CAN GURANTEE THE HIT. SMOOTHLY PRESSING THE TRIGGER IS MOST IMPORTANT.

FEEL WITH THE FOOT TO TEST FOR SECURE FOOTING. ONCE FOOT IS DOWN THEN THE WEIGHT IS SHIFTED TO THAT FOOT. DO NOT SHIFT WEIGHT AS YOU STEP.

84

TACTICAL MOVEMENT IS USED TO CREATE DISTANCE
BETWEEN YOU AND THE THREAT, TO MOVE TO COVER,
OR WHEN IT IS NECESSARY TO MOVE TOWARDS THE
THREAT. TO MOVE SMOOTHLY AND SHOOT ACCURATELY
IT IS NECESSARY TO PRACTICE. YOU CAN PRACTICE THIS
WITHOUT USING YOUR WEAPON - JUST HOLD UP YOUR HANDS
AND USE YOUR "AIR GUN."

THE BIGGEST PROBLEM WITH MOVING IN THIS MANNER IS
THAT MOST PEOPLE WILL BLADE THEIR BODY MORE AS
THEY BEGIN TO MOVE. THIS PUTS YOUR FEET INTO ALIGNMENT
WHICH CREATS AN UNSTABLE STANCE, AND LIMITS THE ACTUAL
DISTANCE YOU CAN STEP BEFORE THE FRONT FOOT HITS
THE REAR FOOT. YOU NEED TO KEEP YOUR FEET SHOULDER
WIDTH APART AS YOU MOVE TACTICALLY. IT SHOULD BE LIKE
WALKING DOWN A RAILROAD TRACK WITH FEET ON THE
OUTSIDE OF BOTH RAILS.

RIGHT FOOT MOVES FIRST, LEFT FOOT
MOVES NEXT, FOLLOWED BY RIGHT FOOT.
FEET STAY SHOULDER WIDTH APART.

FEET TOO
CLOSE

IF YOU BLADE YOUR
BODY AS YOU MOVE
YOU ARE UNSTABLE
AND CAN'T TAKE
LONG STEPS.

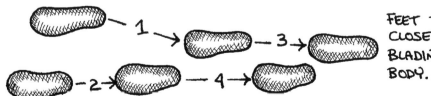

FEET TOO
CLOSE FROM
BLADING THE
BODY.

RAPID MOVEMENT

RAPID MOVEMENT, SOMETIMES CALLED THE "GROUCHO WALK," IS USED TO RAPIDLY MOVE FORWARD. IT SHOULD NOT BE EMPLOYED TO MOVE BACKWARDS BECAUSE IT IS EASY TO TRIP AND FALL. AS YOU MOVE IT IS A HEEL-TOE ACTION AND YOU TAKE SHORT BABY STEPS. THE HEEL IS PLACED DOWN FIRST AND THE FOOT ROLLS FLAT TO THE TOES.

FOR RAPID MOVEMENT THE RIGHT FOOT IS FIRST TO MOVE

SHORT STEPS, FEET ARE CLOSER TOGETHER.

BEND KNEES AND LOWER YOUR CENTER OF GRAVITY.

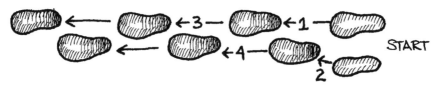

RIGHT MOVES   LEFT MOVES   RIGHT FOOT MOVES FIRST   START

←3—   ←1—   START

←4—   2

A LOT OF PEOPLE WILL USE THE RAPID TYPE MOVEMENT WHEN RETREATING FROM THE THREAT BECAUSE IT IS A LITTLE EASIER TO SHOOT WHILE USING THIS TYPE MOVEMENT. ON THE RANGE, WHERE WE NORMALLY PRACTICE, THIS IS NOT A PROBLEM. BUT WE DON'T FIGHT ON THE RANGE. THE ENVIRONMENT WE FIGHT IN WILL BE FULL OF UNEVEN GROUND, HOLES, CURBS, CHILDREN'S TOYS... EVEN A SMALL OBJECT IS ENOUGH TO UPSET YOUR BALANCE USING RAPID MOVEMENT.

YOUR SITUATION AND ENVIRONMENT WILL DETERMINE THE TYPE MOVEMENT YOU EMPLOY. ALSO REMEMBER THERE MAY BE TIMES WHEN YOU MUST MOVE QUICKLY WITHOUT WORRY ABOUT TRYING TO SHOOT. THE SAME TECHNIQUES APPLY TO THE RIFLE. PRACTICE IS THE KEY TO SUCCESS.

TO PRESENT THE PISTOL AND MOVE WE BEGIN THE PRESENTATION AS WE TAKE OUR FIRST STEP. STEP, AND AT THE SAME TIME YOU SLAP AND GRIP, AND THEN YOU COMPLETE THE PRESENTATION AS THE NEXT STEP IS TAKEN. IF EVERYTHING OCCURS AT ONCE IT SHOULDN'T TAKE YOU ANY ADDITIONAL TIME TO GET THE PISTOL ONTO THE TARGET WHILE YOU ARE MOVING.

IF IT IS A SITUATION WHERE IT IS MORE IMPORTANT TO MOVE QUICKLY, IT IS BETTER TO STEP WITH THE LEFT FOOT FIRST SO THAT THE WAIST, AND PISTOL, ARE NOT SHIFTING AROUND AS YOU TRY TO DRAW THE PISTOL.

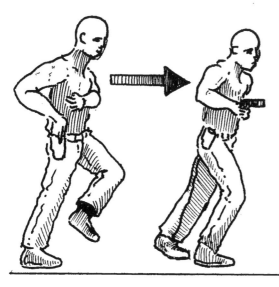

AS YOU STEP WITH THE LEFT FOOT YOU GRIP THE PISTOL WHILE THE SUPPORT HAND SLAPS THE CENTER OF BODY.

AS THE LEFT FOOT IS PLANTED AND RIGHT FOOT BEGINS TO MOVE THE PISTOL IS PULLED FROM HOLSTER AND THE DRAW IS COMPLETED.

WE MOVE AWAY FROM THE THREAT TO CREATE DISTANCE. DISTANCE CREATES TIME FOR US TO GET OUR WEAPON ONTO TARGET AND MAKE HITS ONTO THE THREAT.

MOST PEOPLE WILL ASK WHY BACK AWAY BECAUSE THERE IS NO WAY I CAN BACK UP QUICKER THAN HE CAN RUN AT ME. IT'S NOT A QUESTION OF OUTRUNNING THEM. WE ARE CREATING TIME TO APPLY OUR MARKS-MANSHIP.

DISTANCE = TIME = MARKSMANSHIP

WHEN MOVING AWAY FROM A THREAT TRY TO MOVE
AT ANGLES INSTEAD OF STRAIGHT LINES. THIS FORCES
THE THREAT TO TRACK YOU. FOR A RIGHT HANDED
THREAT YOU SHOULD MOVE TO YOUR LEFT, MAKING IT
MORE DIFFICULT FOR THREAT TO TRACK YOU. OBVIOUSLY
IF YOU HAVE COVER TO USE YOU WOULD MOVE TO IT
IN AS STRAIGHT A LINE AS POSSIBLE. ADDITIONALLY THE
ENVIRONMENT MAY RESTRICT YOUR OPTIONS.

WITH MOST OF THE TACTICS YOU MUST KEEP IN MIND THE
FIGHT AND ENVIRONMENT DETERMINES WHAT OPTIONS ARE
FESIBLE.

PULL ARMS
INWARD

FOR SHOOTING WHILE MOVING I FIND
THAT IF I PULL MY ARMS AND PISTOL
A LITTLE CLOSER TO THE BODY IT
IS EASIER TO KEEP A SIGHT PICTURE.
BRINGING WEAPON CLOSER SHORTENS
THE ARC OF TRAVEL AND BOUNCE IN
THE ARMS AND SIGHTS OF THE WEAPON.

FROM LONGER DISTANCES, AND STABILE
POSITIONS, IT SEEMS TO HELP IF YOU
EXTEND THE ARMS.

MOVING AND SHOOTING WITH THE
PISTOL IS EASIER THAN THE RIFLE.
WITH THE PISTOL THE ARMS CAN
WORK TO STABILIZE THE SIGHTS
REGARDLESS OF WHAT THE BODY IS
DOING. THE RIFLE IS ATTACHED TO THE
BODY, AT THE STOCK/SHOULDER/CHEEKWELD,
WHICH MEANS MOVEMENT IN THE BODY IS
TRANSFERRED TO THE SIGHTS OF THE WEAPON.
PLUS THE LONGER DISTANCE INCREASES ARC OF MOVEMENT.

AS YOU SHOOT YOU MUST SEE THE FRONT SIGHT PRIOR TO PRESSING THE TRIGGER TO CONFIRM WHERE THE SHOT WILL GO. THEN AS YOU PRESS THE TRIGGER AND THE SHOT FIRES YOU SHOULD SEE THE SIGHT AS IT LIFTS OFF THE TARGET. THIS IS THE ONLY WAY TO KNOW WHERE YOU HIT. THERE WON'T BE A BIG HOLE APPEAR ON THE THREAT AND WITH CLOTHES IT WILL BE HARD TO TELL WHERE THE SHOT GOES. WITH MULTIPLE TARGETS YOU MIGHT HAVE TO SHOOT EACH TARGET AND YOU WILL NEED TO KNOW THAT YOU HAVE MADE GOOD HITS. THERE ISN'T TIME TO WAIT FOR RESULTS, YOU MIGHT HAVE TO TRANSITION TO ANOTHER TARGET.

WHEN MOVING AND SHOOTING A LOT OF PEOPLE WILL TRY TO TIME THEIR SHOTS WITH THEIR FOOTWORK. SIGHTS & TRIGGER WORK INDEPENDENT OF THE FEET. THE BEST TIME TO SHOOT IS WHEN ONE FOOT IS UP AND MOVING AND YOU ARE ACTUALLY STANDING, OR BALANCING, ON ONE FOOT. THIS IS THE MOST BALANCED OR STABLE POINT OF THE SIGHTS. AS SOON AS THE FOOT HITS THE GROUND THE BODY SHIFTS AND BOUNCES SOME WHICH AFFECTS SIGHT PICTURE.

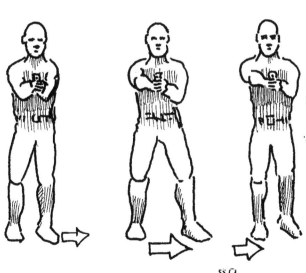

LATERAL MOVEMENT. IF MOVING LEFT YOU MOVE LEFT FOOT FIRST. STEP SIDEWAYS A BIG STEP, THEN A HALF STEP WITH OTHER FOOT. EACH TIME A SEQUENCE OF STEPS IS COMPLETED YOU END UP IN YOUR FIGHTING STANCE.

LATERAL MOVEMENT ALLOWS US TO AVOID THE CENTER LINE OF THE ATTACK. AN ATTACK IS MOST DANGEROUS AT IT'S CENTER CORE OF THE WEAPON BEING USED. WHEN A WEAPON IS BEING USED IT HAS A LIMITED FIELD OF EFFECTIVNESS. A BULLET IS ONLY EFFECTIVE IN THE SMALL AMOUNT OF SPACE IT OCCUPIES AS IT TRAVELS THROUGH SPACE. IF WE AVOID THAT AREA, ALL THINGS OUTSIDE THAT SPACE ARE SAFE. SO IF WE MOVE TO THE SIDE, EVEN 18 INCHES, WE HAVE REMOVED OUR BODY AWAY FROM THE LINE OF ATTACK. THE THREAT MUST EVALUATE, RE-ACQUIRE THE SIGHTS ONTO YOU, AND ACT. DEPENDING ON THE THREAT'S REACTION TIME THIS CREATES A WINDOW FOR YOU TO COUNTER ATTACK. SO YOUR FIRST RESPONSE TO AN ATTACK MIGHT BE TO STEP TO ONE SIDE. EVEN IF SOMEONE IS CHARGING YOU AND AT THE LAST MINUTE YOU MOVE SIDEWAYS THEY WILL MISS YOU OR HAVE TO STOP AND REDIRECT THEIR ATTACK.

WE ALSO MOVE LATERALLY TO GET TO COVER.
ALL FORMS OF MOVEMENT – LATERAL, BACK, FORWARD, ...
ARE COMBINED INTO ONE RESPONSE. LEARN TO FLOW
FROM ONE TO ANOTHER.

IN THE SUMMER MY WIFE PUTS OUT FEEDERS FOR THE HUMMINGBIRDS. THESE BIRDS ARE A GREAT SOURCE OF TACTICAL KNOWLEDGE. THEY ARE CONSTANTLY FIGHTING IN ORDER TO DOMINATE THEIR FEEDERS. SINCE THEY HAVE TO BE CONSTANTLY ON THE LOOKOUT FOR OTHERS THEY NEVER CEASE FROM LOOKING AROUND THEM. EVEN WHEN THEY ARE FEEDING THEY WILL ONLY EAT FOR A SHORT MOMENT AND THEN THEIR HEAD IS BACK UP AND LOOKING AROUND. YOU SHOULD APPLY THE SAME ACTIONS. BE THE HUMMINGBIRD. CONSTANTLY BE LOOKING ABOUT, CHECKING OUT YOUR ENVIRONMENT, CHECKING TO SEE IF ANYONE AROUND YOU MIGHT BE SPOTTING AND CHOOSING YOU AS A VICTIM. WHEN ATTACKED YOU MUST FIGHT BACK WITHOUT HESITATION.

THE PRINCIPLES FOR MANIPULATING THE AR RIFLE ARE THE SAME AS THE PISTOL. THE ACTUAL TECHNIQUES ARE SLIGHTLY DIFFERENT. RIFLE SHOULD STAY IN THE SHOULDER, STRONG HAND ON THE GRIP, EXCEPT FOR CERTAIN MANIPULATIONS.

WITH THE PISTOL ANYTIME THE MAGAZINE IS REMOVED IT GOES INTO THE PINKY FINGER OF THE FIRING HAND. WITH THE AR I PREFER TO HOLD THE MAG WITH THE 3 BOTTOM FINGERS OF THE HAND. THIS FREES UP THE THUMB AND FIRST FINGER TO CYCLE THE BOLT ETC.

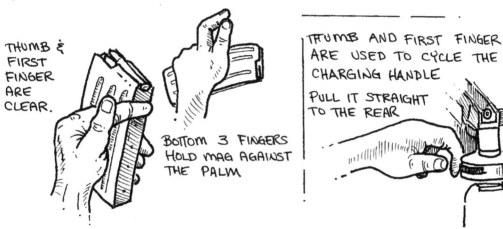

THUMB & FIRST FINGER ARE CLEAR.

BOTTOM 3 FINGERS HOLD MAG AGAINST THE PALM

THUMB AND FIRST FINGER ARE USED TO CYCLE THE CHARGING HANDLE

PULL IT STRAIGHT TO THE REAR

LOADING - WITH THE LEFT HAND HOLDING THE MAG THE FIRST FINGER FEELS THE TOP ROUND TO DETERMINE WHICH SIDE THE TOP ROUND IS ON. DO THIS BY FEEL SO EYES ONLY LOOK AT ENVIRONMENT, NOT THE MAGAZINE. INSERT THE MAG, SEAT IT, AND TUG TO INSURE IT'S SEATED. (NOTE - LOAD MAGS 10% LESS THAN CAPACITY. IF FULLY LOADED THEY WILL NOT SEAT IN THE RIFLE BECAUSE OF SPRING PRESSURE.) ONCE THE MAG IS SEATED THE LEFT HAND CYCLES THE CHARGING HANDLE. AFTER CHARGING YOU WILL DROP THE MAG AND FEEL WITH FINGER TO DETERMINE IF TOP ROUND HAS SWAPPED SIDES. THIS LETS YOU KNOW THERE IS A ROUND CHAMBERED.

TO PERFORM A PRESS CHECK WITH THE AR YOU WILL HAVE TO SUPPORT THE WEAPON WITH LEFT HAND, REACHING AROUND WITH THE FIRST FINGER TO CHECK CHAMBER. THE RIGHT HAND PULLS BACK THE CHARGING HANDLE BY GRABBING THE HANDLE WITH THE FIRST TWO FINGERS IN A SNAKE FANG TYPE ACTION.

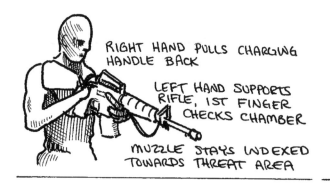

RIGHT HAND PULLS CHARGING HANDLE BACK

LEFT HAND SUPPORTS RIFLE, 1ST FINGER CHECKS CHAMBER

MUZZLE STAYS INDEXED TOWARDS THREAT AREA

WHEN DOING THE PRESS CHECK IS ONE OF THE FEW TIMES THE RIGHT HAND COMES OFF THE GRIP OF THE RIFLE.

AFTER CHECKING THE CHAMBER YOU NEED TO MAKE SURE THE CHARGING HANDLE IS SEATED.

INDENTION IN BOLT CARRIER

YOU ALSO NEED TO MAKE SURE THE BOLT IS SEATED. TO DO THIS THE FIRST FINGER OF LEFT HAND USES THE INDENTION IN THE BOLT CARRIER TO PRESS THE CARRIER FORWARD. THIS IS WHAT THE INDENTION IN THE BOLT CARRIER IS DESIGNED FOR. DO NOT USE THE FORWARD ASSIST. IF THERE IS A PROBLEM, SUCH AS A DIRTY CHAMBER OR FAULTY ROUND OF AMMO, THE FORWARD ASSIST WILL FORCE IT AND COULD JAM THE RIFLE. PLUS UNLESS THE CLAW ON THE ASSIST LINES UP WITH THE TEETH ON THE CARRIER BANGING ON THE ASSIST WON'T DO ANY GOOD.

UNLOADING - TRIGGER FINGER PRESSES THE MAG RELEASE, LEFT HAND REMOVES THE MAG. RETAIN MAG IN LEFT HAND AND CYCLE CHARGING HANDLE, EJECTING THE ROUND. BE SURE TO CHECK THE CHAMBER VISUALLY. IF YOU WANT TO LOCK THE BOLT TO THE REAR YOU WILL AGAIN SUPPORT THE RIFLE WITH LEFT HAND, POSITIONING THE THUMB OF THE LEFT HAND SO IT CAN PRESS THE BOLT LATCH. RIGHT HAND PULLS CHARGING HANDLE TO THE REAR.

IF YOU ARE LOADING THE RIFLE WITH BOLT LOCKED OPEN YOU WILL SEAT MAG AND THE THUMB OF LEFT HAND SLIDES UP TO PRESS THE RELEASE BUTTON. WHEN BOLT IS LOCKED TO THE REAR DON'T USE CHARGING HANDLE. THIS WILL TAKE EXTRA TIME, AND WON'T ALLOW BOLT TO SEAT WITH FULL POWER OF THE SPRING.

AR EMPTY LOAD - AS SOON AS YOU REALIZE THE RIFLE IS EMPTY THE LEFT HAND COMES DOWN TO RETRIEVE FRESH MAG. TRIGGER FINGER PRESSES MAG RELEASE TO DUMP EMPTY MAG. INSERT FULL MAG, SEAT IT, AND TUG TO MAKE SURE MAG IS SEATED. LEFT THUMB SLIDES UP TO PRESS BOLT RELEASE. THE ENTIRE TIME MUZZLE SHOULD BE ON TARGET.

TACTICAL RELOAD - THERE ARE TWO METHODS OF DOING THE TAC RELOAD. WITH THE FIRST TECHNIQUE THE LEFT HAND GETS THE FRESH MAG, GRABBING IT DOWN LOW ON THE MAG. PULL IT OUT OF THE POUCH AND THEN BRING IT UP TO MAG IN THE RIFLE. SANDWICH FRESH MAG BETWEEN HAND AND MAG IN THE RIFLE. GRAB THE MAG IN THE RIFLE AS HIGH AS POSSIBLE. PRESS MAG RELEASE WITH TRIGGER FINGER AND REMOVE THE PARTIAL MAG. AS YOU PULL MAG OUT YOU WILL NOTICE THE MAGS ARE STAGGERED WITH THE FULL MAG BEING THE HIGHEST. INSERT AND SEAT FULL MAG AND SECURE PARTIAL MAG.

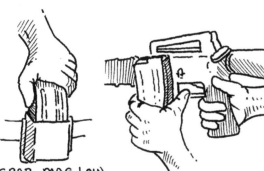

FRESH MAG IS HIGHEST

GRAB MAG LOW, WHICH WITH IT IN MAG POUCH WILL BE GRABBING THE HIGHEST PORTION EXTENDING UP. (BULLET SHOULD BE POINTING TO THE REAR WHILE IN THE POUCH)

BRING FRESH MAG UP AND GRAB THE MAG IN THE RIFLE AS HIGH AS POSSIBLE. FINGERS AND THUMB GRAB MAG, SANDWICHING IT BETWEEN HAND, FRESH MAG, AND OLD MAG.

AS YOU PULL THE OLD MAG OUT THE FRESH MAG WILL BE HIGHEST. THIS IS THE ONE THAT GOES INTO RIFLE. INSERT, SEAT AND TUG. SECURE THE PARTIAL MAG.

THE SECOND TECHNIQUE FOR TACTICALLY RELOADING THE AR IS TO USE THE SAME METHOD AS USED WITH THE PISTOL. AS YOU BRING UP THE FRESH MAG YOU POSITION IT BETWEEN THE FIRST AND SECOND FINGERS. THIS ALLOWS YOUR THUMB AND FIRST FINGER TO REMOVE THE PARTIAL FROM THE RIFLE. THIS TECHNIQUE WORKS ESPECIALLY WELL WHEN WORKING WITH THE 20 ROUND MAGS. WITH THE SHORTER 20 ROUND MAGS THE FIRST TECHNIQUE, WHERE YOU GRAB THE FRESH MAG LOW AND THE PARTIAL MAG HIGH, DOESN'T WORK AS WELL.

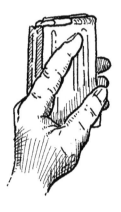

WITH THE TECHNIQUE THE HAND COMES UP, YOU PINCH THE MAG IN THE RIFLE, AND TRIGGER FINGER PRESSES MAG RELEASE. REMOVE PARTIAL, HAND MOVES OVER TO INSERT AND SEAT NEW MAG.

WRAPPING THE AR MAG WITH ATHLETIC OR GRIP TAPE GIVES YOU A MUCH BETTER SURFACE TO GRAB, ESPECIALLY IF THE HANDS ARE WET OR COLD OR YOU ARE WEARING GLOVES.

DON'T WRAP THE TOP HALF OF THE MAG SINCE THIS IS THE PORTION THAT GOES INTO THE MAG WELL.

WITH THE AR, AND PISTOL, IT IS A GOOD IDEA TO HAVE MAGAZINES YOU USE FOR TRAINING AND THEN MAGS THAT ARE ONLY USED FOR SELF DEFENSE OR OPERATIONS. USE COLOR TAPE TO CODE OR MARK THE MAGS DS TO WHICH IS WHICH. BE SURE TO KEEP THEM SEPERATE AS FAR AS GEAR STORAGE. ALTHOUGH SOME PEOPLE WILL KEEP MAGS WHICH DON'T FUNCTION WELL FOR TRAINING PURPOSES IT ISN'T A GOOD IDEA UNLESS THEY ARE PAINTED NEON ORANGE OR SOMETHING. IN THE NORTH HOLLYWOOD ROBBERY ONE OF THE RESPONDING OFFICERS HAD A FAULTY MAG WHICH ENDED UP IN HIS RIFLE DURING THE FIGHT.

• AR MALFUNCTIONS

MALFUNCTION CLEARANCES WITH THE AR ARE BASICALLY THE SAME AS THEY ARE WITH THE PISTOL. AS SOON AS YOU PRESS THE TRIGGER AND THE RIFLE DOESN'T FIRE YOU TAP TO SEAT THE MAG AND TUG TO MAKE SURE IT'S SEATED. THEN CHARGE THE BOLT. AS YOU RELEASE THE CHARGING HANDLE AND IT GOES FORWARD YOU'LL BE ABLE TO TELL IMMEDIATELY IF THE ACTION IS CLEARED OR NOT. IF IT IS CLEAR THEN FIRE. IF THE BOLT DOESN'T SEAT YOU GO INTO THE SECOND CLEARANCE. PRESS THE MAG RELEASE AND STRIP THE MAG OUT OF THE WEAPON. CYCLE THE ACTION TO CLEAR THE OBSTRUCTION. ONCE THE ACTION IS CLEARED RELOAD AND FIRE IF NEEDED.

SOMETIMES YOU WILL HAVE TWO ROUNDS WEDGED TOGETHER AND CYCLING THE ACTION WON'T CLEAR THEM. WHEN THIS OCCURS YOU WILL HAVE TO LOCK THE BOLT CARRIER TO THE REAR AND THEN THE FINGERS OF YOUR LEFT HAND GO UP THE MAG WELL TO DISLODGE THE ROUNDS. REMEMBER THAT TO LOCK BOLT CARRIER TO THE REAR THE LEFT HAND SUPPORTS THE WEAPON, POSITIONED SO THE THUMB CAN PRESS CATCH, AND RIGHT HAND LEAVES THE GRIP TO PULL CHARGING HANDLE TO THE REAR. IF YOU HAVE TO WORK THIS PROCEDURE THE WHEN ROUNDS ARE DISLODGED DON'T FORGET TO CYCLE ACTION AGAIN TO INSURE THE CHAMBER IS CLEAR. OTHERWISE WHEN YOU RELOAD YOU WILL JUST SET UP ANOTHER MALFUNCTION.

WITH THE AR THERE IS ANOTHER MALFUNCTION THAT CAN OCCUR CALLED A BOLT OVER. THIS OCCURS WHEN YOU HAVE A ROUND OR PIECE OF BRASS WIND UP ON TOP OF THE BOLT CARRIER. PULLING THE CHARGING HANDLE TO THE REAR WON'T CLEAR IT BECAUSE IT JUST PULLS THE ROUND BACK WITH THE BOLT CARRIER. TO CLEAR THIS YOU WILL HAVE TO TAKE A KNIFE OR SCREWDRIVER AND FORCE THE BOLT TO THE REAR WHILE MAG WELL IS POINTED DOWN. NORMALLY NOT SOMETHING YOU CAN DO QUICKLY.

BOLT OVER CLEARANCE

YOU WILL HAVE TO USE A TOOL TO PRESS THE BOLT AND CARRIER TO THE REAR.

MAG WELL SHOULD BE POINTED DOWN SO THAT AS THE BOLT IS SHOVED TO THE REAR THE BRASS OR ROUND WILL DROP TO THE GROUND.

WITH THE AR YOU CAN ALSO GET A ROUND STUCK IN THE CHAMBER. WHEN THIS HAPPENS THE CHARGING HANDLE WON'T PULL TO THE REAR. ORIGINALLY I LEARNED TO CLEAR THIS BY DROPPING TO A KNEE AND BANGING THE STOCK AGAINST THE GROUND AS YOU SLAM THE CHARGING HANDLE TO THE REAR. THE TECHNIQUE I CAME UP WITH WAS TO DO THE SAME ACTION BUT TO BANG THE STOCK AGAINST YOUR HIP. THIS WAY YOU DON'T HAVE TO DROP TO A KNEE, MEANING YOU DON'T HAVE TO LOSE MOBILITY, AND WITH THE MUZZLE POINTED AT THE THREAT YOU CAN GET THE RIFLE BACK INTO THE FIGHT QUICKER.

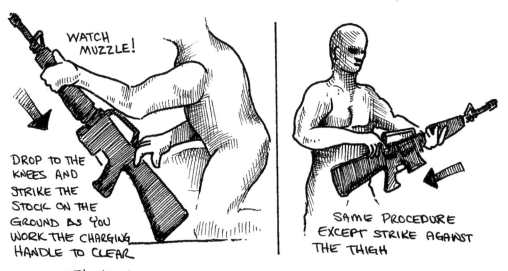

WATCH MUZZLE!

DROP TO THE KNEES AND STRIKE THE STOCK ON THE GROUND AS YOU WORK THE CHARGING HANDLE TO CLEAR

SAME PROCEDURE EXCEPT STRIKE AGAINST THE THIGH

WITH EITHER TECHNIQUE IF YOU HAVE A COLLASPABLE STOCK YOU WILL COLLASPE IT FIRST OR IT WILL BREAK THE STOCK.

WHEN TRAINING THERE ARE A VARIETY OF LOCATIONS
TO PLACE SPARE MAGAZINES FOR THE AR. TACTICAL VESTS,
THIGH RIGS, BELT POUCHES, AND BACK POCKET OF THE PANTS.
YOU SHOULD WORK WITH ALL OPTIONS. EVEN IF WE WORK
WITH TAC VESTS OR THIGH RIGS YOU SHOULD PRACTICE BY
WORKING WITH THE MINIMAL. THERE ARE SITUATIONS WHERE
YOU WON'T HAVE ALL YOUR TACTICAL GEAR. THE SAME IS
TRUE FOR PISTOL OR ANY OTHER FIREARM YOU TRAIN WITH.

MALFUNCTION SETUP

TO SET UP TYPE 1 MALFUNCTION YOU CAN EMPTY THE
CHAMBER, WITH LOADED MAG, OR YOU CAN HAVE A
ROUND IN THE CHAMBER, AND A LOADED MAG IN THE
RIFLE BUT NOT SEATED. WITH THE FIRST OPTION YOU
HAVE MALFUNCTION IMMEDIATELY. WITH THE SECOND
SETUP THE RIFLE WILL FIRE ONE ROUND AND THEN YOU
WILL GET THE MALFUNCTION. WITH THE MAG UNSEATED
YOU MIGHT HAVE TO HOLD IT IN THE MAGWELL WITH YOUR
SUPPORT HAND.

FOR TYPE 2 YOU PULL BOLT CARRIER BACK AND INSERT
A SPENT PIECE OF BRASS IN FRONT OF BOLT AND LET THE
BOLT GO FORWARD.

FOR TYPE 3 YOU LOCK THE BOLT TO THE REAR AND
THEN DROP A PIECE OF SPENT BRASS ALL THE WAY INTO
THE EJECTION PORT. THEN WITH MAG IN THE RIFLE LET
THE BOLT GO FORWARD, WHICH SETS UP A DOUBLE FEED.

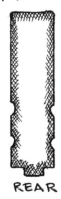

FRONT

FRONT

REAR

REAR

IF YOU LOOK AT CROSS SECTION OF MAGS YOU WILL
NOTICE THE REAR OF AR IS STEPPED, FRONT IS
FLAT. WITH THE 45 MAG REAR
IS FLAT, FRONT IS CURVED. THIS
ALLOWS YOU TO DETERMINE THE
POSITION OF THE MAG WITHOUT
HAVING TO LOOK AT THEM.

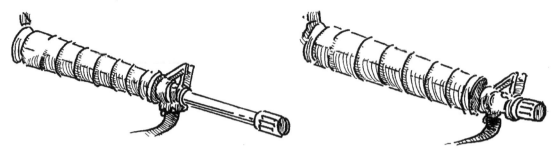

THE 16 INCH BARREL IS THE IDEAL LENGTH, BUT THE SIGHT RADIUS IS SHORTER THAN THE 20 INCH. THE DISSAPATOR HAS AN EXTENDED SIGHT RADIUS, THE SAME AS A 20 INCH, BUT WITH THE 16 INCH BARREL. I TRAINED WITH ONE OF THESE FOR A WHILE AND I LIKED THE WAY THIS SETUP PERFORMS. THE ORIGINAL SP1 BARRELS ARE LIGHWEIGHT AND THE 20 INCH BARREL CAN BE SHORTENED TO 16 INCHES TO CREATE THE DISSAPATOR SETUP.

THE LOW READY IS WITH STOCK IN YOUR SHOULDER AND THE WEAPON DEPRESSED LOW ENOUGH SO YOU CAN SEE THE HANDS OF YOUR THREAT, OR EVERYTHING IN YOUR ENVIRONMENT. THIS IS THE BEST POSITION TO USE WHEN THERE IS A DANGER OF CLOSE RANGES, IE CORNERS A THREAT COULD APPEAR AROUND.

IF YOU ARE SEARCHING A RURAL OR WIDE OPEN AREA THE HIGH READY DOESN'T TIRE YOU OUT AS MUCH AS THE LOW READY. STOCK IS HELD AT WAIST LEVEL WITH MUZZLE HELD UP. FOR CLOSE QUARTER SITUATIONS IT HAS RETENTION PROBLEMS, JUST LIKE HOLDING THE PISTOL WITH MUZZLE UP HIGH.

THE CROSS BODY, OR INDOOR READY, OR ANY OTHER NAME YOU CALL IT IS WHERE THE RIFLE IS COLLASPED INTO THE BODY, STOCK FLAT AGAINST THE SHOULDER AND MUZZLE POINTED OUTWARD OF THE FEET. CAN BE USED WHEN YOU NEED TO MOVE AROUND AND THERE ARE A LOT OF PEOPLE IN THE AREA.

THE PROPER WAY TO SLING THE RIFLE WITH MUZZLE UP IS TO DO IT ON THE RIGHT SIDE, FOR A RIGHT HANDED SHOOTER. RIGHT HAND HOLDS ONTO THE RIFLE OR PUTS TENSION ON THE FRONT OF THE SLING TO KEEP IT FROM SLIDING OFF THE SHOULDER.

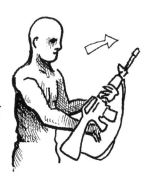

TO DISMOUNT THE RIFLE FROM THIS SLING POSITION THE SUPPORT HAND COMES UNDER THE RIGHT ARM, BETWEEN THE ARM AND BODY, AND GRABS THE HANDGUARD OF THE RIFLE.

SUPPORT HAND BRINGS RIFLE OFF THE SHOULDER AND FORWARD, INDEXING THE MUZZLE TO THE THREAT AS RIFLE COMES OFF THE SHOULDER. RIGHT HAND ACQUIRES A GRIP ON RIFLE AS SOON AS POSSIBLE AND STOCK IS MOUNTED INTO SHOULDER.

TO SLING THE WEAPON FROM READY POSITION THE LEFT HAND GRIPS THE FRONT OF THE SLING, WHERE IT IS ATTACHED TO THE FORWARD PART OF THE RIFLE. RIGHT HAND RELEASES RIFLE AND LETS IT DROP AND THE LEFT HAND GUIDES THE RIFLE OVER THE RIGHT SHOULDER.

THERE ARE SOME DISADVANTAGES WITH THE MUZZLE UP POSITION ON STRONG SIDE. FIRST IS THE FACT THAT IF YOU ARE CARRYING A PISTOL WHEN YOU DISMOUNT THE RIFLE IT CAN GET HUNG UP ON THE PISTOL. ALSO WITH THE RIFLE BLOCKING THE PISTOL IT IS DIFFICULT TO GET TO THE PISTOL IF NEEDED. WITH MUZZLE UP IF THERE IS A DISCHARGE IT GOES UP, WHERE BULLET COMES DOWN SOMEWHERE, AND THE DISCHARGE BLAST IS NEAR YOUR HEAD. WITH THE MUZZLE UP IT ALSO PRESENTS A HIGHER PROFILE WHICH CAN ALERT OTHERS TO THE FACT THAT YOU ARE ARMED.

THE MUZZLE DOWN POSITION, ON THE SUPPORT
SIDE IS THE PREFERRED METHOD OF CARRY.
IT PRESENTS A LOW PROFILE, KEEPS THE MUZZLE
POINTED DOWN AND AWAY FROM YOUR HEAD,
AND LEAVES THE PISTOL - ON YOUR PRIMARY
SIDE, OPEN FOR USE IF NEEDED. KEEP THE
SUPPORT HAND ON THE SLING TO PREVENT RIFLE
FROM SLIDING OFF YOUR SHOULDER.

TO PRESENT RIFLE FROM THIS
POSITION THE SUPPORT HAND COMES
DOWN AND GRIPS THE HANDGUARD.
BRING THE MUZZLE STRAIGHT UP
AND POINT IT IN ON THE THREAT. AT THE SAME
TIME THE RIFLE IS ROTATED COUNTER CLOCKWISE,
THE PRIMARY ACQUIRES A GRIP AND THE RIFLE
IS SEATED INTO THE SHOULDER.

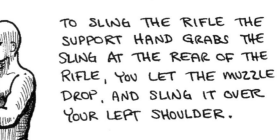

TO SLING THE RIFLE THE
SUPPORT HAND GRABS THE
SLING AT THE REAR OF THE
RIFLE, YOU LET THE MUZZLE
DROP, AND SLING IT OVER
YOUR LEFT SHOULDER.

THE SCRAMBLE CARRY IS USED WHEN
YOU NEED TO FREE UP BOTH HANDS.
WITH THE SLING ADJUSTED PROPERLY
YOU CAN LOOP IT OVER YOUR NECK
BUT STILL BE ABLE TO GET THE
STOCK INTO YOUR SHOULDER TO SHOOT
AND FIGHT. THIS GIVES YOU THE
VERSTILITY OF A TACTICAL SLING
WITHOUT ALL THE EXTRA SLING AND
BUCKLES.

HAVING THE SLING MOUNTED TO THE
SIDE OF THE REAR STOCK, INSTEAD OF
THE BOOTOM, ALLOWS THE RIFLE TO HANG
FLAT AGAINST YOUR BODY REGARDLESS OF HOW YOU
ARE SLINGING THE RIFLE.

100

FOR THE LEFT HANDED SHOOTER TO PERFORM A TACTICAL RELOAD FIRST GRAB THE FRESH MAG LOW WITH THE RIGHT HAND.

POSITION YOUR HAND AS HIGH AS POSSIBLE ON THE MAG IN THE RIFLE AND GRIP IT WITH THE LAST THREE FINGERS OF THE HAND, PRESSING THE 2 MAGS TOGETHER. THIS WILL POSITION THE THUMB TO PRESS THE MAG RELEASE.

AS YOU PULL THE MAG OUT THE FRESH MAG IS POSITIONED HIGHER AND READY TO BE INSERTED INTO THE RIFLE.

WITH THE EMPTY RELOAD THE BOLT CARRIER RELEASE IS PRESSED WITH THE TRIGGER FINGER OF THE LEFT HAND. !

TO LOCK THE BOLT TO THE REAR THE TRIGGER FINGER OF LEFT HAND DEPRESSES CATCH AS THE RIGHT HAND, IN A SNAKE FANG GRIP, PULLS CHARGING HANDLE TO THE REAR.

A GOOD MODIFICATION FOR LEFT HANDED SHOOTERS IS THE AMBI LATCH FOR THE CHARGING HANDLE. SAFETY IS NORMALLY PRESSED WITH THE THUMB AND ENGAGED WITH THE TRIGGER FINGER.

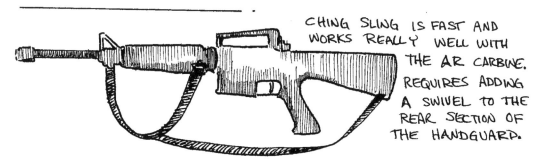

CHING SLING IS FAST AND WORKS REALLY WELL WITH THE AR CARBINE. REQUIRES ADDING A SWIVEL TO THE REAR SECTION OF THE HANDGUARD.

• TRANSISTIONS

SHOULD THE RIFLE MALFUNCTION, AND BECAUSE OF THE DISTANCE BETWEEN YOU AND THE THREAT THERE IS NO TIME TO CLEAR THE MALFUNCTION, IT MAY BE BEST TO TRANSITION TO YOUR PISTOL. WITH THE SUPPORT HAND SIMPLY PULL THE RIFLE INTO YOUR BODY AS YOU LET THE STOCK DROP. PULL THE RIFLE INTO THE BODY SO AS YOU MOVE IT ISN'T FLOPPING AROUND.

SOME PEOPLE WILL USE THE SAME TECHNIQUE EXCEPT WITH MUZZLE DOWN. THIS PUTS THE MAJORITY OF WEIGHT ABOVE THE HAND, WHICH MAKES THE BULK OF THE WEAPON MORE DIFFICULT TO CONTROL.

THE RIFLE CAN ALSO BE LOOPED OVER THE SUPPORT ARM, WHICH ALLOWS YOU TO HAVE A TWO HANDED GRIP ON THE PISTOL.

TO ASSUME THIS POSITION THE RIGHT HAND SUPPORTS RIFLE AS THE LEFT ARM SLIPS THROUGH THE SLING. THE RIGHT ARM LOWERS THE RIFLE DOWN. THE DISADVANTAGE OF THIS TECHNIQUE IS THAT IF YOU ARE MOVING, WHICH IS A GOOD IDEA DURING A FIGHT, THE RIFLE WILL FLOP AROUND.

IF THERE IS TIME YOU CAN ALSO LOOP THE SLING OVER YOUR NECK IN THE SCRAMBLE CARRY MODE. LEFT HAND SIMPLY TAKES SLING OVER THE HEAD AND YOU LOWER THE RIFLE DOWN.

WITH THE TACTICAL SLING THE RIFLE AND SLING SHOULD BE POSITIONED SO THAT AS THE RIFLE IS LOWERED DOWN IT WILL FALL TO THE OPPOSITE SIDE OF THE BODY, AWAY FROM YOUR PISTOL.

DON'T SIMPLY LET THE WEAPON FALL BECAUSE IT WILL WHACK VARIOUS PARTS OF YOUR BODY AS IT DROPS.

ANOTHER TECHNIQUE IS TO SLIDE THE RIFLE BETWEEN THE SUPPORT ARM AND YOUR BODY. CLAMP THE RIFLE AGAINST THE BODY WITH THE ELBOW. ALTHOUGH THIS IS A QUICK TECHNIQUE TO ASSUME IT CAN BE CUMBERSOME TO MOVE ABOUT WITH THE MUZZLE OF THE RIFLE EXTENDING FORWARD.

RIFLE RETENTION

IF SOMEONE ATTEMPTS TO GRAB YOUR RIFLE YOUR FIRST RESPONSE SHOULD BE TO CONSIDER THEM A LETHAL THREAT AND ENGAGE WITH FIRE.

IF IT ISN'T POSSIBLE TO FIRE THERE ARE SEVERAL OPTIONS WHICH PROGRESS FROM ONE TO ANOTHER.

"ROWING" THE RIFLE WILL TWIST THE WRIST AND ARM, BREAKING THEIR GRIP ON THE WEAPON.

THE ROWING ACTION MUST BE INITIATED QUICKLY SO THE THREAT DOESN'T REALIZE WHAT YOU ARE ATTEMPTING TO DO.

IF YOU CLAMP THEIR HAND TO THE RIFLE WITH YOUR HAND AS YOU ROW THE BARREL IT WILL PUT THE INTO A WRIST LOCK AND YOU CAN FORCE THEM TO THE GROUND.

BE SURE WITH ANY ACTION OF THIS TYPE YOU STAY AWARE OF THEIR FREE HAND - IT COULD GO FOR A WEAPON!

103

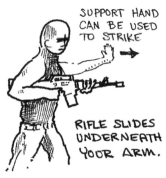

SUPPORT HAND CAN BE USED TO STRIKE

EXTEND

STEP BACK

JERK!

RIFLE SLIDES UNDERNEATH YOUR ARM.

STEP AND JERK - STEP BACK WITH YOUR RIGHT LEG AS YOU EXTEND YOUR ARMS. THEN YOU VIOLENTLY JERK THE RIFLE TOWARDS YOU. THE STOCK OF THE RIFLE WILL SLIDE UNDER YOUR RIGHT ARM TO GET MAXIMUM AMOUNT OF PULL. AGAIN SPEED AND SURPRISE ARE KEYS TO SUCCESS.

AS YOU PERFORM THE STEP AND JERK IF THE THREAT FOLLOWS YOU IN THEN YOU SHOULD SQUAT, DROP, AND ROLL ONTO YOUR BACK, KICKING UP YOUR FEET AS YOU DO TO KEEP THE THREAT OFF. THIS IS THE SAME TECHNIQUE MENTIONED FOR USE WITH THE PISTOL.

 GET TO YOUR FEET AS SOON AS POSSIBLE

IF THE THREAT RUSHES IN YOU CAN USE HIS MOMENTUM TO WORK AGAINST HIM. STEP FORWARD WITH THE RIGHT FOOT, PIVOT ON THE RIGHT AND SWING LEFT FOOT AROUND. MUZZLE RISES UP AND THEN DOWN.

IF THREAT PUSHES MUZZLE DOWN PIVOT ON LEFT FOOT, TURNING MUZZLE CLOCKWISE, REVERSING THROW.

CONTINUED...

TWIST

STEP

PIVOT

THE ACTION DESCRIBED ON THE PREVIOUS PAGE IS SIMILAR
TO AN AKIDO STAFF THROW. THE TECHNIQUE OF USING THE
THREAT'S MOMENTUM CAN BE USED FOR A VARIETY OF
SITUATIONS. THE KEY IS TO REDIRECT THE THREAT'S
DIRECTION OF TRAVEL. REDIRECTION SHOULD BE IN A WAVE
TYPE ACTION.

WAVE

THE WAVE MOVEMENT USES
GRADUAL REDIRECTION TO
GUIDE MOMENTUM.

AS YOU WORK THIS TECHNIQUE, OR ANY OTHER, REMEMBER
TO REDIRECT THE THREAT'S MASS TOWARDS THE THIRD
POINT OF THE TRIPOD REGARDLESS OF WHETHER IT IS TO
THE FRONT OR REAR.

FOR AN ATTACK FROM THE REAR YOU
WANT TO SHOOT THEM OFF OF YOU.
THE SUPPORT HAND SHOULD REVERSE
ITS GRIP ON THE RIFLE AND THEN
PIVOT THE MUZZLE AROUND AND
DOWN. EVEN SHOOTING THEM IN THE
FOOT OR LEG WILL CAUSE THEM TO
RELEASE YOU SO YOU CAN CREATE
DISTANCE AND ENGAGE WITH
ADDITIONAL SHOTS AS NEEDED.

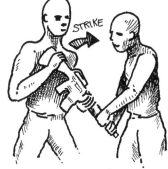

STRIKE

FOR EXTREMELY CLOSE SITUATIONS
WHEN A THREAT CLOSES IN AND FORCES
MUZZLE DOWN YOU CAN REVERSE THE
RIGHT HAND, SLIDING IT TO THE STOCK,
AND STRIKE WITH STOCK. IF THEY
ARE IN THE PROCESS OF PUSHING DOWN
ON MUZZLE THEIR FORCE ASSISTS YOU
WITH THE STRIKE ACTION.

AS SOON AS THEY RELEASE THE RIFLE YOU STRIKE WITH
MUZZLE, ROWING FROM MUZZLE TO STOCK.

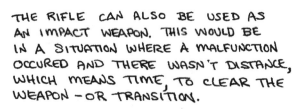

THE RIFLE CAN ALSO BE USED AS AN IMPACT WEAPON. THIS WOULD BE IN A SITUATION WHERE A MALFUNCTION OCCURED AND THERE WASN'T DISTANCE, WHICH MEANS TIME, TO CLEAR THE WEAPON - OR TRANSITION.

FOR A FORWARD STRIKE THE SUPPORT HAND REVERSES THE GRIP, SO THE FINGERS ARE ON TOP OF THE WEAPON, THEN YOU PULL THE RIFLE OVER THE SHOULDER AND BACK. THIS IS THE COCKING STAGE. THE MUZZLE IS THEN DRIVEN INTO THE THREAT.

STRIKE AREAS ARE THE OCULAR CAVITY, THE THROAT, OR THE CENTER OF THE CHEST. I WOULD CONSIDER WEAPON STRIKES TO BE LETHAL FORCE.

THE SAME BASIC TECHNIQUE CAN BE USED FOR A STRIKE TO THE RIGHT SIDE. THE SUPPORT HAND ROLLS OVER AND THE TOP OF WEAPON IS TWISTED SO IT IS POINTED TO THE RIGHT. THE SUPPORT HAND SUPPLIES THE FORCE TO STRIKE.

RIGHT SIDE

LEFT SIDE

FOR THE LEFT SIDE STRIKE THE RIFLE IS ROTATED COUNTER CLOCKWISE SO SIGHT IS POINTED LEFT. SUPPORT HAND CUPS THE HANDGUARD. FOR STRIKES TO THE SIDE THE SIGHT SHOULD BE YOUR POINT OF IMPACT.

STRIKES TO THE SIDE ARE USEFUL WHEN SOMEONE ATTACKS TO YOUR SIDE, OR COMES AROUND A CORNER, AND THERE ISN'T TIME TO INDEX ONTO THE THREAT TO ENGAGE WITH FIRE. AS SOON AS YOU STRIKE YOU SHOULD CREATE DISTANCE AND INDEX ONTO THE THREAT, FIRING IF NEEDED. WEAPON STRIKES SHOULD ONLY BE USED AS A QUICK FIX, AND NOT YOUR FIRST CHOICE.

(SHOWN TO ME BY BENNIE COOLEY)

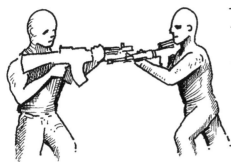

THE RIFLE CAN ALSO BE USED TO PARRY A WEAPON, SAY IN A SITUATION WHERE IT IS CLOSE QUARTERS AND YOU HAVE A MALFUNCTION OR EMPTY WEAPON.

A PARRY SHOULD ALSO BE FOLLOWED UP BY A WEAPON STRIKE. REMEMBER THAT SPEED AND SURPRISE ARE NEEDED TO APPLY THESE TECHNIQUES WITH SUCCESS.

IN EXTREME CLOSE QUARTERS THE RIFLE CAN ALSO BE USED AS A RETENTION DEVICE LIKE A CANE OR STAFF COULD.

DON'T LIMIT YOURSELF BY THINKING THE RIFLE IS ONLY USEFUL AS LONG AS IT WILL FIRE. YOUR ULTIMATE WEAPON IS YOUR MIND, AND YOU ARE LIMITED ONLY BY YOUR IMIGINATION.

SHORT AND QUICK SIDE KICKS CAN ALSO BE USEFUL. THESE ARE ESPECIALLY GOOD WHEN YOU ARE DEALING WITH THREATS WHO DON'T WARRANT SHOOTING.

AS ALWAYS BE AWARE THAT SOMEONE CAN GO FROM A NON-LETHAL THREAT TO A LETHAL THREAT AND BE PREPARED TO RESPOND ACCORDINGLY — AND QUICKLY!

PISTOL STRIKES

THE WEAPON STRIKES CAN ALSO BE PERFORMED WITH PISTOLS. THE POSITION OF THE SUPPORT HAND DEPENDS ON THE DIRECTION OF THE STRIKE. FOR A STRIKE TO THE FRONT YOU CAN USE AN UNDERHAND OR OVERHAND GRIP.

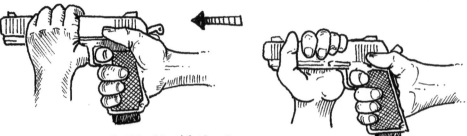

SUPPORT HAND GUIDES MUZZLE
POWER FOR STRIKE COMES FROM
PRIMARY HAND

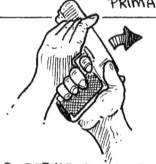

FOR STRIKE TO THE RIGHT
SUPPORT HAND CUPS PISTOL.
STRIKE AREA IS THE TOP
OF THE SLIDE. POWER
COMES FROM SUPPORT HAND.

STRIKE TO LEFT
SUPPORT HAND CUPS
RIGHT SIDE OF PISTOL

THE MUZZLE AND BOTTOM
OF GRIP CAN ALSO BE USED
FOR A FORWARD STRIKE.

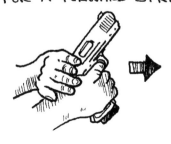

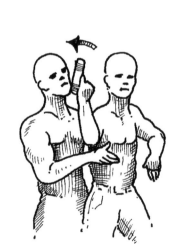

THE PISTOL CAN ALSO BE USED
TO STRIKE OVER YOUR SHOULDER
TO STRIKE A THREAT IN CLOSE
TO THE REAR.

REMEMBER THAT WEAPON STRIKES ARE CONSIDERED LETHAL FORCE!

- USE OF POSITIONS

VARIOUS POSITIONS ARE EMPLOYED TO SHOOT AND FIGHT WITH
FIREARMS EITHER TO TAKE ADVANTAGE OF COVER, SHOOT
AROUND OBSTACLES, OR TO ASSUME A MORE STABLE POSITION
WHEN ACCURATE FIRE IS REQUIRED.

EACH POSITION HAS ADVANTAGES AND DISADVANTAGES. FOR
EXAMPLE SOME ARE QUICK TO ASSUME, BUT DON'T PROVIDE
AS MUCH STABILITY AS POSITIONS WHICH MIGHT BE SLOWER
TO ASSUME. YOU MUST ALSO CONSIDER HOW LONG IT TAKES
TO GET UP AND OUT OF A POSITION. REMEMBER FIGHTS ARE
USUALLY VERY DYNAMIC, PARTICIPANTS CHANGE LOCATIONS, MOVING
OFTEN, AND YOU DON'T WANT TO GET INTO A POSITION WHICH
MIGHT ALLOW YOU TO BE PINNED DOWN OR TRAPPED.

THERE ARE SOME POSITIONS WHICH ARE GOOD FOR SHOOTING,
LIKE SITTING POSITIONS, BUT ARE NOT RECOMMENDED FOR FIGHTING
SINCE THEY ARE SLOW TO GET INTO AND SLOW TO GET OUT OF.

NATURAL POINT OF AIM IS CRITICAL TO WORKING POSITIONS
PROPERLY. NATURAL POINT OF AIM (NPOA) MEANS YOU ARE RELYING
ON BONE STRUCTURE AS OPPOSED TO MUSCLE. MUSCLES, AND THEIR
STRENGTH OR TENSION, WILL VARY ACCORDING TO CIRCUMSTANCES.
BONE SUPPORT IS MUCH MORE CONSISTANT, AND THEREFORE MORE
ACCURATE.

MANY OF THE POSITIONS ARE THE SAME FOR BOTH PISTOL
AND RIFLE. THE KEY TO EMPLOYING POSITIONS EFFECTIVELY,
AS WITH ANY OTHER ASPECT OF FIGHTING, IS REPETITION.
YOU MUST PRACTICE UNTILL ACQUIRING A STABLE POSITION
BECOMES NATURAL AND OCCURS WITHOUT THOUGHT. INITIALLY
YOU WILL HAVE TO GET INTO POSITION AND CHECK YOUR NATURAL
POINT OF AIM, THEN MEMORIZE YOUR BODY'S RELATIONSHIP
TO THE TARGET LOCATION. AFTER PRACTICE, MEANING NUMEROUS
REPETITIONS, YOU CAN DROP INTO POSITION WITHOUT ANY ADJUSTING.

BEGIN YOUR TRAINING WITH THE POSITIONS AND THEN WORK
WITH THEM IN CONJUNCTION WITH THE USE OF COVER. BUT
TO USE POSITIONS WITH COVER YOU MUST BECOME FAMILIAR
WITH THE FUNDAMENTALS OF THE POSITIONS.

IN A FIGHT YOU MAY BE FORCED TO SHOOT FROM MODIFIED
POSITIONS, BUT THE BASIC FUNDAMENTALS WILL STILL APPLY.

THE UNBRACED, OR SPEED KNEELING, IS ACQUIRED BY DROPPING DOWN ONTO THE SUPPORT SIDE KNEE. TRADITIONALLY THIS WAS ACCOMPLISHED BY STEPPING FORWARD AND ACROSS WITH THE STRONG SIDE FOOT. IN A FIGHT IT IS BETTER TO SIMPLY DROP DOWN WITH SUPPORT KNEE. YOU MIGHT NOT WANT TO STEP FORWARD, WHICH MOVES YOU CLOSER TO THE THREAT, OR IF WORKING CLOSE TO COVER YOU MIGHT NOT HAVE DISTANCE TO STEP FORWARD.

FROM THE WAIST UP BODY POSITION IS THE SAME AS STANDING POSITION. TO BE ABLE TO PUSH UP TO STANDING IT IS BEST TO KEEP SUPPORT FOOT BENT WITH TOES ON THE GROUND. POSITION IS THE SAME WITH THE RIFLE.

THIS POSITION IS QUICK TO ASSUME AND TO GET UP AND OUT OF.

AS WITH ANY POSITION YOU SHOULD SEARCH AND SCAN, THEN COME UP, SEARCHING AND SCANNING AS YOU RISE SINCE YOU ARE ENTERING NEW THREAT AREA AS YOU COME UP. FROM THE HIGHER POSITION YOU WILL BE ABLE TO SEE NEW AREAS WHICH MAY CONTAIN THREATS.

THE BRACED KNEELING PUTS YOUR BODY SLIGHTLY LOWER AND CREATES A MORE STABLE POSITION BY BRACING THE SUPPORT ELBOW AGAINST THE KNEE. THE FLAT ON THE BACK OF THE ELBOW SHOULD BE INDEXED AGAINST THE FLAT OF THE KNEE. YOUR REAR END SHOULD BE DROPPED DOWN SO IT IS RESTING ON STRONG SIDE HEEL. SUPPORT SIDE FOOT IS PULLED BACK SLIGHTLY TO ALLOW BODY TO LOWER DOWN.

STRONG SIDE KNEE SHOULD BE POINTED OUTWARD SLIGHTLY SO THAT THE SUPPORT FOOT AND STRONG SIDE KNEE AND FOOT FORM A TRIANGLE FOR STABILITY. IF THE STRONG KNEE IS TOO CLOSE TO THE SUPPORT KNEE THE POSITION WON'T BE AS STABLE.

CHECK AND CONFIRM NATURAL POINT OF AIM!

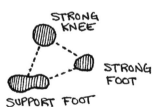

STRONG KNEE

STRONG FOOT

SUPPORT FOOT

110

DURING A FIGHT YOU MAY HAVE TO FLOW FROM ONE
POSITION TO ANOTHER. THIS SHOULD BE PRACTICED. DURING
TRAINING IF YOU DISCOVER POSITIONS THAT WON'T WORK
FOR YOU THEN YOU HAVE STILL LEARNED SOMETHING.

THE DOUBLE KNEE, OR CALIFORNIA
KNEEL, IS DROPPING DOWN TO
BOTH KNEES. THIS IS A QUICK
POSITION TO ASSUME AND GET OUT
OF. IT ALSO ALLOWS YOU TO
RAISE OR LOWER YOUR BODY SOME.

THIS IS A GOOD POSITION FOR SHOOTING
AROUND THE SIDE OF COVER BECAUSE YOU
CAN LEAN OUT TO THE LEFT OR RIGHT.
YOU CAN ALSO ELEVATE OR DEPRESS THE
WEAPON AS NEEDED.

WITH ALL POSITIONS YOU SHOULD PRACTICE
RELOADS AND MANIPULATIONS.

RIGHT   ROLLOUT   LEFT   DEPRESS   ELEVATE

THE SQUAT POSITION IS EITHER A
LOVE OR HATE POSITION. IT EITHER
WORKS GREAT OR DOESN'T BECAUSE
OF BODY BUILD OR FLEXIBILITY.

THE KEY TO STABILITY IS THAT
BOTH HEELS MUST BE FLAT ON
THE GROUND. THIS IS AN EXTREMELY
QUICK POSITION TO GET IN AND
OUT OF.

YOU CAN ALSO BRACE THE ELBOWS
AGAINST THE KNEES FOR STABILITY.
ELBOWS SHOULD BE POSITIONED SLIGHTLY
INSIDE OF THE KNEES.

111

THE MOST ACCURATE PRONE POSITION FOR THE PISTOL IS TO ROLL SLIGHTLY TO THE STRONG SIDE SO THE ARM IS FLAT ON THE GROUND. THIS ALSO ALLOWS YOU TO BUILD THE PUSH-PULL ISOMETRIC TENSION TO RECOVER FROM RECOIL. LEGS SHOULD BE SPREAD APART FOR STABILITY WITH FEET AND HEELS FLAT ON THE GROUND.

IF LAYING FLAT THE ARMS CAN BE RAISED UP, BUT THIS REQUIRES RAISING THE HEAD WHICH CAN BECOMING TIRING.

SUPPORT OR STRONG LEG CAN BE BENT TO RELIEVE PRESSURE ON TORSO.

PRONE POSITIONS, ALTHOUGH STABLE, ARE SLOW TO GET INTO AND SLOW TO GET UP AND OUT OF. THEY DO PROVIDE A STABLE AND ACCURATE BASE TO FIRE FROM AND CAN BE USED WHEN MAKING A LONGER DISTANCE SHOT.

TO ASSUME THE PRONE YOU DROP ONTO BOTH KNEES AND THEN USE THE SUPPORT HAND TO LOWER YOURSELF DOWN. GETTING UP SHOULD BE ACCOMPLISHED BY GOING TO A KNEELING POSITION, USING SUPPORT HAND IF NECESSARY, THEN WORKING YOUR WAY TO STANDING. SEARCHING AND SCANNING AS YOU COME UP.

A VARIATION OF THE KNEELING POSITION IS TO EXTEND THE LEG OUT TO THE SIDE WHICH ALLOWS YOU TO LOWER YOUR BODY MASS AND LEAN OUT TO THE SIDE. THIS CAN BE DONE TO THE STRONG OR SUPPORT SIDE. WORKS WELL WHEN WORKING TO THE SIDE OF COVER.

112

WITH THE RIFLE THE PRONE POSITION CAN HAVE THE BODY DIRECTLY BEHIND THE WEAPON OR IT CAN BE ANGLED TO THE SUPPORT SIDE. WITH A HEAVY RECOIL WEAPON IT SEEMS TO WORK BETTER IF THE RIFLE FORMS A STRAIGHT LINE THROUGH THE BODY AND DOWN THE STRONG SIDE LEG.

WITH PRONE THE LEGS CAN BE STRAIGHT, OR SUPPORT LEG CAN BE BENT, WHICH TWISTS THE TORSO AND ALLOWS YOU TO BREATHE A LITTLE EASIER.

WITH THE RIFLE IT IS VERY CRITICAL TO WORK FROM THE NATURAL POINT OF AIM, RELYING ON BONE STRUCTURE AS OPPOSED TO MUSCLE SUPPORT.

WITH THE AR, WHEN USING A 30 ROUND MAG, THE MAG CAN BE USED AS A MONOPOD TO REST THE WEAPON ON.
YOU SHOULD TEST FIRE USING THIS TECHNIQUE TO INSURE THAT WITH YOUR WEAPON AND MAG COMBO IT DOESN'T CREATE ANY MALFUNCTIONS OR RELATED PROBLEMS.

——— ·ROLL OVER PRONE ———

THE ROLL OVER PRONE IS USED TO SHOOT FROM UNDERNEATH AN OBJECT, FOR EXAMPLE UNDERNEATH A CAR. TO ASSUME THIS POSITION THE STRONG ELBOW IS PULLED INSIDE AND YOU ROLL OVER ONTO THE STRONG SHOULDER. THE SUPPORT HAND IS HELD UNDER THE WEAPON, MUCH LIKE MAKING A BRIDGE WHEN SHOOTING POOL. SUPPORT SIDE LEG IS BENT AND PULLED UP TO ALLOW THE BODY TO TWIST INTO POSITION. ONCE YOU PRACTICE THIS IS IS AN EXTREMELY STABLE POSITION.

A VARIATION OF THE ROLLOVER IS TO LAY PARRALEL TO THE TARGET, ROLL ONTO THE STRONG SHOULDER AND SUPPORT THE RIFLE WITH THE SUPPORT HAND UNDERNEATH. THE REAR END IS RAISED UP AND YOUR KNEES SUPPORT THE LOWER BODY.

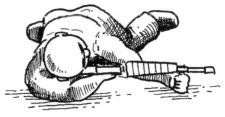

BODY IS PARRALEL TO THE THREAT.

EXTENDED PRONE

THE EXTENDED PRONE IS ANOTHER POSITION WHICH IS USED TO FIRE UNDERNEATH AN OBJECT. THE BODY IS FLATTENED OUT AND THEN THE RIFLE IS EXTENDED OUT AND HELD SIDEWAYS.

WITH THE LIGHT RECOIL OF THE .223 THE RIFLE DOESN'T HAVE TO BE HELD IN THE SHOULDER.

THE HEAD IS HELD LOW TO ALLOW A PROPER SIGHT PICTURE.

WITH ANY OF THE POSITIONS WHERE THE RIFLE IS HELD ON ITS SIDE YOU MUST FACTOR IN THE DIFFERENCE BETWEEN THE POINT OF AIM AND POINT OF IMPACT. THIS IS A FACTOR AT DISTANCES OF 25 YARDS AND CLOSER.

THE SIDE POSITION IS A STABLE PLATFORM FOR ACCURATE SHOOTING. THE HANDGUARDS REST ON THE LEG WHILE THE SUPPORT HAND GRASPS THE REAR OF THE STOCK IN AN OVER-HAND GRIP. THE SIGHT HEIGHT CAN BE CHANGED BY RAISING OR LOWERING THE LEGS.

A VARIATION OF THE SITTING POSITION IS TO EXTEND THE LEGS STRAIGHT OUT IN FRONT AND ROLL THE BODY FORWARD SO THE RIFLE AND SUPPORT HAND ARE RESTING ON THE LEGS.

114

SUPINE POSITION

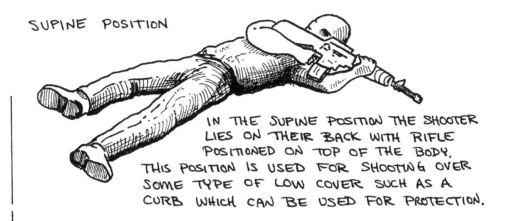

IN THE SUPINE POSITION THE SHOOTER
LIES ON THEIR BACK WITH RIFLE
POSITIONED ON TOP OF THE BODY.
THIS POSITION IS USED FOR SHOOTING OVER
SOME TYPE OF LOW COVER SUCH AS A
CURB WHICH CAN BE USED FOR PROTECTION.

MODIFIED PRONE

THIS IS A
GOOD POSITION
FOR SHOOTING
AROUND CORNERS.
IT EXPOSES THE
LEAST AMOUNT OF
YOUR BODY.

BODY IS POSITIONED AT A
90° ANGLE TO THE TARGET
STRONG ARM IS FLAT ON THE GROUND
IN FRONT WITH RIFLE TURNED SIDEWAYS
AND STOCK POSITIONED IN THE ELBOW OR
AGAINST THE BICEP. HANDGUARD RESTS
ON TOP OF SUPPORT ARM.

WHEN USING THE KNEELING POSITION
STABILITY CAN BE INCREASED BY RESTING
THE BACK OF THE MAGAZINE AGAINST
THE FRONT OF THE KNEE AND
THE STRONG HAND AND RIFLE
GRIP ON THE TOP OF THE SUPPORT
LEG.
THIS CAN ALSO BE DONE FROM SITTING

THE KEY TO USING RIFLE POSITIONS IS
PRACTICE. 1000 REPETITIONS TO LEARN
THE POSITION, 10,000 TO POLISH THEM.
THE MORE POSITIONS YOU HAVE IN YOUR "TOOLBOX" THE MORE
CHOICES YOU HAVE TO FIT THE VARIETY OF SITUATIONS YOU MAY
FIND YOURSELF OPERATING UNDER.

115

FIRING ON THREATS TO THE STRONG SIDE
WITH THE RIFLE CAN BE DIFFICULT
WITHOUT SHIFTING YOUR WHOLE BODY,
ESPECIALLY WITHOUT TWISTING BODY
WHEN SHOOTING ON THE MOVE.

THE BUTTSTOCK ROLLOVER POSITION
WORKS TO SHOOT TO THE STRONG
SIDE. THE STOCK IS LAID ON TOP
OF THE SHOULDER WHILE HELD
SIDEWAYS.

THIS ALLOWS YOU TO TWIST THE MUZZLE TO
THE STRONG SIDE WHILE KEEPING THE BODY
INDEXED TOWARDS THE DIRECTION YOU ARE
MOVING. IT WILL ALLOW YOU TO ROTATE THE
MUZZLE APPROX 60° TO THE RIGHT.

DIRECTION
OF MOVEMENT

TO TRANSITION TO TARGETS
ON YOUR LEFT AND RIGHT
YOU CAN BRING THE SUPPORT
ARM OUT TO THE SIDE, AS
OPPOSED TO THE NORMAL
POSITION WHERE IT IS HELD
UNDERNEATH THE WEAPON. WITH THE ARM
AT THE SIDE IT CAN BE USED TO PUSH THE MUZZLE TO THE
RIGHT OR LEFT WITHOUT SHIFTING THE BODY. TECHNIQUE CAN
BE APPLIED TO PISTOL AS WELL.

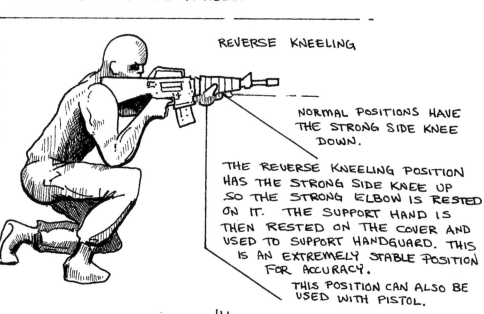

REVERSE KNEELING

NORMAL POSITIONS HAVE
THE STRONG SIDE KNEE
DOWN.

THE REVERSE KNEELING POSITION
HAS THE STRONG SIDE KNEE UP
SO THE STRONG ELBOW IS RESTED
ON IT. THE SUPPORT HAND IS
THEN RESTED ON THE COVER AND
USED TO SUPPORT HANDGUARD. THIS
IS AN EXTREMELY STABLE POSITION
FOR ACCURACY.

THIS POSITION CAN ALSO BE
USED WITH PISTOL.

THE USE OF COVER

FOR MOST COMBATIVE ENGAGEMENTS, AT LEAST IN THE INITIAL FEW SECONDS, THERE WILL NOT BE TIME TO EMPLOY COVER. WE TRAIN TO USE COVER, LEARNING HOW TO PROPERLY TAKE ADVANTAGE OF THE PROTECTION IT PROVIDES, SO WHEN IT IS POSSIBLE WE CAN USE IT PROPERLY.

NORMALLY FIGHTS ARE DYNAMIC AND FLUID, REQUIRING YOU TO CREATE DISTANCE BETWEEN YOU AND THE THREAT - OR THREATS. IF POSSIBLE IT IS BETTER TO REMAIN ON YOUR FEET AND USE COVER. HOWEVER SOME COVER WILL REQUIRE USE OF ONE OF THE FIGHTING POSITIONS SUCH AS KNEELING, SQUAT OR PRONE. KEEP IN MIND THE DIFFERENCE BETWEEN SHOOTING AND FIGHTING POSITIONS. DURING A FIGHT WE MUST EMPLOY POSITIONS WHICH WILL ALLOW YOU TO GET INTO POSITION QUICKLY AND EQUALLY IMPORTANT GET OUT OF POSITION TO CHANGE OR SHIFT YOUR LOCATION AS NEEDED. IF YOU ALLOW YOURSELF TO REMAIN STATIONARY YOU WILL FIND YOURSELF OVER RUN OR FLANKED BY A QUICK THINKING OPPONENT.

REMEMBER THAT COVER IS A TWO WAY STREET; IF IT WORKS FOR YOU IT WILL WORK JUST AS WELL FOR THE THREAT. ALL THEY MUST DO IS REPOSITION THESELVES SO THEIR BODY IS HID BEHIND THE COVER.

TO REACT TO THE THREAT'S ACTIONS YOU MOST REMAIN MOBILE. WHEN YOU DROP INTO A POSITION YOU MUST STILL BE ABLE TO MOVE, RESPONDING TO THE THREAT AS THEY MOVE. A DIFFERENCE OF REPOSITIONING YOUR BODY BY A FOOT CAN BE CRITICAL. SMALL PORTIONS OF TIME, A TENTH OR QUARTER OF A SECOND, CAN BE THE DIFFERENCE BETWEEN WINNING AND LOSING.

CONSIDER THE DIFFERENCES BETWEEN COVER AND CONCEALMENT. COVER PROTECTS YOU FROM INCOMING ROUNDS, BUT IS RELATIVE TO WHAT THE THREAT IS SHOOTING AT YOU. CONCEALMENT ONLY HIDES YOU FROM VIEW. BOTH HAVE THEIR USE IN COMBAT.

SOME OF THE TECHNIQUES FOR USING COVER PROPERLY GO AGAINST OUR NATURAL INSTINCTS. THIS MEANS WE MUST TRAIN UNTIL WE ARE ABLE TO OVERCOME THE NATURAL INSTINCTS AND APPLY THE PROPER TECHNIQUES.

THE ELEMENTS OF THE FIGHT DICTATE WHAT TECHNIQUES SHOULD BE EMPLOYED. THESE DIFFERENCES ARE DISCUSSED IN DETAIL. IF THEY ARE NOT PRACTICED, WITH PLENTY OF THOUGHT, IT WILL ONLY BE LUCK IF YOU SURVIVE. IT IS MUCH BETTER TO RELY ON SKILL.

WHEN USING COVER THE MORE DISTANCE YOU CAN GET BETWEEN YOU AND THE COVER THE BETTER. IF ROUNDS ARE IMPACTING THERE WILL BE FRAGMENTATION OF THE BULLET AND DEBRIS FROM THE COVER ITSELF. THE CLOSER YOU ARE TO THE COVER AND THE IMPACT ZONE THE GREATER YOUR CHANCES ARE OF BEING WOUNDED. DURING GUNFIGHTS THE MAJORITY OF WOUNDS OCCUR FROM THIS. DURING THE NORTH HOLLYWOOD FIGHT OUT OF THE TWENTY PLUS WOUNDED ONLY ONE OF THESE WERE FROM TAKING A DIRECT HIT; THE REST WERE FROM RICHOCETS AND FRAGMENTATION.

WE ALSO KNOW THAT ROUNDS IMPACTING ONTO A SURFACE DO NOT BOUNCE OFF AT A CORRESPONDING ANGLE LIKE A POOL BALL DOES OFF THE BUMPER OF THE POOLTABLE. IF YOU ARE CLOSE TO THE SURFACE THE ROUND IS COMING OFF OF YOU WILL BE IN THE PATH OF THE ROUND. BY CREATING DISTANCE YOU MOVE OUT OF THE BULLET'S PATH.

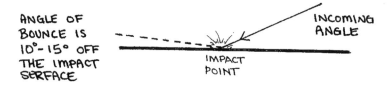

ANGLE OF BOUNCE IS 10°-15° OFF THE IMPACT SERFACE

INCOMING ANGLE

IMPACT POINT

WE ALSO DISTANCE OURSELVES FROM COVER BECAUSE IT ALLOWS US TO SEE MORE OF WHAT IS GOING ON IN OUR ENVIRONMENT. THE CLOSER YOU ARE THE MORE RESTRICTED YOUR ABILITY TO SEE. DISTANCE ALSO ALLOWS MORE FREEDOM OF MOVEMENT.

TO EMPLOY COVER WE SIMPLY NEED TO GET IT BETWEEN US AND THE THREAT. YOU CAN BE THIRTY FEET AWAY AND IT WILL STILL PROVIDE PROTECTION. HOWEVER WE MUST CONSIDER THE GEOMETRY OF THE SITUATION, LOCATIONS OF THE THREATS ETC, AND THE AREAS OF PROTECTION THE COVER WILL PROVIDE.

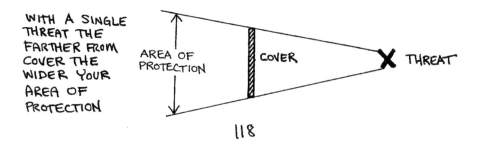

WITH A SINGLE THREAT THE FARTHER FROM COVER THE WIDER YOUR AREA OF PROTECTION

AREA OF PROTECTION

COVER

X THREAT

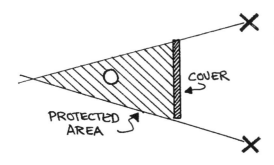

COVER

PROTECTED AREA

WHEN FACING TWO THREATS YOU HAVE A DIMINISHED AREA OF PROTECTION. THE FARTHER YOU GET FROM COVER THE SMALLER THE AREA YOU HAVE TO MOVE PROTECTED FROM THREATS.

IF ONE OR BOTH THREATS REPOSITION THEMSELVES THE AREA OF PROTECTION WILL SHIFT - YOU WILL HAVE TO REPOSITION YOURSELF ACCORDINGLY.

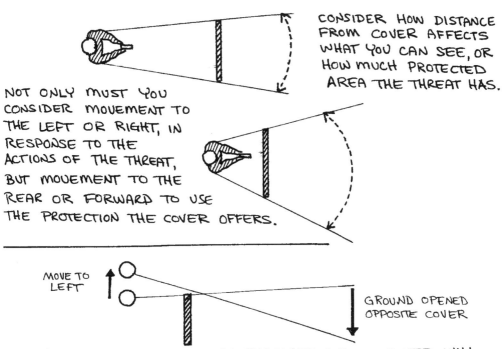

CONSIDER HOW DISTANCE FROM COVER AFFECTS WHAT YOU CAN SEE, OR HOW MUCH PROTECTED AREA THE THREAT HAS.

NOT ONLY MUST YOU CONSIDER MOVEMENT TO THE LEFT OR RIGHT, IN RESPONSE TO THE ACTIONS OF THE THREAT, BUT MOVEMENT TO THE REAR OR FORWARD TO USE THE PROTECTION THE COVER OFFERS.

MOVE TO LEFT

GROUND OPENED OPPOSITE COVER

AS YOU MOVE LATERALLY THE DISTANCE FROM COVER WILL DICTATE HOW MUCH GROUND IS OPENED UP ON THE OTHER SIDE OF THE COVER. ONE STEP LEFT COULD OPEN UP 6 FEET OF GROUND OPPOSITE THE COVER. THE MORE YOU DISTANCE YOURSELF FROM COVER THE LESS GROUND IS EXPOSED OPPOSITE COVER

119

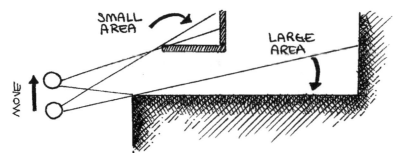

THE SAME AMOUNT OF MOVEMENT OPENS UP MORE GROUND ON THE FURHER WALL AS OPPOSED TO THE SHORT DISTANCE ON THE WALL CLOSER TO YOU. THIS IS VERY IMPORTANT WHEN YOU ARE WORKING ON BUILDING CLEARING.

WHEN USING COVER, IF POSSIBLE, IT IS MUCH BETTER TO WORK FROM THE SIDE AS OPPOSED TO OVER THE TOP OF COVER

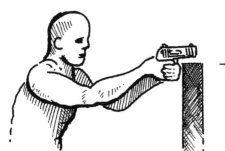

WORKING OVER THE TOP WILL EXPOSE YOU TO THE THREAT FROM THE COLLAR BONE UP. THIS IS WHY DURING VIOLENT BATTLES THE MAJORITY OF LETHAL HITS OCCUR FROM THE NECK UP.

WHEN WORKING FROM THE SIDE MUCH LESS OF YOUR HEAD IS EXPOSED TO THE THREAT.

WHEN DEALING WITH MULTIPLE THREATS MAKE SURE YOU DON'T EXPOSE YOURSELF TO BOTH THREATS AT THE SAME TIME

WORK THREAT "A" THEN ROLL OUT TO DEAL WITH THREAT "B"

120

HOLD HEAD VERTICAL NOT SIDEWAYS!

WHILE WORKING AROUND THE SIDE OF THE COVER YOU NEED TO HOLD YOUR HEAD STRAIGHT UP VERTICAL AS OPPOSED TO LEANING IT OUT. THE BEST WAY TO PRACTICE IT IS TO SHUT THE EYE OPPOSITE THE SIDE YOU ARE WORKING AND THEN WORK WITH ONE EYE OPEN. USE YOUR NOSE AS AN INDEX POINT. THE WALL SHOULD BE EVEN WITH THE TIP OF NOSE.

WITH THE AR RIFLE, OR ANY OTHER SYSTEM WITH SIGHTS HIGHER THAN THE BORE YOU HAVE TO BE AWARE

THE SIGHTS ARE CLEAR BUT THE MUZZLE ISN'T

WHEN KEEPING DISTANCE FROM COVER YOU HAVE TO LOOK TO MAKE SURE MUZZLE IS CLEAR THEN SHIFT YOUR FOCUS TO THE SIGHTS TO OBTAIN A SIGHT PICTURE.

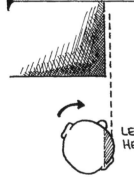

LESS OF THE HEAD EXPOSED

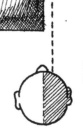

MORE OF THE HEAD IS EXPOSED WITH IT STRAIGHT

POSITIONING THE HEAD BY ROTATING IT SLIGHTLY EXPOSES LESS OF THE HEAD AS OPPOSED TO KEEPING IT INDEXED STRAIGHT FACING THE THREAT.

THE BEST WAY TO FINE TUNE YOUR POSITION FOR WORKING WITH COVER IS TO SET A FULL LENGTH MIRROR OPPOSITE A CORNER SO AS YOU WORK AROUND IT YOU SEE WHAT THE BAD GUY SEES OF YOU IN THE MIRROR.

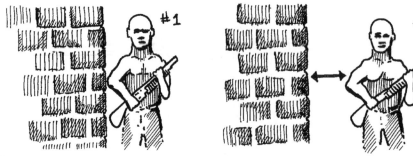

AS YOU USE COVER IT IS BEST TO SEE THE LEAST AMOUNT OF
THE THREAT REQUIRED TO CONFIRM THAT THEY ARE ARMED
AND BE ABLE TO ENGAGE THEM WITH FIRE. IF YOU CAN
SEE A LOT OF SPACE BETWEEN YOUR COVER AND THE THREAT
THEN YOU ARE EXPOSING TOO MUCH OF YOURSELF. EXAMPLE
#1 SHOWS THREAT IS ARMED AND YOU CAN ENGAGE. #2 THERE
IS TOO MUCH SPACE BETWEEN THREAT AND YOUR COVER.

YOU MUST KEEP IN MIND THAT THE THREAT CAN USE THE
COVER TO THEIR ADVANTAGE. IN THIS ILLUSTRATION THE THREAT
DROPS DOWN TO TAKE ADVANTAGE OF THE COVER, THEN HE
MOVES FORWARD AND TO THE SIDE TO ATTACK. ONCE HE
GETS BEHIND COVER AND YOU LOSE SIGHT OF HIM IT IS A
DANGEROUS SITUATION. YOU MUST REPOSITION YOURSELF SO
YOU CAN MAINTAIN VISUAL CONTACT WITH THE THREAT AND
ENGAGE AS REQUIRED.

SWITCHING THE WEAPON TO THE SUPPORT SIDE TO WORK AN
OPPOSITE CORNER OR COVER ISN'T A GOOD IDEA UNLESS YOU ARE
FULLY ABLE TO SHOOT AND MANIPULATE THE WEAPON EQUALLY
WELL WITH THAT HAND - WHICH USUALLY ISN'T THE CASE, EVEN
WITH LOTS OF PRACTICE. PLUS YOU HAVE A TIME DELAY AS YOU
ARE SWAPPING HANDS WHERE YOU ARE UNABLE TO FIGHT.
BEST TO PRACTICE POSITIONS SO YOU EXPOSE THE LEAST
AMOUNT OF YOUR BODY AND USE STRONG SIDE ONLY.

122

MOVING

HIDDEN

REAPPEAR

WHEN MOVING FROM COVER TO COVER YOU NEED TO MINIMIZE
THE TIME YOU ARE EXPOSED TO LESS THAN 3 SECONDS. ANY
LONGER THAN THIS AND THE THREATS HAVE TIME TO SEE YOU,
OBTAIN A SIGHT PICTURE, AND ENGAGE. A USEFUL TECHNIQUE
IS TO MOVE TO COVER, DROP BEHIND IT SO THE THREATS CAN
NOT SEE YOU, THEN MOVE TO ANOTHER POSITION PRIOR TO
COMING UP TO ENGAGE. THE DISADVANTAGE TO THIS IS THAT
YOU LOSE SIGHT OF THE ENVIRONMENT AND ANY THREATS.

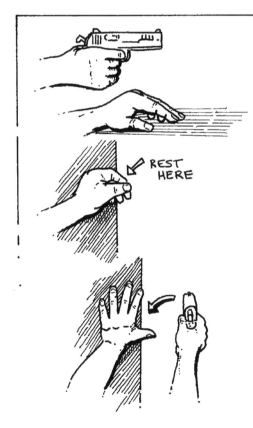

REST
HERE

WHEN YOU ARE FORCED TO
SHOOT LONGER DISTANCES WITH
THE PISTOL YOU CAN BRACE
AGAINST COVER AS AN AID
TO ACCURACY.

THE HAND CAN BE RESTED FLAT
AGAINST SOMETHING, SIMILIAR
TO BRIDGING A POOL CUE.

YOU CAN ALSO BRACE AGAINST
A VERTICAL SERFACE USING
YOUR FIST OR PALM.

THE KEY IS TO REST THE WEAPON
AGAINST THE HAND INSTEAD OF
THE HARD SERFACE OF COVER.

THE SAME TECHNIQUES CAN
BE USED WITH THE RIFLE OR
CARBINE.

BE CAREFUL OF EXTENDING THE
HAND PAST THE COVER TO AVOID
FRAGMENTATION OR DEBRIS.

WHEN USING COVER AS A BRACE THE SUPPORT HAND CAN GRASP THE FRONT OF THE SLING IN A FIST. THIS LOCKS THE WEAPON INTO A STEADY POSITION.

WITH THE LIGHT RECOIL OF THE 223 YOU CAN NORMALLY GET AWAY WITH RESTING THE HANDGUARD AGAINST COVER. YOU CAN USE THE SUPPORT HAND TO BRACE THE REAR OF THE STOCK.

FOR WORKING AROUND CORNERS YOU CAN TILT THE PISTOL OR RIFLE, ROTATING MUZZLE TOWARDS CORNER.

AS YOU WORK COVER EXPOSE THE LEAST AMOUNT OF YOURSELF AS NECESSARY TO THE THREATS. THE EYE, SIGHTS AND MUZZLE SHOULD BE THE ONLY THINGS EXTENDING BEYOND COVER. THIS REQUIRES EXTENSIVE AND CONSTANT PRACTICE!

THE SAME PRINCIPALS APPLY TO CLEARING OR SEARCHING A BUILDING THAT APPLY TO THE USE OF COVER. CONSIDER HOW THE RULES OF GEOMETRY APPLY TO ANY MOVEMENT, USE OF COVER, AND CLEARING/SEARCHING.

124

CLEARING A BUILDING OR STRUCTURE SHOULD BE DONE
SLOWLY AND CAREFULLY. THERE IS NO SAFE WAY TO DO IT
PROPERLY WHEN YOU ARE BY YOURSELF. YOU SHOULD ONLY
ATTEMPT IT WHEN THERE ARE NO OTHER OPTIONS AVAILABLE.
THERE ARE GUIDELINES AND TECHNIQUES YOU SHOULD TRAIN
IN AND USE, BUT REMEMBER THIS PROCESS IS AN ART - NOT
A SCIENCE. EVENTUALLY YOUR TRAINING SHOULD INCLUDE
FORCE-ON-FORCE SCENARIOS AGAINST LIVING REACTIVE
THREATS. THIS IS THE BEST WAY TO PREPARE FOR THE
REALITIES OF COMBAT.

A SUCCESSFUL SEARCH INVOLVES MINIMIZING YOURSELF AS A
TARGET, MAXIMIZING THE DISTANCES BETWEEN YOU AND THE
THREAT OR THREAT ENVIRONMENT AND WHEN NECESSARY
ENGAGING WITH ACCURATE FIRE. REMEMBER THAT EVERY STEP
YOU TAKE INJECTS YOU INTO A NEW THREAT AREA.

WHEN SEARCHING A BUILDING I
PREFER TO USE A READY POSITION
THAT LOCATES THE WEAPON, AND
ARMS AND HANDS, SLIGHTLY LOWER
THAN THE CORNER I'M WORKING.

MUZZLE INDEXED
SLIGHTLY LOWER
THAN CORNER

THIS READY POSITION INSURES
YOUR WEAPON AND BODY PARTS
WON'T BLOCK YOU FROM BEING
ABLE TO SEE ANY TARGET
INDICATORS. OFTEN A FOOT
OR TOES, ETC WILL BE THE
FIRST THING YOU WILL SEE

THE MAJORITY OF MOVEMENT WHEN CLEARING IS
LATERAL OR SIDEWAYS MOVEMENT. THIS IS USED TO
PIE CORNERS. AS YOU SLICE OFF PORTIONS OF THE
CORNER YOU SHOULD ENVISION A WAGON WHEEL AND
ITS SPOKES. THE CORNER IS THE HUB OF THE WHEEL.
YOUR BODY AND ARMS ARE THE SPOKES AND YOU PIVOT
AROUND THE HUB OR CORNER.

125

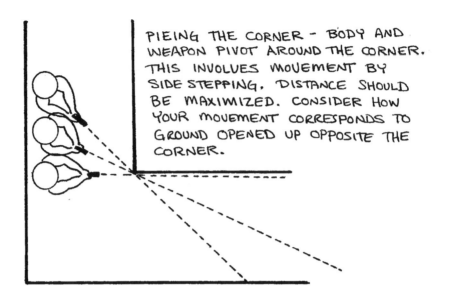

PIEING THE CORNER - BODY AND WEAPON PIVOT AROUND THE CORNER. THIS INVOLVES MOVEMENT BY SIDE STEPPING. DISTANCE SHOULD BE MAXIMIZED. CONSIDER HOW YOUR MOVEMENT CORRESPONDS TO GROUND OPENED UP OPPOSITE THE CORNER.

MOVEMENT SHOULD BE SLOW AND DELIBERATE. BODY POSITIONING IS CRITICAL TO MINIMIZING YOUR EXPOSURE.

 THE POSITION IS BASICALLY THE SAME FOR RIGHT AND LEFT SIDE. THE MAIN DIFFERENCE IS TILTING AT THE WAIST.

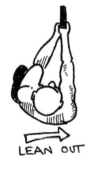
LEAN OUT

TILTING OUT AT WAIST

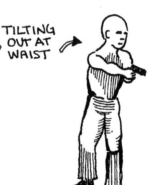

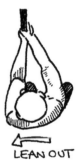
LEAN OUT

STANCE AND POSITION OF THE FEET ARE THE SAME FOR BOTH SIDES

IF YOU ARE CLEARING A LEFT HAND CORNER YOU SHOULD LEAD YOUR MOVEMENT WITH THE RIGHT FOOT. FOR RIGHT CORNER LEFT FOOT LEADS. THINK OF A WAGON WHEEL - THE CORNER IS THE HUB AND YOU PIVOT AROUND THE CORNER LIKE THE SPOKES OF THE WHEEL.

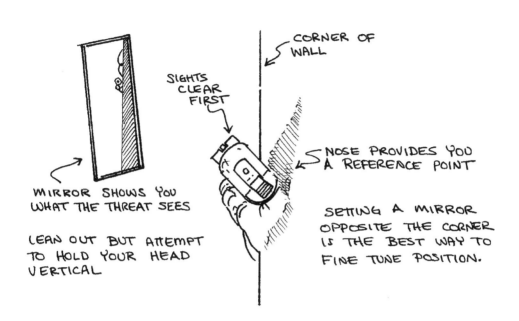

SIGHTS CLEAR FIRST

CORNER OF WALL

NOSE PROVIDES YOU A REFERENCE POINT

MIRROR SHOWS YOU WHAT THE THREAT SEES

LEAN OUT BUT ATTEMPT TO HOLD YOUR HEAD VERTICAL

SETTING A MIRROR OPPOSITE THE CORNER IS THE BEST WAY TO FINE TUNE POSITION.

WORKING DOWN HALLWAYS YOU SHOULD AVOID HUGGING THE WALLS WHEN POSSIBLE. MINIMIZE YOUR TIME IN HALL SINCE THEY RESTRICT YOUR ABILITY TO MOVE. AS YOU WORK DOWN HALL YOU WILL NEED TO MAXIMIZE DISTANCE TO CLEAR CORNER, REQUIRING YOU TO GET CLOSER TO WALL.

AS YOU WORK A "T" INTERSECTION YOU WILL NEED TO GO FROM SIDE TO SIDE WORKING FORWARD. KEEP UP WITH HOW FAR YOU CLEAR AND DON'T BREAK THAT PLANE AS YOU WORK FORWARD.

ONCE YOU HAVE CLEARED AS FAR AS POSSIBLE YOU WILL NEED TO CLEAR THE FINAL PORTION BY ENTERING INTO THE HALLWAY SLIGHTLY. SET UP IN THE MIDDLE AND HEAD EXTENDS FORWARD TO PICK UP ON ANY MOVEMENT.

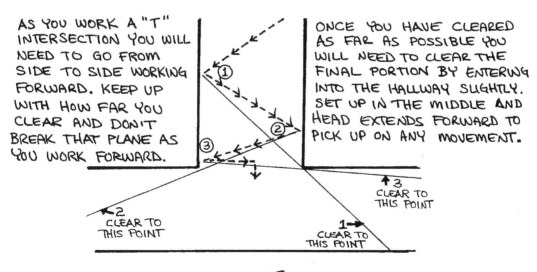

3 CLEAR TO THIS POINT

2 CLEAR TO THIS POINT

1 CLEAR TO THIS POINT

127

IF YOU HAVE NO INDICATORS AS TO LOCATION OF POSSIBLE THREATS YOU SET UP IN THE CENTER, MOVE UP SO YOU CAN SEE BOTH DIRECTIONS OUT OF THE SIDES OF YOUR EYES, LOOKING AND CUEING OFF MOVEMENT.

IF ONE DIRECTION HAS A WALL OR ENDS CLOSER TO YOU THIS MIGHT BE THE DIRECTION YOU WOULD WANT TO CHECK FIRST, SINCE IF THERE WERE A THREAT HERE IT WOULD BE CLOSER TO YOU. THIS SHOULD BE DONE WITHOUT COMPLETELY TURNING YOUR BACK TO THE OPPOSITE DIRECTION.

DYNAMIC ACTIONS SHOULD BE AVOIDED WHENEVER POSSIBLE. IF YOU GO DYNAMIC, AND RUSH INTO A ROOM OR AROUND A CORNER, AND THERE ARE MULTIPLE THREATS LOCATED THERE THEN YOU HAVE EXPOSED YOURSELF TO THEM ALL. DEPENDING ON THE THREATS' REACTIONS YOU MAY OR MAY NOT BE ABLE TO ENGAGE SUCCESFULLY.

- DOORWAYS

AS YOU APPROACH THE DOOR CHECK THE HINGES TO DETERMINE WHAT DIRECTION THE DOOR OPENS IF THE DOOR OPENS TOWARDS YOU THEN YOU SHOULD POSITION YOUR FOOT SO THAT IF SOMEONE ATTEMPTS TO COME OUT THE DOOR IT WON'T SLAM INTO YOU BUT WILL LODGE AGAINST YOUR FOOT. ALSO MAKE SURE YOUR WEAPON WON'T BE KNOCKED OUT OF THE WAY IF THE DOOR IS OPENED.

TRY TO STAND TO THE SIDE OF THE DOOR WHEN POSSIBLE. CHECK THE HANDLE TO SEE IF IT WILL OPEN.

AS YOU OPEN THE DOOR YOU NEED TO FALL BACK TO THE LAST AREA OF SAFETY.

MOST PEOPLE WILL OPEN THE DOOR AND THEN TRY TO LOOK INTO THE ROOM. IF SOMEONE IS WAITING TO AMBUSH YOU, AND YOU STAND THERE AS YOU OPEN THE DOOR YOU WILL BE SHOT. OPEN THE DOOR AND FALL BACK-EITHER TO THE LAST SAFE CORNER OR FALL BACK UNTIL YOU CAN'T SEE INTO THE ROOM. IF YOU CAN'T SEE INTO THE ROOM THEN ANYONE IN THE ROOM WON'T BE ABLE TO SEE YOU. IF THEY CAN'T SEE YOU THEY CAN'T SHOOT YOU. ONE THING AT A TIME. FIRST OPEN THE DOOR AND FALL BACK, CREATING DISTANCE. THEN IF NOTHING HAPPENS YOU CAN BEGIN TO CLEAR THE DOORWAY, WHICH IS BASICALLY A CORNER.

IT DOESN'T MATTER WHICH DIRECTION THE DOOR OPENS FROM. WHAT YOU DON'T WANT TO DO IS PUT YOUR BACK TO AN AREA YOU HAVEN'T CHECKED OR CLEARED.

IN THE ILLUSTRATION BELOW THE DOOR IS BEING CLEARED, PIEING THE CORNER. ONCE YOU REACH POSITION #3 TO GO FURTHER IN PIEING YOU WOULD HAVE TO PUT YOUR

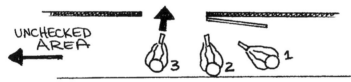

BACK TO THE UNCHECKED AREA. TO CLEAR THE REST OF THE DOORWAY YOU MUST MOVE FORWARD SO THAT YOU CLEAR THE DOOR BUT CAN STILL KEEP AN EYE ON THE UNCHECKED AREA AND RESPOND TO ANY THREATS IN THAT DIRECTION. WEAPON SHOULD BE POSITIONED SO YOU CAN INDEX IT IN EITHER DIRECTION.

ONCE YOU ENTER A ROOM YOU GIVE UP THE AREA YOU CAME FROM. SO WHEN YOU EXIT THE ROOM YOU WILL HAVE TO CLEAR AND SEARCH AS YOU COME OUT. IT IS BETTER THEN, WHEN POSSIBLE, TO CLEAR THE ROOM WITHOUT ENTERING IT AND GIVING UP THE GROUND YOU NOW CONTROL.

ALWAYS SEARCH AS DEEP INTO THE STRUCTURE AS POSSIBLE. REMBER CORNERS ARE NOT CLEAR UNTIL YOU SEE THE EDGE OF THE CORNER WHERE THE TWO WALLS MEET.

129

STAIRS ARE BEST CLEARED BY GOING UP, WHICH ALLOWS THE EYES AND WEAPON TO CLEAR FIRST.

WORKING DOWN STAIRS EXPOSES LEGS AND BODY TO THREATS.

IF POSSIBLE WHEN YOU MUST WORK DOWN STAIRS YOU MAY WANT TO SLIDE DOWN THEM AS OPPOSED TO WALKING.

KNOWING THAT HALLWAYS, DOORS, AND STAIRWELLS ARE DANGEROUS AREAS AND LIMIT YOUR ABILITY TO FIGHT CAN BE APPLIED IN DEFENSIVE SITUATIONS. THESE WOULD BE THE AREAS YOU WOULD WANT TO FIGHT THREATS IN, ENGAGING THE THREATS IN AREAS THAT LIMIT THEIR ABILITY TO MOVE AND FIGHT.

REMEMBER AS YOU CLEAR A STRUCTURE TO PAY ATTENTION TO WINDOWS. THEY SHOULD BE TREATED AS DOORWAYS. IF YOU ARE INSIDE CLEAR THEM, LOOKING OUTSIDE. IF YOU ARE OUTSIDE YOU MUST USE THEM TO LOOK INSIDE. DON'T BECOME SO FOCUSED ON WHAT YOU ARE SEARCHING THAT YOU FAIL TO PAY ATTENTION TO WINDOWS.

SOMEONE WHO IS UNSKILLED AT CLEARING A STRUCTURE WILL OFTEN USE A "QUICK PEEK" AROUND A CORNER, OR ONCE THEY SEE SOMEONE THEY WILL WITHDRAW, HESITATE AND THEN COME BACK AROUND THE CORNER. IF YOU ARE IN A DEFENSIVE SITUATION AND SOMEONE DOES THIS YOU SHOULD CHANGE YOUR LOCATION SO THAT WHEN THEY COME BACK AROUND THE CORNER YOU WON'T BE WHERE THEY EXPECT YOU TO BE. THE CHOICES ARE TO MOVE OUT SO THAT WHEN THEY COME OUT THEY WILL EXPOSE THEMSELVES AND YOU CAN ENGAGE, OR GO DEEPER SO THEY HAVE TO CONTINUE TO SEARCH FOR YOU.

130

ON DOORS THAT HAVE SPRINGS
OR DEVICES TO CLOSE THE DOOR
YOU WILL HAVE TO USE YOUR
FOOT TO KEEP IT OPEN AS
YOU WORK THE DOOR. AS YOU
OPEN THE DOOR YOU WILL FEEL
TENSION, OR A VISUAL INSPECTION
WILL LET YOU KNOW WHAT TO
EXPECT. YOU MAY WANT TO OPEN
IT AND THEN FALL BACK, ALLOWING
IT TO CLOSE AND SEE IF YOU
GET ANY RESPONSE. THEN AS
YOU OPEN IT USE YOUR FOOT
TO BLOCK IT OPEN SO THAT YOU
CAN WORK THROUGH IT.

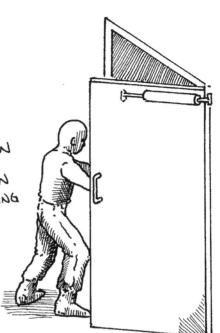

WHEN ENTERING A ROOM THAT IS DARK,
COMING FROM A LIGHTED AREA, YOU
MUST GUARD AGAINST BEING BACKLIT
CREATING AN EASY TARGET FOR A
THREAT TO ENGAGE.
YOU WILL WANT TO STEP TO THE
SIDE, AWAY FROM THE LIGHTED AREA.
SOME SCHOOLS TEACH THAT
YOU SHOULD SHUT THE DOOR
BEHIND YOU, BUT THIS WILL
CUT OFF YOUR ROUTE OF
ESCAPE SHOULD IT BE
NECESSARY FOR YOU TO WITHDRAW.

IF YOU ARE WORKING A CORNER
SOME SCHOOLS ADVOCATE GOING
TO A KNEELING POSITION, TO
COME AROUND AT A DIFFERENT
HEIGHT IN HOPES OF CONFUSING
OPPONENTS. THE PROBLEM IS
YOU LOSE THE ABILITY TO
MOVE - A CRITICAL NECESSITY IN
CLOSE QUARTERS SITUATIONS.

131

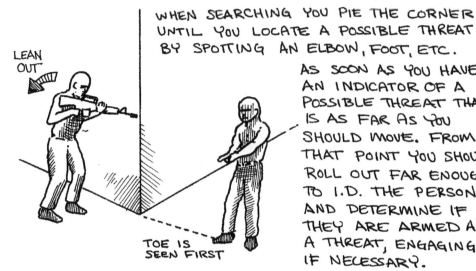

WHEN SEARCHING YOU PIE THE CORNER UNTIL YOU LOCATE A POSSIBLE THREAT BY SPOTTING AN ELBOW, FOOT, ETC.

AS SOON AS YOU HAVE AN INDICATOR OF A POSSIBLE THREAT THAT IS AS FAR AS YOU SHOULD MOVE. FROM THAT POINT YOU SHOULD ROLL OUT FAR ENOUGH TO I.D. THE PERSON AND DETERMINE IF THEY ARE ARMED AND A THREAT, ENGAGING IF NECESSARY.

LEAN OUT

TOE IS SEEN FIRST

DON'T MOVE OR ROLL OUT ANY FARTHER THAN NEEDED TO IDENTIFY THE THREAT AND ENGAGE. AT THE SAME TIME MINIMIZE YOURSELF AS A TARGET.

THE SAME TECHNIQUE IS USED TO CLEAR THE LAST FINAL PORTION OF A CORNER. YOU WILL CLEAR BY PIEING, MOVING BY SMALL STEPS. THE LAST PORTION CAN BE CLEARED BY LEANING OUT SLIGHTLY.

IN MOST ENVIRONMENTS THERE WILL BE MORE THAN ONE AREA OR DIRECTION YOU WILL HAVE TO BE CONCERNED WITH.

YOU SHOULD SET YOUR WEAPON IN THE MIDDLE OF THE AREA, SO YOU CAN RESPOND IN ANY DIRECTION, AND SCAN WITH YOUR EYES.

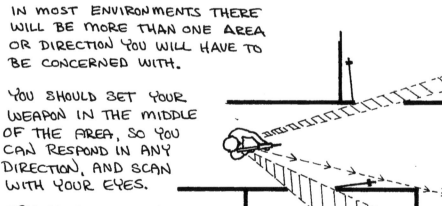

TRY NOT TO PUT YOUR BACK TO ANYTHING UNCHECKED. WHEN YOU HAVE TO TRY TO LIMIT THE AMOUNT OF TIME YOUR BACK IS EXPOSED.

UNDER MOST CIRCUMSTANCES A SLOW AND DELIBERATE SEARCH IS THE BEST TECHNIQUE TO EMPLOY, ESPECIALLY WHEN YOU ARE BY YOURSELF. THE MORE DANGEROUS THE SITUATION IS THE SLOWER AND MORE CAREFUL YOU SHOULD BE. HOWEVER, THERE ARE SITUATIONS WHERE YOU MIGHT HAVE TO DO THINGS QUICKLY. EVEN THOUGH YOU NEED TO DO THE CLEARING WITH SPEED, THE SAME TECHNIQUES SHOULD BE APPLIED WHEN POSSIBLE. THERE ARE ALSO SITUATIONS WHERE I WOULDN'T WANT TO CLEAR EVERY ROOM OR DOOR, SAY WHEN YOU WERE TRYING TO ESCAPE AN AREA OR GET TO AN AREA QUICKLY. JUST REMEMBER WHEN YOU ARE MOVING QUICKLY YOU SHOULD NEVER GO ANY FASTER THAN YOU CAN CONTROL YOUR ACTIONS. FOR EXAMPLE IF YOU ARE MOVING TOO FAST AND RUN INTO A THREAT YOU WOULD EXPOSE TOO MUCH OF YOUR BODY BY NOT BEING ABLE TO STOP DUE TO YOUR MOMENTUM.

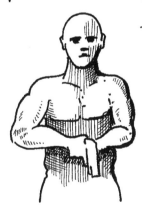

THE SUL POSITION, WHERE THE PISTOL IS HELD FLAT AGAINST THE BODY WITH MUZZLE POINTED DOWN, IS FAVORED BY A LOT OF INSTRUCTORS FOR SEARCHING AND CLEARING.

JEFF GONZALES TEACHES TO POSITION THE SUPPORT HAND SO THAT IT CAN BE USED TO STRIKE IF NECESSARY.

THE PROBLEM WITH THIS POSITION IS THAT IF SOMEONE IS ABLE TO GET IN TIGHT THERE IS A POSSIBILITY OF THEM BEING ABLE TO TRAP THE WEAPON AGAINST YOUR BODY.

IF YOU ARE USING THE SUL POSITION FOR SEARCHING YOU POSITION THE FEET TO THE SIDES, BEND FORWARD AT THE WAIST SO THAT THE EYES ARE THE FIRST THING TO COME AROUND THE CORNER. ONCE YOU LOCATE THE THREAT YOU STEP JUST FAR ENOUGH TO INDEX ONTO THE TARGET AND PUNCH THE PISTOL OUT TOWARDS THE THREAT.

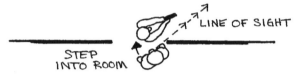

STEP INTO ROOM

LINE OF SIGHT

THIS ACTION REQUIRES DYNAMIC ACTION TO PROVIDE THE SURPRISE NECESSARY. THE PROBLEM IS THAT IF YOU DYNAMICALLY ENTER THE ROOM THERE COULD BE MULTIPLE THREATS. BY WORKING WITHIN THEIR REACTION GAPS YOU MAY BE ABLE TO ENGAGE 2 TO 3 TARGETS BUT ANY MORE THAN THAT AND YOU COULD BE IN TROUBLE.

BRACED AGAINST SIDE OF WALL

TOO MUCH BODY EXPOSED.

UNBRACED POSITION

LESS OF YOUR BODY EXPOSES

WHEN ENGAGING A TARGET FROM BEHIND A WALL, OR COVER, IT IS BEST NOT TO BRACE AGAINST IT TO STABILIZE YOUR POSITION BECAUSE IT WILL EXPOSE TOO MUCH OF YOUR BODY— UNLESS THE DISTANCE IS LONG AND YOU ARE REQUIRED TO MAKE A VERY ACCURATE SHOT.

IF YOU ARE CLEARING A STRUCTURE—AND THERE ARE NO TIME ISSUES TO CONSIDER—AFTER YOU ENGAGE A TARGET IT WOULD BE A GOOD IDEA TO HOLD YOUR POSITION FOR A WHILE TO SEE IF ANY OTHER THREATS THAT MIGHT BE IN THE BUILDING WILL RESPOND IN ANY WAY. IF YOU WAIT LONG ENOUGH THEY WILL LOSE THEIR PATIENCE AND COME LOOKING FOR YOU. NOW YOU HAVE REVERSED ROLES TO YOUR ADVANTAGE.

COMBATIVE TURNS

THREATS CAN COME FROM ANY DIRECTION AND MOST LIKELY AN ATTACKER WON'T LAUNCH THEIR ATTACK FROM YOUR FRONT - IT WILL COME FROM THE SIDES OR REAR. YOU MUST TRAIN FOR THIS BY PRACTICING COMBATIVE TURNS.

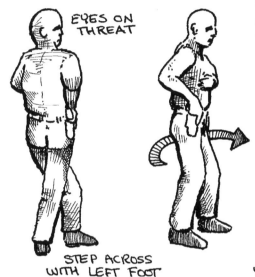

EYES ON THREAT

STEP ACROSS WITH LEFT FOOT

FOR EXAMPLE FOR A THREAT ON YOUR RIGHT SIDE YOU WILL TURN THE HEAD TO OBTAIN A VISUAL ON THE THREAT. AT THE SAME TIME YOU PERFORM THE FIRST STEP- SLAP AND GRIP- OF THE PRESENTATION, AND WITH THE LEFT FOOT STEP FORWARD AND ACROSS. ALL THIS HAPPENS AT ONCE.

AS YOU STEP WITH THE LEFT FOOT IT IS BEST IF POSSIBLE TO STEP SOME DISTANCE.

NEXT YOU RAISE UP YOUR FEET SO YOU ARE ON THE BALLS OF YOUR FEET AND PIVOT SO THE BODY IS INDEXED TO THE THREAT.

ONCE YOUR ARE FACING THE THREAT YOU COMPLETE THE DRAW STROKE. MAKE SURE YOU DON'T PULL THE PISTOL UNTIL YOU ARE FACING THE THREAT. IF YOU DRAW THE PISTOL TOO SOON, AS YOU TURN YOU WILL SWEEP EVERYONE WITH THE MUZZLE. PLUS IF THE WEAPON IS OUT AS YOU TURN THERE IS THE POSSIBILITY SOMONE NEAR COULD EASILY TRAP THE WEAPON. WE ALSO KNOW IF YOU EXTEND THE ARMS WITH THE PISTOL IN HAND AS YOU TURN THE WEIGHT ADDS MOMENTUM WHICH MAKES IT MORE DIFFICULT TO BRING THE WEAPON TO BEAR ONTO THE TARGET.

AS YOU STEP WITH THE LEFT FOOT YOU SHOULD TRY TO GAIN AS MUCH DISTANCE AS POSSIBLE SO THAT AS YOU PIVOT YOU ARE ALSO MOVING YOUR BODY LATERALLY AND OUT OF THE LINE OF ATTACK.

BODY MOVES LATERAL AT SAME TIME

AS YOU PERFORM THE TURNS YOU SHOULD END UP IN
YOUR FIGHTING STANCE UPON COMPLETION OF THE TURN.
THIS MAY REQUIRE YOU TO DRAG THE FOOT THAT YOU
ARE NOT STEPPING WITH. AS YOU PIVOT IF NEEDED
THE FOOT DRAGS INTO POSITION TO ADJUST YOUR STANCE.

THE MOVEMENT AND PIVOT SHOULD BE AS NATURAL AS
POSSIBLE. JUST LIKE YOU WERE TURNING TO WAVE AT A
FRIEND OR SOMETHING LIKE THAT. THE MORE NATURAL
THE MOVEMENT THE SMOOTHER AND QUICKER IT IS.

TARGET TO LEFT SIDE

STEP FORWARD WITH RIGHT
FOOT AS HEAD TURNS AND
YOU BEGIN THE DRAW.

PIVOT ON THE BALLS OF
THE FEET AS YOU SPIN.
DRAG LEFT FOOT INTO
POSITION. PRESENT PISTOL
ONCE YOU ARE FACING
THREAT.

LOOK

SPIN

STEP

FOR A TARGET TO YOUR REAR THE TECHNIQUS ARE THE
SAME EXCEPT YOU ARE SPINNING 180° INSTEAD OF 90°
YOU CAN STEP WITH EITHER RIGHT OR LEFT FOOT. IF YOU
STEP WITH RIGHT FOOT YOU WOULD STEP ACROSS TO THE
LEFT AND SPIN COUNTER-CLOCKWISE. WITHL LEFT FOOT YOU
STEP TO THE RIGHT AND SPIN CLOCKWISE. IF POSSIBLE IT
IS BETTER TO SPIN SO THAT THE PISTOL IS TURNED AWAY
FROM THREAT WHILE IT IS IN THE HOLSTER TO GUARD AGAINST
DISARM ATTEMPTS.

THE COMBATIVE TURNS ARE ALSO USED WHEN THE PISTOL
IS ALREADY IN YOUR HANDS. TO DO THIS THE PISTOL IS
SIMPLY LOWERED INTO A LOW READY POSITION AS YOU TURN.
AS SOON AS YOU COMPLETE TURN PISTOL IS BROUGHT BACK
UP INTO SHOOTING POSITION.

THE SAME METHODS ARE USED FOR THE RIFLE. THE WEAPON
IS COLLASPED AGAINST THE BODY WITH MUZZLE DOWN AS
TURN IS EXECUTED.

A KNEELING POSITION CAN BE USED IN CONJUNCTION
WITH THE COMBATIVE TURN IF YOU ARE WORRIED
ABOUT THREAT REACTION. I COULD TURN AND DROP INTO
KNEELING TO CONFUSE THREAT OR BUY A SMALL AMOUNT
OF TIME.

1   2   3   4
     STEP PIVOT DROP

LATERAL MOVEMENT
CAN ALSO BE USED,
STEPPING LEFT OR
RIGHT AFTER YOU
COMPLETE YOUR TURN.

THE VARIOUS TYPES OF MOVEMENT ARE COMBINED
IN VARIATIONS ACCORDING TO THE SITUATION. YOU MUST
PRACTICE SO THAT YOU CAN FLOW FROM ONE TO ANOTHER.

AS YOU WORK CORNERS MAXIMIZE YOUR DISTANCE.
SOMETIMES THIS ISN'T POSSIBLE. IF THE THREAT
GRABS YOUR WEAPON FROM AROUND A CORNER USE
THE CORNER TO RAKE THEIR HANDS FROM THE WEAPON
BY STEPPING BACK AND PULLING.

REMEMBER TO KEEP THE
MUZZLE LOW AND NEVER
AT A HIGH READY IN
CLOSE QUARTERS SITUATIONS.

IF THE THREAT CLOSES GROUND
AND CAN FORCE MUZZLE UP
IT IS DIFFICULT TO CONTROL
THE WEAPON.

IN SITUATIONS WHERE SOMEONE
IS ATTEMPTING TO DISARM YOU
YOUR RESPONSE MUST BE
IMMEDIATE AND LETHAL.
DO NOT HESITATE!

MUZZLE UP

AS YOU MOVE UP TO COVER MAKE SURE TO GET THE MUZZLE UP SO AS YOU ARE MOVING YOU CAN ENGAGE IF NEEDED. A COMMON MISTAKE PEOPLE MAKE IS TO LEAVE THE MUZZLE DOWN UNTIL THEY GET TO COVER, THEN THEY HAVE TO SWING THE MUZZLE TO THE SIDE TO GET ON TARGET.

IF YOU CLOSE UP ON THE COVER AND HAVE TO REPOSITION YOU MUST SWING MUZZLE AROUND OR BACK UP TO CREATE DISTANCE. THIS APPLIES TO PISTOL AND CARBINE.

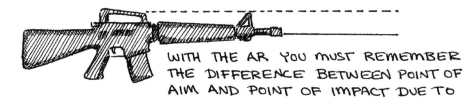

WITH THE AR YOU MUST REMEMBER THE DIFFERENCE BETWEEN POINT OF AIM AND POINT OF IMPACT DUE TO OFFSET OF SIGHTS AND BORE.

THIS APPLIES TO DISTANCES LESS THAN 25 YARDS OR WHEN USING COVER. FOR EXAMPLE TO MAKE AN EFFECTIVE HEAD SHOT AT CLOSE RANGE YOU MUST AIM 2½ INCHES HIGH. WHEN USING COVER YOU CAN HAVE A SIGHT PICTURE BUT THE MUZZLE BE BLOCKED BY THE COVER. AS YOU MOVE TO COVER YOU MUST VISUALLY CHECK TO MAKE SURE MUZZLE IS CLEAR THEN OBTAIN A SIGHT PICTURE.

AR ZERO

THERE IS A TREND WITH THE AR TO ZERO AT 25 YARDS, BUT WITH A 25 ZERO RIFLE WILL SHOOT 5½ INCHES OR HIGHER AT 100. THIS MAKES IT DIFFICULT TO MAKE A HEAD SHOT AT 100.

ZERO	25	50	75	100	DISTANCE
25	O	2½ H	4½ H	5½ H	
50	1 L	O	1½ H	2 H	
75	1½ L	¼ L	O	1½ H	
100	2½ L	1 L	½ L	O	

REGARDLESS OF ZERO AT 25/CLOSER YOU MUST COMPENSATE FOR SIGHT/BORE OFFSET.

ONE HAND MANIPULATIONS - PISTOL

EMPTY RELOAD - WITH PISTOL HELD OUT TOWARDS THE TARGET THE MAG RELEASE IS PRESSED SO MAG DROPS. IF THE MAG WON'T DROP FREE IT CAN BE HOOKED ONTO HOLSTER OR BELT AND STRIPPED OUT OF PISTOL. WEAPON MUST THEN BE SECURED SO THAT THE HAND CAN ACCESS FRESH MAG AND GET IT INTO PISTOL. THE SIMPLEST PLACE TO STOW PISTOL IS IN THE HOLSTER. IF YOU ARE USING STRONG HAND PISTOL IS PUT INTO HOLSTER NORMALLY. WITH SUPPORT HAND PISTOL IS SLIPPED INTO HOLSTER BACKWARDS. MAG IS THEN SEATED INTO THE WEAPON, PISTOL IS PULLED OUT OF HOLSTER, AND SLIDE RELEASED. RELEASING THE SLIDE IS ACCOMPLISHED BY DEPRESSING SLIDE LOCK OR BY HOOKING SLIDE AGAINST BIT OF HOLSTER, BELT, ETC- OR PRESSING TOP OF SLIDE TIGHTLY AGAINST HIP- AND FORCING WEAPON FORWARD SO IT RELEASES SLIDE.

PISTOL CAN BE SECURED IN HOLSTER TO RELOAD. WITH SUPPORT HAND IT IS SLIPPED IN BACKWARDS. FRONT OR REAR POCKETS, OR YOUR WAISTBAND, CAN ALSO BE USED.

THE WEAPON CAN ALSO BE TUCKED UNDER THE ARM. USE CAUTION AND BE AWARE OF WHERE THE MUZZLE IS POINTING. SOME PEOPLE TEACH PUTTING IT BETWEEN THE LEGS, BUT THIS CAUSES YOU TO LOSE THE ABILITY TO MOVE.

NOT A GOOD IDEA!

WHEN TEACHING IT IS A GOOD IDEA TO ONLY USE HOLSTER FOR SECURING PISTOL SINCE YOU DON'T WANT STUDENTS COVERING THEMSELVES WITH MUZZLE OR POINTING IT AT OTHERS.

139

THE TACTICAL RELOAD IS ACCOMPLISHED USING THE SAME TECHNIQUES EXCEPT THE WEAPON IS SECURED, PARTIAL MAG IS REMOVED AND STOWED, AND THEN FRESH MAG IS ACQUIRED AND INSERTED INTO WEAPON.

RELOADS SHOULD BE PRACTICED WITH BOTH PRIMARY AND SUPPORT HAND IN THE EVENT THAT YOU ARE WOUNDED OR INJURED.

TO MAKE IT EASIER TO ACCESS THE SPARE MAGAZINE WITH THE PRIMARY HAND IT IS A GOOD IDEA TO BE ABLE TO SHIFT THE MAG POUCH AROUND ON THE BELT TOWARDS THE FRONT OF THE BODY.
IT MAY ALSO BE A GOOD IDEA TO CARRY A SPARE MAG IN THE REAR POCKET OF THE PRIMARY SIDE.
REMEMBER THAT MAGAZINES PUT IN FRONT POCKETS WILL BE HARD TO GET TO WHEN YOU ARE IN A KNEELING POSITION.

TO DRAW THE PISTOL FROM THE HOLSTER WITH THE SUPPORT HAND THE PISTOL IS PULLED PARTWAY FROM THE HOLSTER THEN TWISTED 180° SO THAT YOU CAN GET THE PROPER GRIP ON THE WEAPON. THIS TECHNIQUE IS USED WHEN THE HAND COMES AROUND THE FRONT OF THE BODY.
THE ALTERNATIVE METHOD IS FOR THE HAND TO COME AROUND THE BACK OF THE BODY BUT THIS IS A MORE DIFFICULT TECHNIQUE FOR MOST PEOPLE.

IT IS A GOOD IDEA TO PRACTICE THE SINGLE HAND MANIPULATIONS FROM VARIOUS POSITIONS SUCH AS KNEELING, ETC. SO THAT YOU ARE ABLE TO PERFORM THESE ACTIONS FROM BEHIND COVER. REMEMBER THERE IS ALWAYS THE POSSIBILITY THAT YOU WILL BE INJURED DURING A FIGHT. EXPECTING NOT TO BE INJURED IS LIKE GOING INTO A BOXING MATCH AND THINKING YOU WILL NEVER BE HIT.

MALFUNCTION CLEARANCES WITH ONE HAND REQUIRE THE SAME ACTIONS AS WHEN USING BOTH HANDS. THE PROCESS OR SEQUENCE IS THE SAME - WHEN THE WEAPON WON'T FIRE YOU TAP TO SEAT THE MAG, CYCLE THE SLIDE TO CLEAR OR LOAD THE WEAPON. IF THIS DOESN'T CLEAR THE PISTOL YOU MUST UNLOAD, CLEAR THE OBSTRUCTION, AND RELOAD.

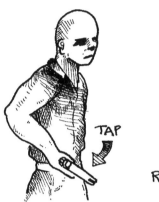

TAP

RACK

THE MAGAZINE IS SEATED BY TAPPING THE WEAPON AGAINST PART OF YOUR BODY.

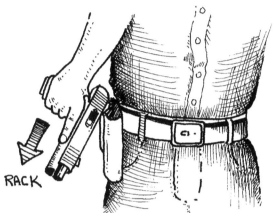

THE SLIDE IS CYCLED BY HOOKING THE REAR SIGHT AGAINST PART OF YOUR GEAR, SUCH AS YOUR HOLSTER, AND FORCING THE WEAPON FORWARD.

FOR A TYPE 3 MALFUNCTION YOU WILL NEED TO STRIP THE MAG FROM THE PISTOL. THIS IS WHERE A SHORT LIP ON THE FRONT OF THE MAG, WHICH EXTENDS PAST THE FRONT OF THE PISTOL, IS A GOOD IDEA. YOU WILL NEED TO HOOK THIS LIP ONTO THE HOLSTER AND AS YOU PRESS THE MAG RELEASE STRIP THE MAG FROM THE PISTOL, THEN CYCLE THE SLIDE TO CLEAR THE BLOCKAGE. ONCE CLEARED THE PISTOL IS HOLSTERED, OR SECURED IN A POCKET OR SUCH, AND RELOADED. IF YOU ONLY HAVE ONE MAG, THE ONE STRIPPED FROM THE PISTOL, YOU WILL NEED TO RETRIVE IT TO RELOAD THE PISTOL.

IF YOUR MAG DOESN'T HAVE A LIP ON IT YOU WILL HAVE TO LOCK THE SLIDE TO THE REAR TO REMOVE THE MAG. THIS IS ACCOMPLISHED BY HOOKING SIGHTS, PRESSING SLIDE TO THE REAR AND ENGAGING SLIDE LOCK. THEN HOLSTER, PRESS MAG RELEASE AND REMOVE MAG. BRING WEAPON BACK OUT TO CYCLE AND CLEAR BLOCKAGE. HOLSTER TO RELOAD.

141

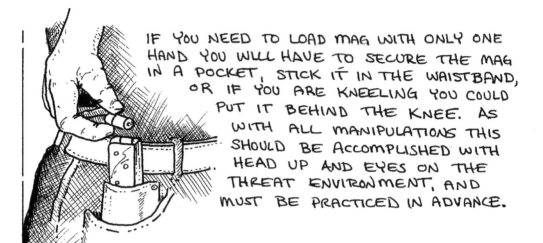

IF YOU NEED TO LOAD MAG WITH ONLY ONE
HAND YOU WILL HAVE TO SECURE THE MAG
IN A POCKET, STICK IT IN THE WAISTBAND,
OR IF YOU ARE KNEELING YOU COULD
PUT IT BEHIND THE KNEE. AS
WITH ALL MANIPULATIONS THIS
SHOULD BE ACCOMPLISHED WITH
HEAD UP AND EYES ON THE
THREAT ENVIRONMENT, AND
MUST BE PRACTICED IN ADVANCE.

SINGLE HAND MANIPULATIONS, SUCH AS THE TAP-RACK
SEQUENCE, COULD ALSO COME INTO PLAY WHEN YOU ARE
USING A FLASHLIGHT. FOR EXAMPLE WITH THE LIGHT
IN THE SUPPORT HAND YOU COULD TAP AND RACK USING
THE ONE HAND TECHNIQUE. WITH PRACTICE THIS COULD
BE ACCOMPLISHED QUICKER THAN SECURING THE LIGHT
AND RUNNING THE MANIPULATION, PLUS IF NECESSARY YOU
COULD KEEP THE LIGHT ON WHILE MANIPULATING.

SINGLE HAND MANIPULATIONS MUST ALSO BE WORKED
WITH THE CARBINE. THE SEQUENCE OF ACTIONS
IS THE SAME. WITH THE RIFLE THE DIFFERENCE
IS THAT YOU WILL NORMALLY NEED SOMETHING TO
REST OR SUPPORT THE RIFLE AGAINST TO BE ABLE
TO PERFORM THE MANIPULATIONS.

IF YOU ARE WORKING BEHIND COVER
YOU MAY BE ABLE TO WEDGE THE
WEAPON BY APPLYING PRESSURE
WITH YOUR SHOULDER AND
WEDGING THE BAYONET LUG ON
THE EDGE OF THE COVER.
THEN YOU CAN HOLD THE RIFLE
UP WHILE RELOADING OR
CLEARING MALFUNCTION.

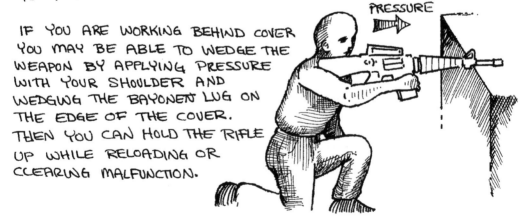

PRESSURE

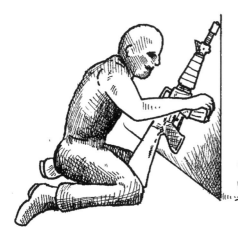

THE OTHER OPTION IS TO REST THE RIFLE AGAINST THE COVER AND THEN HOLD THE WEAPON'S STOCK WITH THE KNEES BY CLINCHING IT BETWEEN THEM. DEPENDING ON WHAT TYPE OF MANIPULATION YOU'RE PERFORMING YOU MAY WANT TO TURN THE WEAPON UPSIDE DOWN AND BACK TO BE ABLE TO WORK IT BEST.

TO SEAT THE MAG DURING A RELOAD OR MALFUNCTION CLEARANCE YOU CAN TURN THE WEAPON UPSIDE DOWN AND TAP OR USE THE THUMB POSITIONED ON THE LIP OF THE MAG WELL AND HAND TO SEAT MAG. ONCE MAG IS SEATED REMEMBER TO TUG TO MAKE SURE IT'S SEATED PROPERLY.

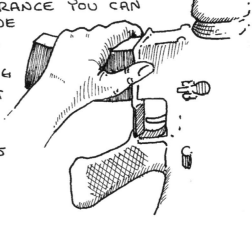

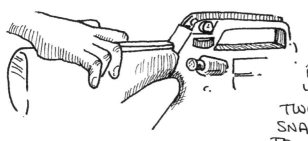

WHEN CYCLING THE CHARGING HANDLE WITH ONE HAND ONLY YOU SHOULD POSITION RIFLE SO TOP IS FACING YOU AND USE FIRST TWO FINGERS IN A SNAKE FANG LIKE GRIP TO CYCLE THE ACTION.

IF YOU ARE USING A TACTICAL SLING CLEARING MALFUNCTIONS WITH ONLY ONE HAND IS DIFFICULT. IT IS BEST TO HAVE A QUICK RELEASE SO THE RIFLE CAN BE REMOVED FROM THE SLING.

WITH A TACTICAL SLING YOU CAN WORK SOME MANIPULATIONS BY LETTING THE WEAPON HANG AND WORKING WITH ONE HAND. TO CYCLE THE ACTION YOU CAN HOOK THE STOCK UNDER THE ARMPIT TO TRAP WEAPON.

USE QUICK FORCEFUL ACTIONS TO WORK THE WEAPON SO THE RIFLE'S MASS WILL HELP HOLD IT STATIONARY.

PRACTICE UNTIL THIS CAN BE DONE WITH HEAD AND EYES UP.

THIS ACTION CAN ALSO BE DONE WITH RIFLE LAYING FLAT ON THE GROUND - PUTTING END OF THE STOCK AGAINST KNEE

TO LOCK THE BOLT OPEN, WHEN CLEARING A TYPE 3 MALFUNCTION, YOU WILL NEED TO USE THE MAGAZINE TO PRESS THE CHARGING HANDLE BACK AND THEN DEPRESS THE BOLT CATCH.

WHEN YOU CYCLE THE ACTION TO CLEAR THE OBSTRUCTION MAKE SURE MAG WELL IS DOWNWARD. THIS MAKES SURE THE LARGEST OPEAING IS POINTED WHERE GRAVITY WILL ASSIST AND INSURES YOU DON'T CREATE A BOLT OVER MALFUNCTION WHERE BRASS OR AMMO FALLS ON TOP OF THE BOLT.

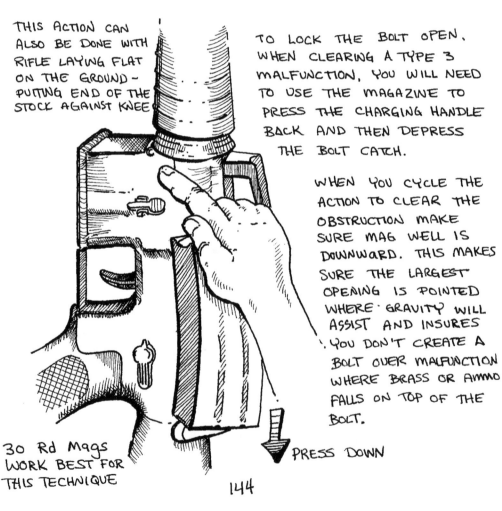

30 Rd Mags WORK BEST FOR THIS TECHNIQUE

PRESS DOWN

144

LOW LIGHT

DOCUMENTATION SHOWS US THAT THERE IS A 70% OR GREATER CHANCE THAT VIOLENT ACTIONS WILL OCCUR IN LOW LIGHT CONDITIONS. REMEMBER THAT LOW LIGHT CONDITIONS EXIST 24 HOURS A DAY. STEP INTO A BUILDING WHICH IS DARK DURING THE BRIGHT LIGHT OF DAY AND IT WILL BE EXTREMELY HARD TO SEE.

TO PROPERLY PREPARE FOR LOW LIGHT CONDITIONS YOU MUST TRAIN WITH A VARIETY OF FLASHLIGHT TECHNIQUES. THE SITUATION WILL DETERMINE WHICH TECHNIQUE WILL WORK BEST. EACH LIGHTING TECHNIQUE HAS ADVANTAGES AND THESE ARE DISCUSSED, AS WELL AS THE DISADVANTAGES OF EACH.

BESIDES THE SPECIFIC LIGHTING TECHNIQUES YOU MUST ALSO LEARN LOW LIGHT PRINCIPLES. THESE ARE MAXIMS WHICH WILL APPLY TO ALLMOST ALL LOW LIGHT OPERATIONS. THE PRINCIPLES MUST BE STUDIED AND PRACTICED JUST LIKE THE SPECIFIC TECHNIQUES.

REMEMBER THERE IS NO SUBSTITUTE FOR TRAINING. ALSO REMEMBER THAT ALL TRAINING DOESN'T HAVE TO INCLUDE LIVE FIRE. WHEN IT COMES TO WORKING WITH THE VARIOUS LIGHT TECHNIQUES, MOVING, CLEARING AND SEARCHING BUILDINGS, A LOT OF IT CAN BE ACCOMPLISHED WITH DUMMY WEAPONS OR NO WEAPON AT ALL.

YOU SHOULD ALSO CONSIDER EQUIPMENT ISSUES. PROPER FIGHTING LIGHTS SHOULD BE SMALL ENOUGH TO CARRY, FIT YOUR HAND, HAVE A LONG RUNNING TIME, AND BE VERY BRIGHT SO THAT WHEN YOU SHINE IT IN AN OPPONENT'S EYES IT WILL BLIND THEM. CARRY A SPARE! TEST FIRE AMMO SO THAT YOU CAN USE ONE WHICH WILL HAVE THE LEAST AMOUNT OF MUZZLE FLASH. YOU SHOULD ALSO THINK ABOUT THE COLOR OF CLOTHING WORN. LIGHT COLORS WILL STAND OUT. BLACK ALSO STANDS OUT BECAUSE IT IS TOO DARK. DARK GRAYS, KHAKI, BROWNS AND GREENS ARE BEST.

STUDY AND THINK ABOUT WHEN TO USE THE LIGHT AND WHEN NOT TO, WHEN YOU SHOULD MOVE AND WHEN YOU WOULD WANT TO REMAIN STATIONARY.

LOW LIGHT PRINCIPLES - FROM SUREFIRE COURSE

- LEARN TO READ LIGHTING CONDITIONS, BOTH FROM YOUR VIEWPOINT AND FROM THAT OF THE BAD GUY. THIS WILL ALLOW YOU TO AVOID BEING BACKLIT AND AVOID CASTING SHADOWS.
- USE THE LIGHT AS LITTLE AS POSSIBLE WHEN SEARCHING AND AS MUCH AS POSSIBLE WHEN YOU LOCATE A THREAT.
- POSITION YOURSELF IN DARK AREAS. TRY TO FORCE YOUR THREAT TO OPERATE IN LIGHTED AREAS.
- USE THE LIGHT TO PROVIDE MISINFORMATION TO THE THREAT BY VARYING YOUR LIGHTING SEQUENCE, RYTHM AND DURATION.

THE LIGHT IS USED TO LOCATE AND IDENTIFY THREATS. IT IS ALSO USED TO NAVIGATE THROUGH UNKNOWN AREAS AND AS A COMMUNICATION TOOL. FOR EXAMPLE I CAN SHINE MY LIGHT ON AN AREA OR SPECIFIC DOOR TO SHOW MY PARTNER WHERE A THREAT IS LOCATED.

HARRIES TECHNIQUE

THE HARRIES TECHNIQUE IS ONE OF THE MOST COMMON LIGHTING METHODS. THE SUPPORT HAND IS BROUGHT UNDER AND AROUND TO THE RIGHT SIDE OF PRIMARY HAND AND THE WRISTS ARE LOCKED TOGETHER. TO KEEP WRISTS LOCKED TOGETHER THE SUPPORT ELBOW SHOULD BE HELD AS VERTICAL AS POSSIBLE AND THE LEFT HAND ROLLED SO THAT IS ON TOP OF PRIMARY HAND. IT NORMALLY HELPS IF YOU BLADE YOUR STANCE, STEPPING FORWARD WITH THE LEFT FOOT SLIGHTLY MORE THAN NORMAL. ISOMETRIC TENSION IS NECESSARY TO KEEP THE WRISTS FROM SEPERATING DURING RECOIL. THIS ISOMETRIC TENSION MAKES IT DIFFICULT TO MAINTAIN FOR EXTENDED PERIODS OF TIME.

146

THE HARRIES TECHNIQUE WORKS WELL WHEN YOU ARE
CLEARING A CORNER TO THE LEFT OR WORKING AROUND
THE RIGHT SIDE OF COVER. IT DOESN'T WORK GOOD
FOR A RIGHT HAND CORNER OR LEFT SIDE OF COVER
SINCE IT WILL REFLECT LIGHT BACK AT YOU. WHEN CLEARING
A CORNER YOU WILL WANT TO POSITION THE LIGHT SO IT IS
THE FIRST THING TO COME AROUND THE CORNER.
ANOTHER CONSIDERATION WITH HARRIES IS THAT ANYWHERE
YOU POINT THE LIGHT THE MUZZLE IS ALSO POINTED. THIS
MEANS ANYONE YOU LIGHT, EVEN THOUGH THEY MIGHT NOT BE
A THREAT, WILL BE COVERED BY THE MUZZLE.

TO PRESENT THE PISTOL FOR HARRIES YOU NEED
TO PULL THE LIGHT IN AGAINST THE CENTER OF
THE CHEST TO PREVENT YOU FROM COVERING
YOURSELF WITH THE MUZZLE. THEN ONCE
THE PISTOL IS EXTENDED FORWARD YOU CAN
FLOW INTO THE HARRIES LIGHT TECHNIQUE.

IT WILL RARELY BE
NECESSARY TO PRESENT
BOTH LIGHT AND PISTOL
AT THE SAME TIME.
YOU WILL EITHER ALREADY
HAVE THE LIGHT OUT AND
NEED TO GET PISTOL OUT,
OR THE THREAT WILL BE
SUDDEN AND YOU WILL NEED
TO GET THE PISTOL OUT AS
SOON AS POSSIBLE.

PRESENT PISTOL THEN FLOW
INTO THE HARRIES.
YOU COULD FIRE WITH PISTOL EXTENDED
AND LIGHT HELD AGAINST THE CHEST.

PRESS BACK OF WRISTS
TOGETHER TO LOCK THEM
IN SO THEY DON'T
SEPERATE DURING
RECOIL.

IF YOU WEAR A LARGE
WRIST WATCH IT CAN
GET IN THE WAY
WHEN USING HARRIES.

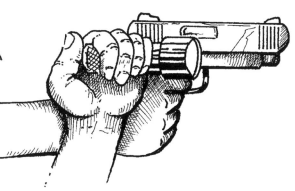

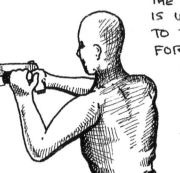

THE REVERSE HARRIES, OR UN-CROSSED, IS WHERE THE LIGHT IS REPOSITIONED TO THE LEFT SIDE OF THE PISTOL - FOR A RIGHT HAND SHOOTER.

THIS IS USED WHEN WORKING A RIGHT HAND CORNER OR FOR SHOOTING AROUND THE LEFT SIDE OF COVER.

THE LEFT SIDE OF THE PISTOL SHOULD HAVE AN AREA THAT THE LEFT HAND CAN MATE UP TO. APPLY ISOMETRIC TENSION TO KEEP HANDS FROM SEPERATING DURING RECOIL.

WHEN USING THE LIGHT THE COMMON TENDENCY IS FOR OUR EYE TO BE ATTRACTED TO WHERE THE LIGHT IS SHINING INSTEAD OF FOCUSING ON THE FRONT SIGHT. PLUS IF THE THREAT IS MOVING OUR EYES ARE DRAWN TO THE MOVEMENT. FLASHLIGHT SHOULD BE AIMED AT THE THREAT'S EYES. THERE WILL BE ENOUGH LIGHT TO STILL SEE WHAT THE HANDS ARE DOING.

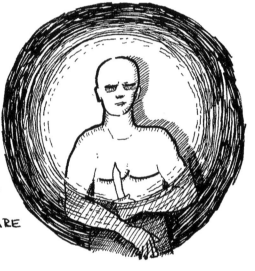

BE CAREFUL WHEN WORKING CORNERS OR COVER TO CLEAR THE LIGHT SO YOU DON'T GET A LOT OF BOUNCE BACK OR REFLECTION WHICH WILL LIGHT YOU UP AND REVEL YOU TO THE THREAT.
TO AVOID THIS MAKE SURE YOU SWITCH THE LIGHT FROM SIDE TO SIDE.

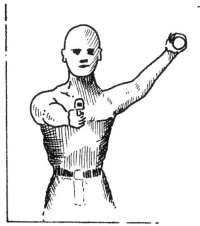

THE F.B.I. TECHNIQUE IS WHERE THE LIGHT IS HELD OUT TO THE SIDE OF THE BODY. THE ADVANTAGE OF THIS IS THAT IF SOMEONE ATTEMPTS TO SHOOT AT THE LIGHT THEY WILL MISS YOU. IT ALSO ALLOWS YOU TO HOLD THE WEAPON ON ONE AREA OR SPECIFIC THREAT AND SCAN IN ANOTHER AREA OR DIRECTION WITH THE LIGHT. IT IS ALSO VERY QUICK TO ASSUME IF YOU ALREADY HAVE THE LIGHT OUT. THE DISADVANTAGE IS THAT YOU MUST SHOOT WITH ONE HAND.

IF IT IS POSSIBLE TO DROP BELOW THE HORIZON YOU WILL BE ABLE TO SEE THREATS EASIER BECAUSE OF THE CONTRAST BETWEEN THEM AND THE SKY.

THIS SAME PRINCIPLE CAN ALSO BE USED TO ACQUIRE A SIGHT PICTURE. YOU CAN RAISE THE WEAPON UP, ALIGN THE SIGHTS, AND THEN

BRING THEM DOWN TO INDEX THEM ONTO THE TARGET.

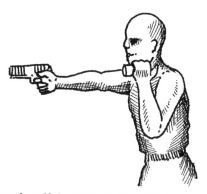

THE NECK INDEX IS A GOOD TECHNIQUE BECAUSE IT ALIGNS THE LIGHT BY POSITIONING IT AGAINST THE JAW AND NECK. THIS IS A QUICK POSITION TO ASSUME. DISADVANTAGE IS THAT YOU ARE SHOOTING WITH ONE HAND. WORKS BEST IF YOU DROP THE SUPPORT FOOT BACK.

BOTH THE FBI AND NECK INDEX TECHNIQUE WORK WELL IF YOU ARE USING THE LEFT SIDE OF COVER OR A RIGHT CORNER OR WORKING OUT IN THE OPEN. IDEALLY YOU SHOULD LEARN TO FLOW FROM ONE TECHNIQUE TO ANOTHER SO YOU CAN USE THE TECHNIQUE BEST SUITED. FOR EXAMPLE WHEN CLEARING YOU WILL HAVE RIGHT AND LEFT CORNERS TO WORK.

WHEN SEARCHING YOU MAY WANT TO CHANGE THE ORIGIN
OF THE LIGHT SO YOU DON'T ESTABLISH AI SET PATTERN
THE THREAT CAN USE TO ENGAGE. FADING VERTICALLY IS
ONE TECHNIQUE WHICH WORKS WELL. THIS IS DONE BY DROPPING
DOWN TO A KNEELING POSITION.

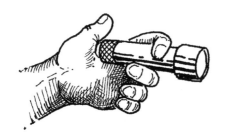

YOU CAN ALSO USE THE
DIFFERENT LIGHTING
TECHNIQUES TO VARY THE
SOURCE OF LIGHT.

YOU MAY ALSO VARY THE
TIME THE LIGHT IS ON,
USING INTERMETENT
LIGHT, OFF AND ON. BUT
MAKE SURE YOU DON'T
MOVE FORWARD OR AROUND
CORNERS DURING CLEARING
WITH LIGHT OFF. IT IS VERY
EASY IF YOU CAN'T SEE TO
STEP OUT INTO THREATS,
AND THEN THEY MAY BE
ABLE TO AMBUSH YOU.

ANOTHER THING TO REMEMBER
IS THAT WITH POWERFUL LIGHTS
THERE WILL BE SO MUCH REFLECTION
GOING ON THAT THE THREAT WILL
KNOW FROM SEVERAL ROOMS AWAY
THAT YOU ARE IN THE AREA.

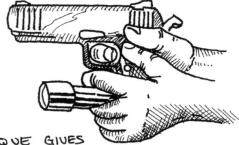

THE ROGERS, OR SYRINGE TECHNIQUE GIVES
YOU A TWO HANDED GRIP ON THE PISTOL BUT HAS A FEW
DISADVANTAGES. IF YOU HAVE SMALL HANDS IT DOESN'T
WORK THAT WELL. IT TAKES SOME TIME TO CONFIGURE THE
LIGHT, HANDS AND WEAPON PROPERLY, PLUS WITH THE WAY
THE LIGHT IS HELD IT DOESN'T FLOW WELL INTO THE OTHER
TECHNIQUES. THERE IS ALSO THE POSSIBILITY THAT THE
LIGHT CAN PRESS AGAINST THE MAG RELEASE.

REMEMBER THE FARTHER AWAY THE LIGHT IS FROM
COVER THE MORE REFLECTION OR BOUNCE BACK WILL
OCCUR OFF THE COVER OR SERFACE.

LANYARDS

WHEN USING A LAYNARD IT IS BEST TO LOOP IT OVER YOUR THUMB VS. LOOPING IT AROUND YOUR WRIST. THIS WAY IF YOU NEED TO GET RID OF IT YOU CAN DROP THE LIGHT. YOU WOULD WANT TO DO THIS IF YOUR LIGHT STUCK ON AND YOU NEEDED TO DITCH IT. THIS ALSO MAKES SURE IF SOMEONE GRABS THE LIGHT THEY CAN'T USE IT TO TAKE CONTROL OF YOU.

THE "O-RING" LANYARD IS THE BEST SYSTEM TO USE. THIS IS SIMPLY A LARGE RUBBER O-RING ATTACHED TO THE LIGHT WHICH IS LOOPED AROUND A FINGER OR THUMB.

THE LANYARD IS USED DURING RELOADS OR MALFUNCTION CLEARANCES WHEN THE SUPPORT HAND IS NEEDED TO WORK THE WEAPON. DROP THE LIGHT OR FLIP IT OUT OF THE WAY, WORK THE CLEARANCE OR RELOAD

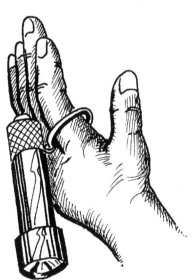

THE OTHER OPTIONS FOR FREEING UP THE SUPPORT HAND FOR MANIPULATIONS IS TO STOW THE LIGHT UNDER THE ARMPIT OF THE PRIMARY ARM. YOU CAN ALSO SECURE IT IN YOUR WAISTBAND, IN A POCKET, OR IN A FLASHLIGHT HOLSTER ON YOUR BELT. IF YOU STICK IT IN A POCKET OR THE WAISTBAND IT IS A GOOD IDEA TO STICK THE LIGHT END IN FIRST SO THAT IF THE LIGHT IS ACTIVATED IT WON'T ILLUMINATE YOU.
FOR LIGHT HOLSTERS I PREFER A HORIZONTAL POUCH. IT RIDES EASIER ON THE BELT, AND I'VE SEEN MANY PEOPLE IN TRAINING PULL THEIR FLASHLIGHT AND TRY TO LOAD IT INTO THEIR PISTOL DURING A RELOAD.

LIGHT USE WITH THE RIFLE

THE LIGHTING PRINCIPLES ARE THE SAME WITH PISTOL OR
RIFLE. THE LIGHTING TECHNIQUES ARE SIMILAR AS WELL.
WEAPON MOUNTED LIGHTS ARE NOT A NECESSITY, AND EVEN
IF YOU DO HAVE A WEAPON MOUNTED LIGHT YOU SHOULD
TRAIN WITH A HAND HELD LIGHT IN CASE THE MOUNTED
LIGHT SHOULD FAIL. JUST AS WITH THE PISTOL YOU WILL NEED
A LEFT AND RIGHT SIDE TECHNIQUE.

THE HARRIES TECHNIQUE CAN ALSO BE USED WITH
THE RIFLE. THE SUPPORT HAND CROSSES UNDER THE
RIFLE AND SUPPORTS THE WEAPON WHILE OPERATING
THE LIGHT. AS WITH THE PISTOL THIS TECHNIQUE
IS USED FOR LEFT CORNER OR WORKING THE
RIGHT SIDE OF COVER.

ONE OF THE DISADVANTAGES
OF THIS TECHNIQUE, OR ANY
OTHER HAND HELD METHOD
IS THAT IF YOU MUST USE
THE SUPPORT HAND, SAY
WHEN OPENING A DOOR, YOU
LOSE USE OF THE LIGHT.

LANYARDS SHOULD BE USED FOR THE SAME REASONS YOU
USE THEM WITH THE PISTOL.

YOU CAN ALSO USE AN UNCROSSED TECHNIQUE BY POSITIONING
THE LIGHT ON THE LEFT SIDE OF THE WEAPON AND USING
THE HEEL OF THE PALM TO HOLD UP THE WEAPON.

UNCROSSED TECHNIQUE WITH
RIFLE SUPPORTED BY HEEL
OF THE PALM. THE THUMB
CAN BE HELD UNDER THE
WEAPON TO LOCK IN THE
WEAPON USING TECHNIQUE
BELOW.

OR THUMB IS
USED TO
WORK TAILCAP
SWITCH TO
ACTIVATE
LIGHT.

ANOTHER TECHNIQUE TO
POSITION THE LIGHT ON THE
RIGHT SIDE IS TO ADJUST
THE TAILCAP UNTIL THE
LIGHT COMES ON AND

THEN BACK IT OFF SLIGHTLY. PRESSURE AGAINST THE BODY AND CAP
WILL THEN ACTIVATE THE LIGHT. GRIP LIGHT IN HAND AGAINST
HANDGUARD. WHEN YOU SQUEEZE IT WILL ACTIVATE LIGHT.

THE LIGHT CAN ALSO BE POSITIONED UNDER THE HANDGUARD SO THE TAILCAP SWITCH IS IN LINE WITH THE MAG WELL. THE LIGHT CAN THEN BE PRESSED REARWARD SO THE CAP IS ACTIVATED AGAINST THE RIFLES RECEIVER. WHEN USING THIS TECHNIQUE YOU SHOULD MAKE SURE THE SLING DOESN'T BLOCK THE LIGHT.

THE SYRINGE TECHNIQUE CAN ALSO BE USED WITH THE RIFLE. THE LIGHT IS GRIPPED BETWEEN THE FIRST TWO FINGERS WHILE THE OTHER FINGERS ASSIST IN SUPPORTING THE RIFLE. THE DOWNSIDE TO THIS TECHNIQUE IS THAT WITH LIGHT POSITIONED IN THIS MANNER IT DOESN'T FLOW WELL INTO THE OTHER TECHNIQUES.

IF YOU ARE MOUNTING A LIGHT TO YOUR RIFLE I FEEL IT IS BETTER TO MOUNT IN A 2 O'CLOCK OR 10 O'CLOCK LOCATION AS OPPOSED TO THE BOTTOM OF THE WEAPON. WITH IT MOUNTED TO THE BOTTOM IT MEANS YOU MUST RAISE THE RIFLE HIGHER TO WORK OVER COVER, PLUS IT CAN MAKE IT DIFFICULT TO REST THE HANDGUARD ON COVER IF YOU ARE USING COVER AS AN AID TO ACCURACY. WITH A SIDE MOUNT AS YOU ROLL OUT FROM COVER OR WORKING A CORNER THIS POSITIONS THE LIGHT TO COME OUT FIRST. REMEMBER THE RIFLE DOESN'T HAVE TO BE HELD VERTICAL WHEN ROLLING OUT TO THE SIDE.

EVEN IF YOU DO HAVE A WEAPON MOUNTED LIGHT IT IS A GOOD IDEA TO WORK WITH A HAND HELD LIGHT.

WORKING WITH THE RIFLE IT MAY BE NECESSARY TO TRANSITION TO THE PISTOL DURING TIMES WHEN THE RIFLE CEASES TO FUNCTION. WITH LOW LIGHT CONDITIONS YOU WILL NEED TECHNIQUES THAT ALLOW YOU TO SHIFT TO THE PISTOL, RETAIN THE RIFLE, AND STILL BE ABLE TO USE THE LIGHT, WHETHER IT IS A HANDHELD OR WEAPON MOUNTED LIGHT.

THE SIMPLEST TECHNIQUE IS TO HUG THE RIFLE AGAINST YOUR BODY BY CLAMPING IT WITH THE FOREARM WHILE THE SUPPORT HAND STILL HOLDS THE FLASHLIGHT. THE RIFLE IS LOWERED DOWN WITH THE PRIMARY HAND. ONCE THE RIFLE IS SECURED THE PRIMARY HAND PRESENTS THE FLASHLIGHT.

RIFLE CAN ALSO BE TUCKED UNDERNEATH THE SUPPORT ARM AND THE FOREARM WRAPS UNDER RIFLE TO SUPPORT IT WHILE HAND HOLDS FLASHLIGHT.

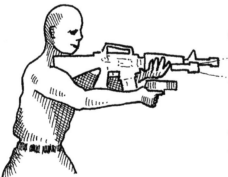

WITH A WEAPON MOUNTED LIGHT THE RIFLE CAN BE HELD IN THE NORMAL FIRING POSITION WITH THE SUPPORT HAND, WHICH CAN STILL ACTIVATE LIGHT, WHILE PRIMARY HAND ACESSES THE PISTOL.

RIFLE CAN ALSO BE TUCKED UNDER THE ARM, AS ABOVE, BUT WITH LIGHT ON RIFLE POINTING TOWARDS THREAT SO IT CAN STILL BE USED TO ILLUMINATE THREAT.

154

YOU HAVE A LIGHT ON YOUR RIFLE
BUT IT GOES OUT. THE ONLY OTHER
LIGHT YOU HAVE IS ON YOUR PISTOL,
BUT YOU DON'T WANT TO GIVE UP
THE ADVANTAGES OF THE RIFLE.
SOLUTION: SLIP THE SUPPORT
HAND UNDER THE RIFLE SO YOU
ARE HOLDING IT IN THE CROOK
OF THE SUPPORT HAND. THE
PRIMARY HAND PRESENTS
THE PISTOL, THEN TRANSFERS
THE PISTOL TO THE SUPPORT
HAND. APPLY PRESSURE TO
THE REAR ON THE MAG AND
MAG WELL WITH SUPPORT
ARM TO LOCK THE RIFLE IN.

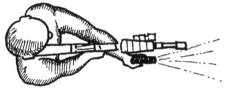

WITH A WEAPON MOUNTED
LIGHT ON THE RIFLE YOU
MAY STILL NEED TO USE
THE HAND HELD LIGHT.

FOR INSTANCE IF THE MOUNTED
LIGHT GOES OUT. OR YOU MAY
NEED TO HOLD A THREAT WITH
THE RIFLE BUT SCAN WITH THE
LIGHT IN ANOTHER DIRECTION
FOR ADDITIONAL THREATS.
FLEXIBILITY IS THE KEY. PRACTICE
FOR EVERY POSSIBLE VARIATION.

THERE MAY BE A SITUATION WHERE
IT WOULD BENEFIT YOU TO PLACE
THE LIGHT IN A STATIONARY
LOCATION WHILE YOU PERFORMED
MANIPULATIONS OR MOVED TO
ANOTHER LOCATION. THIS IS ALSO
A REASON TO CARRY MORE
THAN ONE LIGHT.

155

PRACTICE WORKING THE DIFFERENT LIGHT TECHNIQUES AS YOU MOVE FORWARD AND BACKWARD. NOTICE ON THE DRAWINGS ABOVE HOW THE FOOT AND LEG POSITIONS CHANGE ACCORDING TO THE LIGHT TECHNIQUE USED, OR HOW THE FEET ARE POSITIONED AS YOU ARE MOVING AND WHICH LIGHT TECHNIQUE WORKS BEST.

MOST PEOPLE WHEN THEY ARE SEARCHING WITH THE LIGHT WILL CONSTANTLY MOVE THE LIGHT FROM AREA TO AREA, USING THE ACTUAL BEAM ON THE EXACT LOCATION THEY ARE LOOKING. WITH THE INTENSITY OF THE LIGHTS AVAILABLE NOW THERE IS PLENTY OF LIGHT REFLECTED AROUND TO ACTUALLY BE ABLE TO SEE A LARGE AREA, MAKING IT UNECESSARY TO MOVE THE LIGHT AROUND A LOT.

TRITIUM SIGHTS HELP ALIGN THE SIGHTS IN LOW LIGHT BUT I DON'T BELIEVE THEY ARE REQUIRED. YOU MUST STILL IDENTIFY THE THREAT, AND FOR THIS YOU MUST HAVE A LIGHT SOURCE, OR THERE IS ENOUGH AMBIENT LIGHT TO I.D. THE THREAT WHICH MEANS ENOUGH LIGHT TO SEE THE SIGHTS. PLUS IF YOU GO FROM LIGHT INTO DARK, ENTERING A DARK BUILDING DURING THE DAY, YOUR EYES WON'T ADJUST ENOUGH TO SEE THE TRITIUM.
IF IT IS AN EXTREMELY QUICK ACTION IN CLOSE QUARTERS YOU CAN USE BODY INDEXING TO MAKE THE HITS.
IT IS ALSO POSSIBLE TO USE THE MUZZLE FLASH FROM YOUR FIRST SHOT TO CHECK AND ALIGN THE SIGHTS, ESPECIALLY WITH THE PISTOL.
ALSO REMEMBER WHEN USING A FLASHLIGHT IT IS IMPORTANT TO FOCUS ON THE FRONT SIGHT AND NOT THE AREA WHERE THE FLASHLIGHT BEAM IS SHINING, WHICH IS WHERE THE EYE IS NATURALLY ATTRACTED.

156

THERE IS ONE SCHOOL OF THOUGHT THAT AFTER YOU HAVE USED THE LIGHT AND ENGAGED A THREAT YOU SHOULD TURN THE LIGHT OUT AND MOVE TO AVOID BEING TARGETED BY YOUR LIGHT AND MUZZLE FLASH. THE PROBLEM WITH THIS IS THAT YOU MAY TURN THE LIGHT OUT, MOVE AND THEN WHEN YOU TURN THE LIGHT BACK ON THE THREAT HAS MOVED AND NOW YOU DON'T KNOW WHERE THE THREAT IS. IT IS BETTER TO LIGHT AND ENGAGE, FOLLOW THE THREAT DOWN, AND THEN HOLD ON THE THREAT TO INSURE IT IS DOWN AND ONLY THEN LIGHT OUT AND MOVE. OF COURSE IF INCOMING FIRE OCCURS THEN YOU WOULD WANT TO GET THE LIGHT OUT AND MOVE.
ONCE YOU'VE CONFIRMED THE THREAT IS DOWN YOU WOULD WANT TO TURN THE LIGHT OUT, CHANGE YOUR LOCATION AND SEARCH, LIGHT OUT AND MOVE THEN LIGHT ON TO SEARCH. AFTER EVERY TIME THE LIGHT IS USED YOU SHOULD TURN IT OFF AND MOVE IF POSSIBLE. ALSO WHEN POSSIBLE YOU SHOULD ONLY HAVE THE LIGHT ON FOR 3 SECONDS OR LESS, IN ORDER TO AVOID BEING TARGETED.

MOST PEOPLE FEEL UNEASY ABOUT FIGHTING IN LOW LIGHT ENVIRONMENTS BUT THIS IS DUE TO A LACK OF KNOWLEDGE OR EXPERIENCE. WITH PRACTICE YOU CAN OVERCOME THIS FEAR. ALSO REMEMBER THAT IN A LIGHTED ENVIRONMENT EVERYONE IS ON EQUAL FOOTING AND CAN SEE EACHOTHER. WITH TRAINING YOU CAN TURN THE DARK INTO AN ADVANTAGE FOR YOU.

IF YOU ARE IN A DARK ENVIRONMENT AND NOT FAMILIAR WITH LOW LIGHT OPERATIONS AND IT IS POSSIBLE YOU CAN TURN THE LIGHTS ON. OR IF YOU ARE IN A LIGHTED ENVIRONMENT AND IT'S POSSIBLE THEN TURN THE LIGHTS OFF TO GIVE YOU THE ADVANTAGE.

SINCE WE KNOW THE MAJORITY OF VIOLENT ENCOUNTERS OCCUR IN LOW LIGHT CONDITIONS THIS SHOULD DICTATE THAT THE MAJORITY OF YOUR TRAINING SHOULD OCCUR IN LOW LIGHT. HOWEVER THIS IS NOT THE CASE. IF YOUR TRAINING DOESN'T INCLUDE A LOT OF LOW LIGHT WORK YOU ARE CHEATING YOURSELF. REMEMBER MOST OF THE TECHNIQUES CAN BE PRACTICED WITH A DUMMY WEAPON IN YOUR HOME, OR DUMMY AMMO TO WORK MANIPULATIONS ETC.

GROUND FIGHTING

REGARDLESS OF YOUR POSITION YOU NEED TO BE ABLE TO ENGAGE THE THREAT.

THESE ARE POSITIONS THAT MUST BE WORKED AND PRACTICED IN ADVANCE.

SHOOT FROM ALL POSITIONS, AND PRACTICE WORKING RELOADS AND MALFUNCTION CLEARANCES.

LEGS ACT AS STABILIZERS TO PROVIDE A' GOOD FIRING PLATFORM.

MAKE SURE TO KEEP LEGS DOWN SO THAT YOUR KNEES ARE CLEAR OF THE MUZZLE.

AS SOON AS IT IS POSSIBLE WORK YOUR WAY UP TO A STANDING POSITION.

PRACTICE WORKING UP TO STANDING, FIRING FROM EACH POSITION AS YOU WORK YOUR WAY UP.

AS YOU COME UP YOUR FINGER SHOULD BE OFF THE TRIGGER TO AVOID NEGLIGENT DISCHARGE.

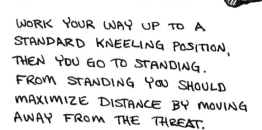

WORK YOUR WAY UP TO A STANDARD KNEELING POSITION, THEN YOU GO TO STANDING. FROM STANDING YOU SHOULD MAXIMIZE DISTANCE BY MOVING AWAY FROM THE THREAT.

SAME TECHNIQUES APPLY TO THE CARBINE.

158

CROSS
LEG

ALTHOUGH THE SITTING POSITION
IS NOT A FIGHTING POSITION
NORMALLY USED IT IS SOMETHING
YOU SHOULD PRACTICE IN CASE
IT IS NECESSARY FOR USE
BEHIND COVER OR AS AN AIDE
FOR MAKING AN ACCURATE SHOT.
ONCE YOU HAVE PRACTICED IT
THE SITTING POSITION IS A
FAIRLY ACCURATE AND STABILE
POSITION.

THERE ARE THREE VARIATIONS
OF SITTING. THE CROSSED LEG,
CROSSED ANKLE, AND OPEN LEG.
YOU MUST TRY EACH IN ORDER
TO DETERMINE WHICH WILL WORK
BEST FOR YOU.

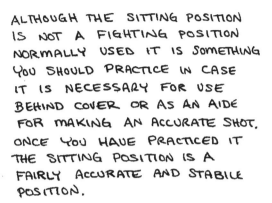

EXPERIMENT BY ALTERNATING
WHICH LEG IS ON TOP, IN THE
CROSSED LEG AND ANKLE, SO
YOU WILL FIND OUT HOW IT WILL
ELEVATE AND DEPRESS THE
MUZZLE.

C. ROSS
ANKLE

YOU WILL NEED TO APPLY
ISOMETRIC TENSION WITH THE
LEGS TO SUPPORT AND STABILIZE
THE ELBOWS.

OPEN
LEG

WITH ANY OF THE POSITIONS IT IS
NECESSARY TO CHECK YOUR NATURAL
POINT OF AIM TO DETERMINE YOUR
BODY'S RELATIONSHIP TO THE TARGET.

THE SITTING POSITION IS EXTREMELY USEFUL WHEN FIRING
FROM A SLOPE ON A TARGET DOWNHILL FROM YOUR POSITION.

AS WITH ANY POSITION YOU SHOULD PRACTICE WORKING FROM
SITTING AND FLOWING INTO OTHER POSITIONS, RELOADING AND
CLEARING MALFUNCTIONS.

DEALING WITH THREATS

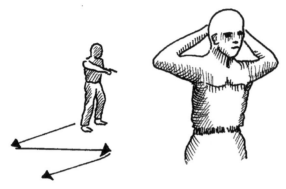

IF YOU HAVE TO DEAL WITH A THREAT YOU SHOULD HAVE THEM FACE AWAY FROM YOU, IN A POSITION WHERE YOU CAN ALWAYS KEEP AN EYE ON THEIR HANDS. AS YOU GIVE THEM VERBAL COMMANDS YOU SHOULD CHANGE LOCATIONS SO THEY CAN'T GET A FIX ON YOUR POSITION.

IT IS A GOOD IDEA INITIALLY TO HAVE THEM FREEZE. ANY OPPORTUNITY FOR THEM TO MOVE IS A CHANCE FOR THEM TO INTIATE AN ATTACK. THEN YOU NEED TO SEE THE HANDS. REMEMBER THE THREAT COMES FROM THE HANDS.

ALWAYS STAY AS FAR AWAY FROM THE THREAT AS POSSIBLE. DON'T APPROACH A THREAT, EVEN IF THEY ARE DOWN, UNLESS YOUR JOB REQUIRES IT.

THE BEST POSITION TO HAVE THE THREAT IS TO MAKE THEM LAY DOWN, FACE AWAY FROM YOU, ARMS EXTENDED WITH THE PALMS UP. NEVER LOSE SIGHT OF THE HANDS. IF YOU HAVE TO MOVE THEM MAKE THEM CRAWL ON THEIR HANDS AND KNEES.

IF POSSIBLE FORCE THE THREAT TO LEAVE THE SCENE. THE LESS TIME YOU ARE FORCED TO DEAL WITH THEM THE BETTER OFF YOU WILL BE.

REMEMBER THAT A LOT OF BAD GUYS PRACTICE DISARMING TECHNIQUES, SO THE CLOSER YOU GET THE MORE OPPORTUNITY THE HAVE TO GO HANDS ON.

IF POSSIBLE YOU SHOULD WORK FROM COVER WHEN DEALING WITH THREATS SO IF THEY DO ATTEMPT AN ATTACK AT LEAST YOU HAVE SOME PROTECTION.

160

VEHICLE DEFENSE.

DON'T EXIT OR LEAVE YOUR VEHICLE UNLESS IT IS TRAPPED OR DISABLED. WHENEVER POSSIBLE YOU SHOULD DRIVE OUT OF THE AREA, USING YOUR AUTO IF NECESSARY AS A LARGE CALIBER RAM.

SHOULD YOUR CAR BE DISABLED OR BLOCKED IN IT MAY BE NECESSARY TO VACATE THE VEHICLE. THE VERY FIRST THING YOU SHOULD DO IN THIS CASE IS MAKE SURE THE CAR IS IN PARK, OR THE TRANSMISSION OF THE CAR IS IN GEAR WITH ENGINE OFF FOR A MANUAL SHIFT VEHICLE. YOU DON'T WANT TO BE RUN OVER BY YOUR OWN CAR.

IT MAY BE NECESSARY TO EXIT FROM THE OTHER SIDE OF THE VEHICLE, FRONT OR REAR, TO CREATE DISTANCE OR COVER BETWEEN YOU AND YOUR ATTACKERS. OR DOORS COULD BE DAMAGED TO WHERE THEY WON'T OPEN. YOU SHOULD PRACTICE EXITING FROM EVERY DOOR ON YOUR VEHICLE.

WHEN POSSIBLE IT IS BEST TO TRY TO POSITION THE ENGINE BETWEEN YOU AND THE THREAT. YOU SHOULD ALSO STAY AWAY FROM THE REAR OF THE VEHICLE WHERE THE GAS TANK IS LOCATED.

IF YOU ARE UNABLE TO EXIT THE AUTO IT MAY BE NECESSARY TO SHOOT FROM WITHIN THE AUTO. IF YOU ARE SHOOTING THROUGH THE WINDSHIELD KEEP IN MIND THE BULLET WILL DEFLECT SLIGHTLY, FOLLOWING THE PLANE OF THE WINDOW. TO MAKE HITS YOU CAN'T SHOOT PAST 5 yds OR SO.

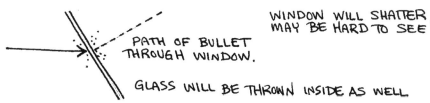

WINDOW WILL SHATTER, MAY BE HARD TO SEE'

PATH OF BULLET THROUGH WINDOW.

GLASS WILL BE THROWN INSIDE AS WELL

161

FIGHTING OUT OF A VEHICLE

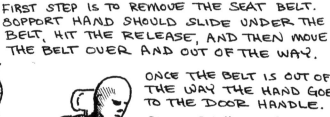

FIRST STEP IS TO REMOVE THE SEAT BELT. SUPPORT HAND SHOULD SLIDE UNDER THE BELT, HIT THE RELEASE, AND THEN MOVE THE BELT OVER AND OUT OF THE WAY.

ONCE THE BELT IS OUT OF THE WAY THE HAND GOES TO THE DOOR HANDLE.

PRIMARY HAND GOES TO THE PISTOL. AT THE SAME TIME THE KNEES ARE TWISTED SO THAT AS THE PISTOL IS DRAWN THE MUZZLE DOESN'T SWEEP ANY PART OF YOUR BODY.

FOR A LEFT HANDED SHOOTER YOU WOULD USE THE LEFT HAND TO UNDO THE SEAT BELT, SWEEPING IT OUT OF THE WAY, WHICH POSITIONS THE HAND AT YOUR PISTOL, THE SUPPORT HAND OPENS THE DOOR PRIOR TO DRAWING THE PISTOL. OR YOUR RIGHT HAND CAN UNDO THE BELT AND CARRY IT OVER AND OUT OF THE WAY, THEN THE LEFT HAND OPENS THE DOOR PRIOR TO DRAWING THE PISTOL.

THE MAIN THING IS TO GET THE BELT UNLATCHED, AND CLEAR OF YOUR BODY PRIOR TO DRAWING THE PISTOL. AS YOU PRESENT THE PISTOL YOU NEED TO GET IT INDEXED ONTO THE THREAT. FOR THE DRIVER, AND A RIGHT HANDED SHOOTER, BRING THE PISTOL STRAIGHT UP FROM THE HOLSTER TO THE 3 O'CLOCK POSITION, THEN FOLLOWING THE CURVE OF THE STEERING WHEEL AND KEEPING THE MUZZLE FORWARD MOVE THE PISTOL TO THE LEFT AND PAST THE WINDOW AND DOORPOST.

FOR THE PASSENGER SIDE, BRING THE WEAPON UP, ABOVE THE DASH, AND THEN OVER TO THE RIGHT.

THESE TECHNIQUES ARE USED TO INSURE WE DON'T COVER OURSELVES WITH THE MUZZLE.

162

AS YOU WORK YOUR WAY OUT OF THE DOOR BE CAREFUL ABOUT EXTENDING THE PISTOL OUT PAST THE DOOR AND THE DOOR FRAME. IF THE DOOR IS SLAMMED OR PUSHED IT WILL TRAP YOUR WEAPON OR INJURE YOUR HANDS OR ARMS.

ALSO BE CAREFUL ABOUT USING YOUR FOOT TO SHOVE OR HOLD THE DOOR OPEN. SAME THING IF THE DOOR IS FORCED CLOSED.

ONCE YOU HAVE EXITED THE VEHICLE WORK YOUR WAY FROM THE THREAT, CREATING AND MAXIMIZING YOUR DISTANCE AND MINIMIZING YOURSELF AS A TARGET.

TRAVELING WITH CHILDREN PRESENTS ADDITIONAL PROBLEMS YOU MUST CONSIDER. IF THEY ARE SMALLER YOU WILL HAVE TO CONSIDER HOW TO GET THEM CLEAR OF THE VEHICLE, OR WILL IT BE BETTER TO HOLD YOUR GROUND AND DEFEND.

IF YOU KEEP A WEAPON IN A BRIEFCASE OR PURSE AND YOU CRASH WHERE WILL IT END UP AFTER THE IMPACT. WHAT IF YOU LOSE YOUR GLASSES? ALL THIS HAPPENED IN FIREFIGHT WITH THE F.B.I. IN MIAMI.

PRACTICING THESE TECHNIQUES IS SOMETHING THAT MUST BE DONE IN ADVANCE. YOU SHOULD ALSO CONSIDER THESE SAME ISSUES FOR EVERY ENVIRONMENT WHERE YOU SPEND LOTS OF TIME. WHERE ARE THE CLOSEST EXITS, WINDOWS YOU COULD ESCAPE FROM, OR AREAS EASILY DEFENDED. IF YOU CAN'T CARRY FIREARMS IN A BUILDING WHAT OTHER ITEMS COULD YOU HAVE THAT WOULD BE USEFUL IN DEFENDING YOURSELF? THERE ARE A LOT OF ITEMS THAT CAN BE USED IN A PINCH IF YOU USE YOUR IMIGINATION. THE KEY IS TO THINK ABOUT IT IN ADVANCE SO THAT YOU ARE PREPARED.

EVERY DAY HAS OPPORTUNITIES TO PRACTICE YOUR TECHNIQUES. FOR EXAMPLE EVERY TIME YOU EXIT YOUR VEHICLE YOU CAN PRACTICE YOUR BELT REMOVAL AND EXIT STRATIGIES. NEVER PASS UP A CHANCE TO REHEARSE.

NATURAL INSTINCT

TO FIGHT WITH FIREARMS CORRECTLY A LOT OF WHAT WE DO GOES AGAINST NATURAL INSTINCT. MAN WAS CREATED TO FIGHT WITH HIS HANDS, USING ROCKS, STICKS AND CLUBS, ETC. TO FIGHT WITH FIREARMS WE MUST LEARN TECHNIQUES WHICH MAXIMIZE THE WEAPON'S POTENTIAL.

FOR EXAMPLE - CROUCHING DOWN, SINGLE HAND OR UNAIMED FIRE, RUNNING WHILE SHOOTING, - ALL THESE ARE ACTS OF INSTINCT. INSTEAD OF TRAINING FOR METHODS WHICH ARE NOT EFFECTIVE WE SHOULD MODIFY OUR BEHAVIOR, GO AGAINST NATURAL INSTINCT, AND PROGRAM OURSELF FOR TECHNIQUES THAT WILL MAXIMIZE THE FIREARM'S ABILITIES. WE MUST USE A STANCE THAT ALLOWS US TO MOVE SMOOTHLY SO WE CAN SHOOT WHILE MOVING, USE BOTH HANDS AND SIGHTED FIRE TO MAKE MULTIPLE HITS ON THE TARGET, MAXIMIZE DISTANCE FROM COVER TO AVOID FRAGMENTATION...

WE MUST TRAIN TO RISE TO THE OCCASION INSTEAD OF DEFAULTING TO INSTINCT. REMEMBER RELIEVING OURSELFS IS A NATURAL INSTINCT BUT WE LEARN TO CONTROL IT AND DO IT IN THE APPROPRIATE TIME AND PLACE.

RANGE MENTALITY

THE BIGGEST PROBLEM I SEE WHEN TEACHING OTHERS IS THE "RANGE MENTALITY." THIS OCCURS WHEN PEOPLE DON'T TAKE THEIR TRAINING SERIOUS, AND DO THINGS ON THE RANGE THAT THEY WOULDN'T DO, OR WANT TO DO, IN AN ACTUAL FIGHT. FOR EXAMPLE IF THE DRILL CALLS FOR 3 SHOTS, THEN AFTER THE THIRD SHOT THEY DROP OF THE TARGET INSTEAD OF RESETTING THE TRIGGER, REACQUIRING THE SIGHTS, AND PREPARING TO SHOOT AGAIN. OR THEY NEGLECT TO SEARCH AND SCAN. ANOTHER BIG MISTAKE IS WHEN WE STOP IN THE MIDDLE OF A DRILL AND WANT TO START OVER.
YOU SHOULD TREAT EVERY DRILL AS THOUGH YOUR LIFE DEPENDED ON YOUR ACTIONS. DO IT THE WAY YOU WOULD IN A FIGHT WHERE FAILURE MEANS DEATH. DON'T CHEAT YOURSELF DURING TRAINING BY TAKING SHORTCUTS.
THIS IS MUCH MORE IMPORTANT THAN MOST PEOPLE REALIZE.

DEFENSE/OFFENSE

I THINK A LOT OF PEOPLE ARE CONFUSED WHEN IT COME TO DEFENSIVE AND OFFENSIVE COMBAT. MOST WILL DEFEND WITH RESERVATION BUT ATTACK ALL OUT. I BELIEVE THE OPPOSITE SHOULD BE THE WAY. YOU MUST DEFEND YOURSELF ALL OUT WITHOUT HOLDING BACK. YOU ARE DEFENDING AGAINST A LETHAL THREAT; YOU HAVE BEEN ATTACKED AND ARE ALLREADY BEHIND THE CURVE. WHEN YOU ATTACK IT IS YOUR PLAN, AND YOU SHOULD BE CAREFUL TO FACTOR IN ROOM TO MODIFY OR REDIRECT YOUR ATTACK AS NECESSARY.

FIGHTS WILL LIKELY COMBINE BOTH DEFENSIVE AND OFFENSIVE ACTIONS. WHEN ATTACKED YOU BEGIN WITH DEFENSIVE ACTIONS, THEN WHEN YOU HAVE BEATEN BACK YOUR OPPONENTS YOU MUST SWITCH TO OFFENSIVE ACTS TO WIN THE FIGHT. THE ABILITY TO RECOGNIZE THE WINDOW OF OPPORTUNITY WHICH ALLOWS YOU TO TRANSITION FROM DEFENSE TO OFFENSIVE ACTIONS IS CRITICAL.

REMEMBER THAT IT IS YOUR PHYSICAL SKILLS, WEAPONS, AND MIND THAT MUST BE USED TO THEIR GREATEST POTENTIAL AS A GROUP, NOT INDIVIDUALLY. THE SUM SHOULD BE GREATER THAN THE PARTS.

SPIRITUAL WARRIOR

THE SPIRIT MUST BE TRAINED JUST LIKE WE PREPARE OUR BODIES. REGARDLESS OF THE BATTLE THE MAN WITHOUT ANY RELIGIOUS BELIEF IS CLOSER TO DEFEAT. IF YOU EXAMINE THE GREAT FIGHTERS OF THE PAST THE ONE THING THEY ALL HAVE IN COMMON IS A STRONG RELIGIOUS BACKGROUND. TO FIGHT YOU MUST NOT FEAR DEATH, AND HAVE CONVICTION THAT YOU ARE RIGHT IN YOUR BELIEFS. . HAVING GOD ON YOUR SIDE, AND THE KNOWLEDGE THAT LIFE ON THIS EARTH IS TEMPORARY, WITH ETERNAL LIFE AFTERWARDS, IS DIFFICULT TO DEFEAT.

THE OTHER SIDE OF THE COIN IS THE MAN WHO BELIEVES IN NOTHING. THIS MAN MAY BE DANGEROUS, SINCE HE IS NOT AFRAID TO GIVE HIS LIFE, BUT HE SELLS IT TOO CHEAP.

THIS IS ONE AREA THAT MOST FAIL TO CONSIDER WHEN THEY ARE PREPARING FOR COMBAT, BUT YOU WOULD DO WELL TO THIS ISSUE IN ADVANCE.

" PRAISE BE TO THE LORD MY ROCK, WHO TRAINS MY HANDS FOR WAR, MY FINGERS FOR BATTLE." PSALM 144:1

SPEED

WHEN MOST PEOPLE BEGIN TRAINING THEY ATTEMPT TO DO EVERYTHING AS FAST AS POSSIBLE. INSTRUCTORS STRESS THE NEED FOR SPEED, AND OBVIOUSLY WE WANT TO STOP OUR ATTACKERS AS SOON AS POSSIBLE.

THE PROBLEM IS THAT IF WE GO TOO FAST WE WILL MAKE MISTAKES. WE SHOULD ONLY OPERATE AT THE SPEED WE CAN GURANTEE THE RESULTS. THIS APPLIES TO MOVEMENT, SHOOTING, MANIPULATIONS...

FOR EXAMPLE MOST PEOPLE SHOOT TOO FAST TO MAKE GOOD HITS. THEY FIRE FAST BECAUSE THEY ARE SCARED, THEY ARE IN A REACTIVE MODE, AND SHOOTING MAKES THEM FEEL GOOD. SHOOTING 7 SHOTS, AND MAYBE HITTING THE TARGET, TAKES LONGER THAN SLOWING DOWN, FOCUSING ON THE SIGHTS AND TRIGGER WORK, AND MAKING 2 GOOD HITS ON THE THREAT.

ONCE THE FIGHT BEGINS YOU MUST REMAIN CALM AND REGULATE YOUR ACTIONS. EVALUATE THE SITUATION, CREATE A PLAN OF RESPONSE, AND IMPLEMENT WITHOUT DELAY. IF YOU SIMPLY REACT, THROW THE WEAPON UP AND JERK THE TRIGGER, SLINGING SHOTS TOWARDS THE GENERAL AREA OF THE THREAT, YOU ARE WASTING TIME.

THE TIME YOU HAVE IN A FIGHT IS PRECIOUS, DON'T WASTE IT! USE YOUR TIME WISELY TO OBTAIN THE GREATEST RETURN.

MISTAKES

THERE ARE VERY FEW FIGHTS WHERE EVERYTHING GOES PERFECT. YOU WILL MAKE MISTAKES. THE DIFFERENCE BETWEEN CAPABLE OPERATORS AND THE EVERY DAY MAN IS WHAT THEY DO WHEN A MISTAKE OCCURS.

DURING A FIGHT, AND WHEN TRAINING, WHEN A MISTAKE OCCURS YOU SHOULD ACKNOWLEDGE IT, CORRECT AND COMPENSATE, AND CONTINUE WITH THE FIGHT. FIGHTS CONTAIN NOU TIME TO STOP, CURSE, OR ANYTHING ELSE THAT'S UNPRODUCTIVE.

MISTAKES ARE EXCESS LUGGAGE. DROP IT AND MOVE ON. DURING THE FIGHT YOU MUST FOCUS ON THE PRESENT AND FUTURE - NOT THE MISTAKE YOU JUST MADE. AFTER THE ACTION IS THE TIME TO EVALUATE YOUR MISTAKES AND TO LEARN FROM THEM.

YOU WILL MAKE MISTAKES. TRAIN TO OVERCOME THEM.

INTERNAL ENERGY

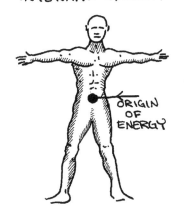

ORIGIN OF ENERGY

IN WESTERN THOUGHT THE MIND AND BODY ARE USUALLY CONSIDERED TO BE SEPERATE ENTITIES. BUT THE CLOSER TOGETHER THE MIND AND BODY THE MORE FLUID WE SHIFT FROM PERCEPTION TO ACTION. THE LESS GAP THERE IS BETWEEN INTENTION (THE MENTAL) AND ACTION (THE PHYSICAL) THE BETTER.

WE SHOULD ALSO USE OUR INTERNAL ENERGY TO ASSIST US WITH FIGHTING, EVEN WHEN USING FIREARMS. YOU SHOULD ACTUALLY VISUALIZE YOUR ENERGY FLOWING FROM THE CENTER OF YOUR BODY, THROUGH THE ARMS AND INTO THE WEAPON, FORCING THE BULLET TOWARDS THE TARGET. ALTHOUGH THIS MAY SEEM UNREAL TO THE WESTERN MIND, THE WESTERN MIND REMEMBER SEPERATES MIND AND BODY, EASTERN MARTIAL ARTIST HAVE RELIED ON PROJECTING ENERGY FOR VICTORY IN COMBAT.

THIS IS FIGHTING IN ITS MOST ADVANCED FORM, AND CAN ONLY BE APPLIED AFTER ALL BASICS HAVE BEEN MASTERED. VERY FEW INDIVIDUALS REACH THIS POINT IN THEIR TRAINING. IF THIS LEVEL OF APPLICATION ISN'T ACHEIVED YOU CAN CERTAINLY DEFEND YOURSELF AND FIGHT EFFECTIVELY, BUT YOU WILL NEVER FEEL COMPLETELY COMFORTABLE IN A COMBATIVE ENVIRONMENT, BUT THEN AGAIN THIS ISN'T EVERYONE'S OBJECTIVE.

DEFENSIVE TACTICS

THE ORIGINAL MANUSCRIPT CONTAINED A SECTION ON WEAPON DISARMING TECHNIQUES WHICH I TRAINED WITH. HOWEVER THIS ISN'T THE FOCUS OF THIS BOOK, AND IS SOMETHING WHICH MUST BE STUDIED IN DEPTH, SO I HAVE ELECTED TO LEAVE IT OUT OF THE PUBLISHED EDITION.

I DO BELIEVE YOU SHOULD STUDY DEFENSIVE, OR UNARMED, TACTICS SINCE THERE MAY BE SITUATIONS WHERE THERE ISN'T TIME, AT LEAST INTIALLY, TO EMPLOY YOUR FIREARM. BUT THAT IS A SUBJECT BEST RESERVED FOR ANOTHER BOOK.

RECOMMENDED READINGS

THE MODERN TECHNIQUE OF THE PISTOL
   MORRISON

PRINCIPLES OF PERSONAL DEFENSE
   COOPER

THE BOOK OF FIVE RINGS
   MUSASHI

NO SECOND PLACE WINNER
   JORDAN

GUNSHOT INJURIES
   LA GARDE

SHOOTING FROM WITHIN
   PLAXCO

TAO OF JEET KUNE DO
   LEE

TO RIDE, SHOOT STRAIGHT, AND SPEAK THE TRUTH
   COOPER

A RIFLEMAN WENT TO WAR
   McBRIDE

SNIPING IN FRANCE
   PRICHARD

BLACKHAWK DOWN
   BOWDEN

SHOOTING TO LIVE
   FAIRBAIRN & SYKES

WITH BRITISH SNIPERS TO THE REICH
   SHORE

LEAD POISONING
   PFOUTS

KILL OR GET KILLED
   APPLEGATE

THE ART OF WAR
   SUN TZU

THE ART OF THE RIFLE
   COOPER

PHASE LINE GREEN
   WARR

STALINGRAD
   BEEVOR

ON KILLING
   GROSSMAN

THE TRANSFORMATION OF WAR
        VAN CLEVELD

TRIGGERNOMERTY
        CUNNINGHAM

THE DEADLIEST MEN
        KIRCHNER

FAST AND FANCY REVOLVER SHOOTING
        McGIVERN

TALES OF AMERICAN VIOLENCE
        PFOUTS

TACTICAL REALITY
        AWERBUCK

THE GIFT OF FEAR
        DE BECKER

ON WAR
        CLAUSEWITZ

WARRIOR DREAMS
        GIBSON

AIKIDO, THE DYNAMIC SPHERE
        WESTBROOK & RATTI

THE CODE OF THE SAMURAI
        SHIGESUKE

I'M FRANK HAMER
        JENKINS & FROST

PRACTICAL SHOOTING
        ENOS

COMBATIVE FUNDAMENTALS
        GONZALES

THE GUNFIGHTER
        ROSA

BLACK MAGIC
        FEAMSTER

HIT OR MYTH
        AWERBUCK

WILD AT HEART

THE BIBLE

THERE IS AN ABUNDANCE OF READING MATERIAL. YOU SHOULD
EDUCATE YOUR MIND BY STUDYING EVERYTHING YOU CAN.
BY THE TIME YOU READ THIS CLINT SMITH'S BOOK SHOULD BE
AVAILABLE - BUY IT!

LEVELS OF TRAINING

THERE ARE 3 LEVELS OF TRANG, WITH A COUPLE OF VARIATION IN EACH LEVEL. RANGE DRILLS, COMBATIVE SHOOTING, AND FORCE-ON-FORCE (FOF) RANGE DRILLS ARE THE BASIC LEVEL. THEY ARE PERFORMED ON THE SQUARE RANGE, AGAINST A SINGLE TARGET, AND MAY INVOLVE THE SHOOTER MOVING. COMBATIVE TRAINING INCLUDES MULTIPLE SHOOT-NO SHOOT TARGET WHICH ARE MOVING, THE USE OF COVER AND LOW LIGHT WORK, JUST TO NAME A FEW OF THE SUBJECTS COVERED. THE HIGHEST LEVEL OF TRAINING, AND INVOLVES MAN AGAINST MAN DRILLS USING TRAING WEAPONS AND AMMO.

STUDENTS BEGIN WITH RANGE DRILLS, LEARNING THE BASICS OF MARKSMANSHIP, MANIPULATIONS, AND THE COMBATIVE MINDSET, IN OTHER WORDS THE FUNDAMENTALS. INCLUDED AND STRESSED ARE SAFETY ISSUES. THESE SKILLS ARE ESENTIAL, AND SERVE AS THE FOUNDATION FOR EVERYTHING ELSE. REPETITION IS THE ONLY WAY TO DEVELOPE AND IMPROVE.

ONCE THE FUNDAMENTALS HAVE BEEN ACQUIRED IT IS TIME TO BEGIN ADVANCED OR COMBATIVE TRAINING. THIS IS WHERE THE STUDENT ACTUALLY BEGINS TO LEARN HOW TO FIGHT WITH THE FIREARM. MOVEMENT, USE OF COVER, ENGAGING MULTIPLE AND MOVING TARGETS, AND SEARCHING AND CLEARING BUILDINGS IS PRACTICED. YOU MUST LEARN TO APPLY THE FUNDAMENTALS UNDER ANY TYPE CONDITIONS OR ENVIRONMENT.

FOF IS WHERE THE STUDENT APPLIES THEIR TACTICS AND PRINCIPLES UNDER CONDITIONS AS REALISTIC AS POSSIBLE. THIS MEANS OPERATING AGAINST LIVE THREATS. THREATS WHO MOVE, REACT, AND THINK. THE JUMP TO FOF IS EXTREME, AND MOST STUDENTS DON'T PERFORM WELL AT FIRST, WHICH IS WHY IT IS SO ESENTIAL TO PREPARING FOR ARMED COMBAT. IT IS LIKE ANY MARTIAL ART — YOU CAN WORK OUT ON THE PUNCHING BAG ALL YOU LIKE, BUT IT ISN'T ANYTHING LIKE SPARRING AGAINST A LIVE OPPONENT.

FOF TRAINING IS DISCOURAGING AT FIRST BECAUSE THE STUDENT BELIEVES THEY KNOW HOW TO FIGHT BASED ON THEIR EXPERIENCE ON THE SQUARE RANGE. IT IS A LITTLE UNSETTLING TO FACE OPPONENTS WHEN YOU CAN'T PREDICT HOW THEY WILL REACT.

FOF IS WHERE WE LEARN HOW TO ISSUE VERBAL COMMANDS. IF YOU AREN'T EFFECTIVE YOU SEE THE RESULTS. WE LEARN TO WATCH THE HANDS WHILE COMMUNICATING AS OPPOSED TO LOOKING AT THE FACE. YOU DISCOVER AND DEVELOP AN UNDERSTANDING OF THE RYTHM OF COMBAT. MOVEMENT AND THE USE OF COVER BECOME CRITICAL KEYS TO SUCCESS.

ALL THESE THINGS COME WITH FOF TRAINING. HOWEVER, DON'T FORGET SAFETY CONCERNS. THERE HAVE BEEN TOO MANY DEATHS DURING FOF DUE TO RELAXED SAFETY ISSUES. CARE MUST BE TAKEN TO INSURE NO ONE IS ARMED WITH ANY WEAPONS. UNLESS REDMAN PROTECTIVE SUITS ARE WORN YOU MUST AVOID ALL PHYSICAL CONTACT. ROLE PLAYERS MUST UNDERSTAND THEIR SCRIPTS, AND FOLLOW THE PRECISELY. FOF CAN BE A USEFUL TOOL IF PROPERLY OVERSEEN OR IT CAN JUST BE MAYHEM WHERE NO LESSONS ARE LEARNED.

DRY PRACTICE

I BELIEVE DRY PRACTICE IS THE BEST WAY TO IMPROVE YOUR SKILLS. THE KEY IS SAFETY. THERE IS PLENTY OF REFERENCE MATERIAL AVAILABLE ON THE SAFETY ISSUES - FOLLOW THEM!

I ACTUALLY DO MY DRY PRACTICE ON THE RANGE. I DEVELOPE AND IMPROVE MY SKILLS DRY, THEN SHOOT A FEW DRILLS JUST TO CONFIRM THAT I HIT THE TARGET WHEN I FIRE. THERE IS A LOT OF MATERIAL I CAN PRACTICE WITHOUT EVEN USING A REAR WEAPON. I HAVE PISTOLS SAWN OUT OF WOOD AND OLD WOODEN RIFLE STOCKS I USE FOR CLEARING MY HOUSE. YOUR EVERY DAY ROUTINE HAS COUNTLESS OPPORTUNITIES FOR YOU TO PRACTICE TECHNIQUES AND APPLY COMBATIVE THEORY. DON'T MISS A CHANCE TO PRACTICE!

FUNDAMENTALS WIN FIGHTS! IF YOU CAN APPLY THE BASICS — COMMUNICATE, MOVE, USE COVER, AND SHOOT ACCURATELY — UNDER ANY TYPE CONDITIONS AND ON DEMAND, WITHOUT WARNING, YOU ARE READY. TO REACH THIS POINT REQUIRES A HEALTHY INVESTMENT OF TIME FROM YOU.

ATTEND AS MUCH TRAINING AS YOU CAN. PRACTICE EVERY OPPORTUNITY YOU HAVE. YOU SHOULD TRAIN AND PRACTICE AS THOUGH YOU ARE GOING TO BE ATTACKED THIS EVENING, OR SOONER.

IF YOU'VE BEEN INVOLVED IN A VIOLENT ATTACK THEN YOU KNOW WHY YOU NEED TO BE PREPARED. IF YOU HAVEN'T BEEN ATTACKED THEN THE CHANCES OF IT OCCURING TO YOU ARE INCREASED... SOONER OR LATER IT WILL HAPPEN. UNLESS YOU ARE EXTREMELY LUCKY, AND I WOULD RATHER RELY ON SKILL AS OPPOSED TO LUCK. REMEMBER THAT PERSONAL PROTECTION IS AN INDIVIDUAL RESPONSIBILITY!

REMEMBER THAT THE 2ND AMMENDMENT GUARANTEES ALL OTHER RIGHTS. IF YOU HAVE FRIENDS WHO ARE NOT SHOOTERS THEN INTRODUCE THEM TO THE ASPECTS OF PERSONAL PROTECTION. THE MORE LAW ABIDING GUN OWNERS WE HAVE WHO VOTE THE BETTER.

WHEN YOU DO HAVE TO USE YOUR FIREARM YOU NEED TO REMBER TO FIGHT SMART!

SHOOT OFTEN
SHOOT WELL
SHOOTRITE!

Tig McK
2004

Made in the USA
Charleston, SC
27 August 2010